The Hidden Places of
DEVON

By
David Gerrard

© Travel Publishing Ltd.

Published by:
Travel Publishing Ltd
7a Apollo House, Calleva Park
Aldermaston, Berks, RG7 8TN

ISBN 1-902-00754-9

© Travel Publishing Ltd

First Published:	1989	Fourth Edition:	1998
Second Edition:	1992	Fifth Edition:	2000
Third Edition:	1996		

HIDDEN PLACES REGIONAL TITLES

Channel Islands	Cheshire
Chilterns	Cornwall
Derbyshire	Devon
Dorset, Hants & Isle of Wight	East Anglia
Essex	Gloucestershire & Wiltshire
Heart of England	Hereford, Worcs & Shropshire
Highlands & Islands	Kent
Lake District & Cumbria	Lancashire
Norfolk	Northumberland & Durham
North Wales	Nottinghamshire
Potteries	Somerset
South Wales	Suffolk
Surrey	Sussex
Thames Valley	Warwickshire & West Midlands
Yorkshire	

HIDDEN PLACES NATIONAL TITLES

England	Ireland
Scotland	Wales

Printing by: Scotprint, Haddington
Maps by: © Maps in Minutes ™ (2000)
Editor: David Gerrard
Cover Design: Lines & Words, Aldermaston
Cover Photographs: Berry Head, nr Brixham; Cottages, Buckland-in-the-Moor; Dartmoor stream - courtesy of © Britain on View/Stockwave

Foreword

The Hidden Places is a collection of easy to use travel guides taking you, in this instance, on a relaxed but informative tour of Devon - Britain's third largest county of rolling hills, bright fresh streams tumbling through wooded valleys, white thatched cottages, bleak upland moors and beautiful rugged coastlines.

This edition of *The Hidden Places of Devon* is the second title to be published *in full colour*. All Hidden Places titles will now be published in colour which will ensure that readers can properly appreciate the attractive scenery and impressive places of interest in Devon and, of course, in the rest of the British Isles. We do hope that you like the new format.

Our books contain a wealth of interesting information on the history, the countryside, the towns and villages and the more established places of interest in the county. But they also promote the more secluded and little known visitor attractions and places to stay, eat and drink many of which are easy to miss unless you know exactly where you are going.

We include hotels, inns, restaurants, public houses, teashops, various types of accommodation, historic houses, museums, gardens, garden centres, craft centres and many other attractions throughout Devon, all of which are comprehensively indexed. Most places are accompanied by an attractive photograph and are easily located by using the map at the beginning of each chapter. We do not award merit marks or rankings but concentrate on describing the more interesting, unusual or unique features of each place with the aim of making the reader's stay in the local area an enjoyable and stimulating experience.

Whether you are visiting the area for business or pleasure or in fact are living in the county we do hope that you enjoy reading and using this book. We are always interested in what readers think of places covered (or not covered) in our guides so please do not hesitate to use the reader reaction forms provided to give us your considered comments. We also welcome any general comments which will help us improve the guides themselves. Finally if you are planning to visit any other corner of the British Isles we would like to refer you to the list of other *Hidden Places* titles to be found at the rear of the book.

Travel Publishing

iv

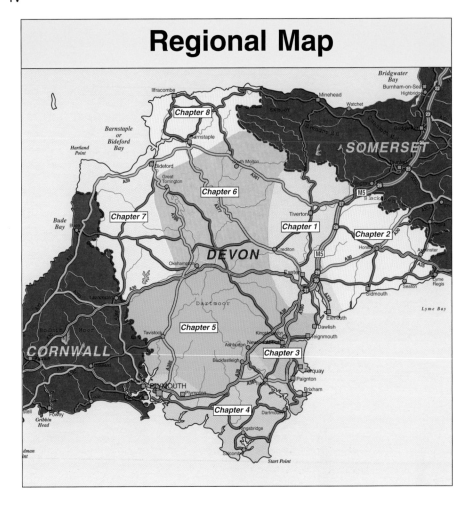

Contents

1 Exeter and the Exe Valley

When Adam and Eve were dispossessed
Of the garden hard by Heaven,
They planted another one down in the west,
'Twas Devon, glorious Devon.

This nostalgic ballad by Sir Harold Edwin Boulton was immensely popular around the turn of the century, and a generation later the travel writer Arthur Mee expressed the same kind of sentiment when he exclaimed, "What do they know of England who do not Devon know?"

Asked to describe the "ideal" English countryside, many people would conjure up a landscape of green, rolling hills, of bright, fresh streams tumbling through wooded valleys, of white thatched cottages clustering around a venerable church, with a picturesque inn nestling beside it. Devon, of course, but only part of it. There are also the bleak uplands of Dartmoor, and the busy port of Plymouth; a rugged coastline to the north which contrasts with the almost Mediterranean character of Torbay - the "English Riviera". There are hundreds of picture postcard villages, of which Clovelly and Inner Hope are perhaps the most famous, and scores of delightful small towns such as Totnes and Dartmouth.

The county also boasts some outstanding buildings. The Gothic masterpiece of Exeter Cathedral has been described as "one of the supreme architectural pleasures of England" and it was a 14th century Bishop of Exeter who built the glorious parish church of Ottery St Mary. The sumptuous mansion of Saltram House near Plymouth contains fine work by Robert Adam, Sir Joshua Reynolds and Thomas Chippendale, while Buckland Abbey is famed as the home of the Drake family and their most famous son, Sir Francis.

Part of Devon's enormous charm derives from the fact that it is so lightly populated. Just over a million people, roughly equivalent to the population of Birmingham, occupy the third largest county in England, some 670,000 acres in all. And most of those million people live in towns and resorts along its coastline, leaving huge tracts of countryside where the villages, the lanes and byways, even in these days, are still magically peaceful.

We begin our tour of this beguiling county at its most ancient and historic city, Exeter.

Exeter Cathedral

EXETER AND THE EXE VALLEY

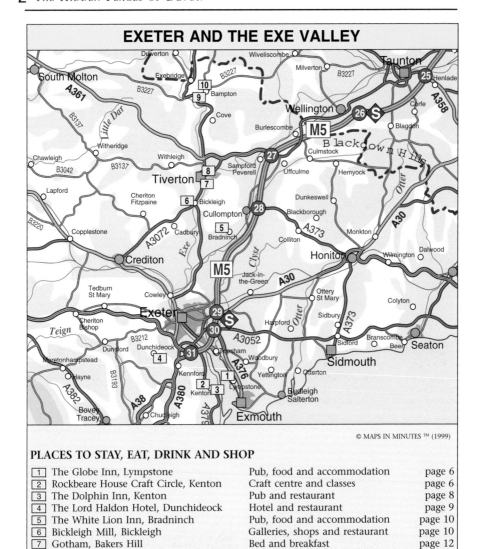

© MAPS IN MINUTES ™ (1999)

PLACES TO STAY, EAT, DRINK AND SHOP

EXETER

A lively and thriving city with a majestic Norman cathedral, many fine old buildings, and a wealth of excellent museums, Exeter's history stretches back for than two millennia. Its present High Street was already in place some two centuries or more before the

Cathedral Close, Exeter

Romans arrived, part of an ancient ridgeway striking across the West Country. The inhabitants then were the Celtish tribe of the *Dumnonii* and it was they who named the river Eisca, "a river abounding in fish".

The Romans made Isca their south-western stronghold, surrounding it with a massive defensive wall. Most of that has disappeared, but a spectacular *caldarium,* or **Roman Bath House** was uncovered in the Cathedral Close in 1971.

In the Dark Ages following the Roman withdrawal, the city was a major ecclesiastical centre and in 670 AD King Cenwealh founded an abbey on the site of the present cathedral. That, along with the rest of Exeter, was ransacked by the Vikings in the 9th century. They occupied the city twice before King Alfred finally saw them off.

The Normans were next on the scene, although it wasn't until twenty years after the Battle of Hastings that William the Conqueror finally took possession of the city after a siege that lasted eighteen days. He ordered the construction of **Rougemont Castle**, the gatehouse and tower of which still stand at the top of Castle Street.

During the following century, the Normans began building **St Peter's Cathedral,** a work not completed until 1206. Half a century later, however, everything except the two sturdy towers was demolished and the present cathedral took shape. These years saw the development of the Decorated style, and Exeter is a sublime example of this appealing form of church architecture. In the 300ft long nave, stone piers like a forest rise 60ft and then fan out into sweeping arches. Equally impressive is the west front, a staggering display of more than sixty sculptures, carved between 1327 and 1369. They depict a curious mix of Biblical characters, soldiers, priests and a royal flush of Saxon and Norman kings.

Other treasures include an intricately-carved choir screen from about 1320, an astronomical clock built in 1376 which is one of the oldest

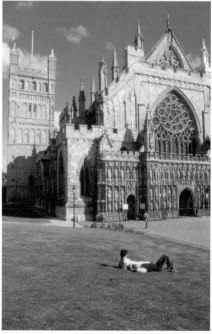

Exeter Cathedral West End

timepieces in the world, a minstrels' gallery with a wonderful band of heavenly musicians, a monumental organ, and a colossal throne with a canopy 59ft high, carved in wood for Bishop Stapledon in 1316.

Such is the grandeur of the Cathedral that other ecclesiastical buildings in Exeter tend to get overlooked. But it's well worth seeking out **St Nicholas' Priory**, an exceptional example of a small Norman priory. It is now an interesting museum where visitors can view the original Prior's cell, the 15th century kitchens, and the imposing central hall with a vaulted ceiling and chunky Norman pillars. The **Church of St Mary Steps** also repays a visit just to see its beautifully-preserved Norman font, and its ancient "Matthew the Miller" tower clock, named after a medieval

Clock at St Mary Steps

miller noted for his undeviating punctuality. The church stands in Stepcote Hill, a narrow cobbled and stepped thoroughfare which until as late as 1778 was the main road into Exeter from the west.

The remarkable **Guildhall** in the High Street has been in use as a Town Hall ever since it was built in 1330, making it one of the oldest municipal buildings in the country. Its great hall was remodelled around 1450, and the Elizabethans added a striking, if rather fussy, portico, but the interior is still redolent of the Middle Ages.

Another interesting medieval building is **The Tucker's Hall** in Fore Street, built in 1471 for the Company of Weavers, Fullers and Shearmen. Inside there is some exceptional carved panelling, a collection of rare silver, and a huge pair of fulling shears weighing over 25lbs and almost 4ft long. Nearby Parliament Street claims to be the world's narrowest street.

Exeter's one-time importance as a port is reflected in the dignified **Custom House,** built in 1681, and now the centrepiece of **Exeter Historic Quayside**, a fascinating complex of old warehouses, craft shops, cafes, and the **Seahorse Nature Aquarium** which is specially dedicated to these beautiful and enigmatic creatures. There are riverside walks, river trips, Canadian canoes and cycles for hire, and a passenger ferry across the river to

Quayside and Maritime Museum

the **Piazza Terracina** which explores five centuries of Exeter's trading connections around the world. The museum contains an extraordinary collection of boats, amongst them an Arab dhow, a reed boat from Lake Titicaca in South America, and a vintage steam launch. A special attraction of the museum is that visitors are positively encouraged to step aboard and explore in detail the many craft on show.

Other excellent museums in the city

include the **Royal Albert Memorial Museum** in Queen Street, (local history, archaeology and paintings); the **Devonshire Regiment Museum** (regimental history); and the **Rougemont House Museum** near the castle which has a copious collection of costumes and lace.

One of the city's most unusual attractions lies beneath its streets: the maze of **Underground Passages** constructed in the 14th and 15th centuries to bring water from springs beyond the city walls. A guided tour of the stone-vaulted caverns is an experience to remember.

River Exe, Topsham

AROUND EXETER

Within a few miles of Exeter, you can take your pick of a remarkable variety of scenery. Northwards, the Exe Valley runs up to Tiverton, and on one of its tributaries, the River Creedy, is the ancient town of Crediton, once the most important ecclesiastical centre in the West Country. To the east rise the Woodbury Hills which tumble down to the broad estuary of the Exe and the small town of Topsham with its fine Dutch-style architecture recalling the days when it was a major port. To the southwest, rolling wooded hills run up to the edge of Dartmoor, with small, somnolent villages tucked away in their folds. In this section, we explore the area, travelling around it in a clockwise direction, starting to the east of Exeter.

A short drive from Junction 30 of the M5 is **Crealy Park**, a large all-weather entertainment centre offering a wide range of attractions for children, including the largest indoor PlayZone in the country, bumper boats and go-karts, a farm nursery and pony rides. The park is open 363 days a year: for further details, call 01395 233200.

TOPSHAM
3 miles SE of Exeter, on minor road off the A376

It's not surprising to find that the whole of the old town of Topsham has been declared a conservation area. Its narrow streets are lined with fine examples of 17th and 18th century merchants' houses, many built in the Dutch style with curved gable ends, there's a wealth of specialist and antique shops, and some stunning views over the Exe estuary.

WOODBURY
7 miles SE of Exeter on the B3179

St Swithin's Church at Woodbury has achieved a rather sad kind of fame because of the Revd. J. Loveband Fulford who in 1846 cut great chunks out of its medieval rood screen so that his parishioners could see him more clearly. Fortunately he left untouched the fine 15th century font made from Beer stone, the Jacobean pulpit, and the interesting memorials.

A mile or so to the east of the village is the famous **Woodbury Common** viewpoint. More than 560ft high, it provides spectacular vistas across the Exe estuary to Dartmoor, and along the south Devon coast. It's easy to understand why an Iron Age tribe chose this spot to build their massive fort whose huge ramparts lie close to the viewpoint.

LYMPSTONE
8 miles SE of Exeter off the A376

Set beside the estuary of the River Exe, Lympstone looks across the water to the impressive outline of Powderham Castle. There's a tiny harbour with a slipway and, on the beach, an Italianate clock tower erected in 1885 by a Mr W. H. Peters in commemoration

THE GLOBE INN,

The Strand, Lympstone, Devon EX8 5EY
Tel: 01395 263166

Located in the heart of the old town and only 30 yards from the estuary beach, **The Globe Inn** is a traditional 18th century building, originally three cottages. The inn sign shows the Earth supported by a lobster, crab and a fish, a good indication of the speciality of the house. The message continues inside with some colourful murals depicting the denizens of the deep. The appeal is also enhanced by the exposed brickwork, wooden panelling and floors.

The inn is run by Christine and Liam Matthews who came here from London and have fallen in love with the area, vowing that they will never leave The Globe! The inn is understandably popular with local fishermen since the fish dishes are prepared from the day's fresh catch.

The Matthews have also introduced a Tapas menu for bar snacks and they offer a traditional roast on Sunday lunchtimes. Three real ales are always on tap and naturally Devon cider is also available. The Matthews organise regular music nights with entertainment by local people and if you are planning to stay in this enchanting corner of Devon, a self catering flat is available throughout the year.

ROCKBEARE HOUSE CRAFT CIRCLE,

Rockbeare House, Kenton, Exeter EX6 8LA
Tel: 01626 890738

The delightful village of Kenton is home to the Rockbeare House Craft Circle, a fascinating enterprise that developed from the local Women's Institute Home Economics classes. The leading spirit of the Circle is Alma Harding whose name in ancient Arabic means a 'woman well-versed in the arts', especially music and dance. For her 50th birthday present, Alma's husband Derek bought Rockbeare House to try and cope with her craft activities and as a future retirement home. Because the retirement was 5 years in the future, the crafts had the opportunity to take over the house. Even now the Hardings have 'retired', crafts still tend to infiltrate rooms supposed to be for living in.

A wide range of crafts are taught - patchwork and quilting, every kind of embroidery imaginable, soft toys, painting on silk, glass, pottery or paper, recycling crafts such as mosaics, straw marquetry, paper-making or rag rugs. The Circle is not a commercial enterprise, students either bring their own materials or buy them at the Centre as required: a lot cost almost nothing. The morning coffee/tea break usually includes some of Alma's home baking and there might even be some poetry reading or dance demonstrations. For visitors who do not want to do craft work, Derek is happy to guide them to interesting walks in the area or even allow sampling of his renowned home-brewed beer!

of his wife, Mary Jane, who was noted for her good works amongst the poor of the village. It's a delight to wander around the old part of Lympstone with its narrow streets, small courts and ancient cottages.

EXMOUTH
10 miles SE of Exeter on the A376

With its glorious coastal scenery and splendid beach, Exmouth was one of the earliest seaside resorts to be developed in Devon, "the Bath of the West, the resort of the tip-top of the gentry of the Kingdom". Lady Byron and Lady Nelson came to stay and found lodgings in The Beacon, an elegant Georgian terrace overlooking the Madeira Walk and Esplanade. This early success suffered a setback when Brunel routed his Great Western line along the other side of the estuary, (incidentally creating one of the most scenic railway journeys still possible in England), and it wasn't until a branch line reached Exmouth in 1861 that business picked up again. The town isn't just a popular resort. Exmouth Docks are still busy with coasters and in summer a passenger ferry crosses the Exe to Starcross.

While in Exmouth, you should make a point of visiting what has been described as "the most unusual house in Britain". A La Ronde is a fairy-tale thatched house built in 1765 by the sisters Jane and Mary Parminter who modelled it on the church of San Vitale in Ravenna. Despite its name, the house is not in fact circular but has 16 sides with 20 rooms set around a 45ft high octagon. The sisters lived here in magnificent feminist seclusion, forbidding the presence of any male in their house or its fifteen acres of grounds.

KENNFORD
5 miles S of Exeter off the A38

Set on the slopes of Great Haldon Hill, beside the River Kenn, Kennford is a good example of a "street village", almost all its houses standing alongside the one road. This used to be the main road to the far southwest until, thankfully, the dual-carriageway A38 was built and siphoned off most of the traffic.

About five miles southeast of Kennford, set in a deer park beside the River Exe, is **Powderham Castle**, home of the Earls of

Devon since 1390. The present building is mostly 18th century and contains some fine interiors, a breathtaking Grand Staircase, and historic family portraits - some of them by Sir Joshua Reynolds, a Devon man himself. The Castle's oldest resident, Timothy, has recently celebrated his 150th birthday. He was rescued in his youth from Portuguese brigands and after some forty years at sea as a ship's mascot was brought to **Powderham Castle** in 1892. For the last hundred years, he has spent his summers on the lawns here, displaying an insatiable appetite for dandelions and strawberries. When winter approaches, Timothy, like any sensible tortoise, takes refuge between the roots of the wistaria tree beside the terrace. Sadly, Timothy has no family. "Slow Date", a tortoise dating agency, was set up specially by nearby Crealy Adventure Park to provide him with partners but these liaisons proved fruitless.

KENTON
7 miles S of Exeter on the A379

Founded in Saxon times, this picturesque village is famed for its glorious 14th century church. The tower stands over 100ft high and is decorated with a wonderful assortment of ornate carvings. Inside, there is more rich carving in the south porch and in the Beer stone arcades of the nave. The pulpit is a 15th century original which was rescued and restored after it was found in pieces in 1866, and the massive rood screen, one of the finest in Devon, is a magnificent testimony to the 15th century woodcarver's art.

DUNCHIDEOCK
7 miles SW of Exeter on minor road off the A30

A beautifully located village, Dunchideock hugs the sides of a deeply-sloping combe. At the northern end, the modest red sandstone church of St Michael has an unusual number of noteworthy internal features. There's a medieval font, a set of carved pew ends and a richly-carved rood screen which at one point makes a surprising diversion around three sides of an octagonal roof column. Amongst the monuments is one to Major-General Stringer Lawrence, the "Father of the Indian Army", who in 1775 left a legacy of £50,000 to his lifelong friend, Sir Robert Palk. Palk proceeded to build himself a mansion,

THE DOLPHIN INN,

Fore Street, Kenton, Exeter EX6 8LD
Tel/Fax: 01626 891371

With its colourful hanging baskets and creamwashed walls **The Dolphin Inn** is a sight to gladden the heart of any weary traveller. Standing in the heart of this picturesque village close to the Exe estuary, The Dolphin is a 17th century building with an enclosed courtyard garden and the eye-catching exterior of this grand old inn makes it hard to miss. Much larger inside than the road frontage would initially suggest, the interior displays a wealth of beams and gleaming brassware. The key feature of the comfortable lounge bar is the magnificent cast iron open fire range, complete with bread oven, that adds a warm glow and homely touch to this pleasant place during the winter. Here, visitors and locals alike can enjoy not only the relaxed atmosphere but also an excellent pint or two of real ale from the bar.

Whilst ensuring that all the drinks here reach her customers in tip top condition, landlady Helen Savory has also gained an enviable reputation for the inn's restaurant. Head chef Keith Ratcliffe, who is well known locally, offers menus which are particularly inviting. As the inn is so close to the sea, fish and seafood are specialities although the menu also includes an interesting and imaginative choice of both meat and vegetarian dishes. Everything is cooked to order and the selection of home made sweets is too tempting to miss. For less formal dining, there is the equally appetising bar snacks menu and also a carvery area on Wednesday and Sunday lunchtimes and on Saturday evenings. In good weather, customers can enjoy their refreshments in the attractive courtyard garden.

The well-kept village itself is a pleasant place to wander around and its grand 14th century church is one of the glories of Devon. With its battlements, turrets and pinnacles, the exterior looks something like a castle (the numerous gargoyles excepted). Inside there's a wonderful carved and painted screen of 1455 which, it's been estimated, has an eighth of a mile of intricate carving and 150 bosses. Another treasure is the beautifully carved pulpit, also 15th century, which incredibly was discarded in the early 1800s and only re-installed a century later.

Also well worth a visit is nearby Powderham Castle, home of the Earls of Devon since 1390. Set in a deer park beside the River Exe, the present castle is mostly 18th century and contains some fine interiors, a breathtaking Grand Staircase and historic family portraits, some of them by Sir Joshua Reynolds, a Devon man himself.

Haldon House, half a mile to the south, along with a folly in memory of his benefactor. Known locally as Haldon Belvedere, or Lawrence Castle, this tall triangular structure stands on the summit of Haldon Ridge and can be seen for miles around.

CREDITON
8 miles NW of Exeter on the A377

Very few Britons have managed to become fully-fledged Saints, so Crediton is rather proud that one of this small and distinguished group was born here in 680AD. The infant was baptised with the name Wynfrith but on becoming a monk he adopted the name Boniface. He rose swiftly through the ranks of the Benedictine Order and in 731 was sent by the Pope to evangelise the Germans. Boniface was remarkably successful, establishing Christianity in several German states. At the age of 71, he was created Archbishop of Mainz but three years later, he and 53 members of his retinue were ambushed and murdered. They were on their way to the great monastery at Fulda in Hesse

Statute of St Boniface, Crediton

THE LORD HALDON COUNTRY HOUSE HOTEL,

Dunchideock, Exeter, Devon EX6 7YF
Tel: 01392 832483 Fax: 01392 833765

An historic building, magnificent countryside and superb cuisine make a stay at **The Lord Haldon Country House Hotel** an experience to remember. The original house was built in 1737 and became the country seat of the Lords of Haldon. The present building is a fragment of that huge mansion but the beautiful views created by Capability Brown can still be enjoyed, as can the peace and tranquillity of this quiet corner of Devon. The house was acquired by the Preece family in 1978 and since then it has been sympathetically refurbished to provide its guests with the service and hospitality of a quality 3-star country house hotel.

Superb cuisine, boasting an AA red rosette and served at night by candlelight, is on offer in The

Chandelier Restaurant where many of the tables overlook the courtyard and the countryside beyond. Menu selections are changed daily to ensure only the freshest products are used. All bedrooms at the Lord Haldon are en suite and have been individually furnished and tastefully decorated, with many of them enjoying lovely views over the Devon countryside. For that extra touch of luxury and romance, book one of the 4-poster bedrooms and make your stay even more memorable.

THE WHITE LION INN,

26 High Street, Bradninch, Exeter,
Devon EX5 4QL
Tel: 01392 881263

Once an important town, larger than Exeter, built on the wealth of the woollen trade and lace industry, Bradninch is also a popular place with American visitors as Daniel Boone was christened here. Now a quiet place, well situated in the heart of the glorious Devon countryside yet close to the motorway and numerous places of interest, Bradninch is also the home of **The White Lion Inn**. Built in 1640, this attractive centrally placed pub has a long frontage that makes it hard to miss. Inside, it is as cosy as every country pub should be. It is owned by Chris and Maggie Stobbart-Rowlands who have not only created a warm and pleasant atmosphere since they arrived here in October 1999 but are also fast gaining a reputation for the good food that is on offer.

In the delightful surroundings of the pub's large open bar, complete with a splendid inglenook fireplace and a display of pictures and paintings by local artists, visitors can enjoy a quiet drink from the wide-ranging selection. The delicious home cooked food includes game dishes in season and a full à la carte menu. Fresh local produce is an essential ingredient although there are many different styles of cuisine on offer - from old-fashioned steak pie to Thai curry. With equally excellent accommodation available and a charming terraced beer garden, this is definitely a place to seek out.

BICKLEIGH MILL,

Bickleigh, Tiverton, Devon EX16 8RG
Tel: 01884 855419 Fax: 01884 855416

Since it was acquired in June 1999 by Ann and Nigel Way (who also own the well known Royal Castle Hotel in Dartmouth, **Bickleigh Mill** has become one of the area's most popular out of town eating and shopping venues. The Mill stands in an idyllic wooded valley in an area of outstanding natural beauty which also happens to be the almost exact centre of Devonshire. There was a mill here when the Domesday Book was compiled but the present building dates back to 1840. The waterfall and its mechanics are still in perfect working order and open, free, to the public. Bickleigh Mill provides a perfect day out for all the family. There's a thriving Restaurant, a Gift Shop stocked with all kinds of crafts,gifts and clothing, a resident potter, and an exhibition gallery. Children love the pets farm with its pony rides and the 'Amazing Maze in Maize' and there are some delightful riverside and woodland walks.

The cosy and welcoming restaurant is managed by Hilary Saunders who has earned an excellent reputation for her catering and culinary expertise. She and her team prepare meals based on local produce - game, meat and seasonal vegetables, and their home made cakes and puddings are out of this world. During the warmer months, the garden lawn by the river is an ideal place to relax and enjoy al fresco eating as the resident tame peacocks strut by. On Friday and Saturday evenings, the restaurant is open for candlelit suppers and the menu changes regularly.

Church of the Holy Cross, Crediton

from the time of Edward VI until 1859 when it moved to its present site at the west end of the High Street.

CADBURY
10 miles N of Exeter off the A3072

To the north of this delightful hamlet is **Cadbury Castle**, actually an Iron Age fort. It was built high on the hilltop, about 700ft above sea level, and it's claimed that the views here are the most extensive in Devon. On a good day Dartmoor and Exmoor are in full view, and the Quantocks and Bodmin Moor can also be seen. A little more than a mile away stands **Fursdon House** which has been lived in by the Fursdon family since around 1260. The varied architecture reflects the many additions made over the centuries. Some fascinating family memorabilia, including old scrapbooks, are on display, there's an excellent collection of 18th century costumes and textiles, and amongst the family treasures is a letter from Charles I written during the Civil War. Opening times are restricted: for more details phone 01392 860860.

BRADNINCH
9 miles N of Exeter on minor road off the B3181

This pleasant little village stands on what used to be the main Exeter to Taunton road but that traffic now sweeps past on the M5, about a mile to the east. It has a striking parish church with a crenellated tower spouting gargoyles and, inside, a magnificent 16th century rood screen. Beautifully coloured in gleaming red, blue and gold, it stretches right across the building.

BICKLEIGH
12 miles N of Exeter on the A396

Running due north from Exeter, the Exe Valley passes through the heart of what is known as "Red Devon". The soil here has a distinctive colour derived from the red Permian rocks that underlie it. Unlike most Devon land, this is prime agricultural land, fertile, easily-worked and, for some reason, particularly favourable to growing swedes to which it gives a much sought-after flavour.

One of the most charming villages in the Exe Valley is Bickleigh. With its riverside

which Boniface had founded and where he was now laid to rest.

Boniface was greatly revered throughout Germany and a few years later the Pope formally pronounced his sanctification, but it was to be almost 1200 years before the town of his birth accorded him any recognition. Finally, in 1897, the people of Crediton installed an east window in the town's grand, cathedral-like **Church of the Holy Cross** depicting events from his life. A few years later, a statue of the saint was erected in the gardens to the west of the church.

The interior of the early-15th century church is especially notable for its monuments which include one to Sir John Sully who fought alongside the Black Prince and lived to the age of 105, and another to Sir William Peryam, a commissioner at the trial of Mary, Queen of Scots. Most impressive of all, though, is the richly ornamented arch in memory of Sir Henry Redvers Buller, commander-in-chief during the Boer War and the hero of the Relief of Ladysmith. Also of interest is the Lady Chapel of 1300 which housed Crediton's famous grammar school

GOTHAM,

Bakers Hill, Tiverton, Devon EX16 5NE
Tel: 01884 253568

A traditional 15th century Devon farmhouse, **Gotham** is set in delightful surroundings less than a mile from the market town of Tiverton. With its thatched roof and whitewashed walls, Gotham is as pretty as a picture, but practical with it. Part of the property has been converted into self catering facilities - the 3 bedrooms can accommodate 5 people and an extra bed or a cot is available if required. There's a kitchen/dining room with oil-fired Aga, a comfortable sitting room with TV and video, a bathroom with bath and shower, and a small back room with washing machine and drier. And for sunny days, there's a lawn for sitting out.

LOWER COLLIPRIEST FARM,

Tiverton, Devon EX16 4PT
Tel/Fax: 01884 252321
e-mail: linda@lowercollipriest.co.uk
website: www.lowercollipriest.co.uk

Although only a mile or so from Tiverton town centre, Lower Collipriest Farm is wonderfully peaceful and relaxing. The lovely old farmhouse is one of the largest thatched buildings in the area and is unique in being built around a courtyard garden, unlike most Devon longhouses. It's the home of Linda Olive who has been offering quality bed and breakfast accommodation here since the mid-1970s. The spacious, warm and comfortable bedrooms are all en suite, enjoy views over the farm and down the valley, and are well-equipped with radio alarm, toiletries, magazines and books. The lounge also has a marvellous view and for colder evenings, a glowing log fire. Dinner is optional but strongly recommended - delicious fresh cooking based on local produce, especially prize-winning cheeses and cream.

Guests can take a Land Rover ride over the working dairy farm, travelling past woodland with many tree varieties and abundant wildlife, and a pond with wild ducks, moorhens and visiting Canada geese. Exmoor and Dunkery Beacon are visible from the highest point on the farm. The farmhouse faces the River Exe where 2 stretches of fishing are available to guests and they are also encouraged to see the cows being milked and all aspects of the farm. The farm also has goats, calves, chickens, dogs and a cat for those not brave enough to visit the cows!

setting and picturesque thatched cottages with lovingly-tended gardens, Bickleigh is one of Devon's most photographed villages. It also boasts two of the area's most popular attractions. Bickleigh Mill has been developed as a craft centre and farm stocked with rare breeds, while across the river is **Bickleigh Castle,** actually a moated and fortified manor house with an impressive gatehouse dating back to the late 1300s. Even older is the detached chapel which was built in the 11th century. Exhibits include Tudor furniture, (including a massive 4-poster), some fine oil paintings, and a Civil War Armoury. The nearby 17th century farmhouse is very atmospheric with its inglenook fireplaces, oak beams and ancient bread ovens. The castle is open daily from the late spring Bank Holiday until the first Sunday in October, and at any time for pre-booked groups.

TIVERTON
16 miles N of Exeter on the A396

The only town of any size in the Exe valley is Tiverton, originally *Twyfyrde*, or two fords, for here the Exe is joined by the River Lowman. The town developed around what is now its oldest building, **Tiverton Castle,** built at the command of Henry I in 1106. Unfortunately, the castle found itself on the wrong side during the Civil War. General Fairfax himself was in charge of the successful onslaught in 1645. A few years later Parliament decreed that it should be "slighted", destroyed beyond any use as a fortification. Cromwell's troops observed the letter of their instructions, sparing those parts of the castle which had no military significance, and leaving behind them a mutilated, but still substantial, structure.

During the Middle Ages, the citizens of Tiverton seem to have had a very highly-developed sense of civic and social

responsibility. Throughout the town's golden age as a wool town, from the late 1400s until it reached its zenith in the 18th century, prosperous wool merchants put their wealth to good use. Around 1613, George Slee built himself a superb Jacobean mansion in St Peter Street, the **Great House,** and in his will bequeathed the huge sum of £500 to establish the **Slee Almshouses** which were duly built right next door. Later almshouses, founded by John Waldron (in Welbrook Street), and John Greenway (in Gold Street) are still in use. As well as funding the almshouse, John Greenway also devoted another sizeable portion of his fortune to the restoration of **St Peter's Church** in 1517. He added a sumptuous porch and chapel, their outside walls richly decorated with carvings depicting sailing ships of the time.

Peter Blundell chose a different method of demonstrating his beneficence by endowing Tiverton with a school. It was in the **Old Blundell's School** building of 1604, by the Lowman Bridge, that the author R.D. Blackmore received his education. He later used the school as a setting for the first chapter of his novel, *Lorna Doone.* Now a highly-regarded public school, "Blundell's" moved to its present location on the edge of town in 1880.

The more one reads of Devon in the early to mid-18th century, the more one becomes convinced that there must have been a serial arsonist abroad. So many Devonshire towns

Knighthayes Court

MANOR MILL HOUSE,

Bampton, Devon EX16 9LP
Tel: 01398 332211 Fax: 01398 332009
e-mail: stay@manormill.demon.co.uk
website: www.manormill.demon.co.uk

Offering a choice of bed & breakfast or self-catering accommodation, **Manor Mill House** is a delightful place to stay. It was built originally as a miller's house in the early 1600s and boasts a wealth of character with features such as old beams, inglenook fireplaces and log fires. To add to the appeal, it also enjoys a riverside location. The house stands virtually in the centre of Bampton, a typical Devon village famous for its floral displays and annual Pony Fair in October. Manor Mill House is now the home of Chris and Kathy Ayres who assure their visitors that "whatever your desire, whatever the weather" a warm welcome and a pleasant stay is guaranteed!

The Ayres have carefully restored the house to provide some really cosy, comfortable accommodation. There are 3 luxury en suite bedrooms with a choice of twin, double, king-size beds - or even a four

poster bed. Each room has a colour TV and tea/coffee-making facilities and a laundry room is available. There are good eating places close by so the Ayres do not offer evening meals unless they are specifically requested. For those who prefer self-catering, Mill Cottage is also very cosy and comfortable, with a double bedroom, bathroom, beamed lounge/dining room and fully equipped kitchen with dishwasher. Electricity and central heating is included in the price and there is ample parking. Please note that all rooms in Manor Mill House and Mill Cottage are non-smoking.

THE WHITE HORSE,

Fore Street, Bampton, Devon EX16 9ND
Tel: 01398 331245

Bampton is a peaceful little place set beside the River Batherm, a tributary of the Exe. The village regularly wins awards for its floral displays and the surrounding countryside is rich pasture land grazed by sheep and cattle. Atop a hill to the north once stood Bampton Castle but the site is now marked only by a stand of trees. Bampton's normally tranquil atmosphere is disrupted for a while in late October when the Exmoor Pony Sales take place.

Located at the heart of this appealing village **The White Horse Inn** is also at the heart of the community. It was once a coaching inn and the old courtyard is now an inviting beer garden where you can enjoy one of the real ales, perhaps, and tuck into the wholesome, value for money pub food on offer - a good range of choices that includes pies, pasties and sandwiches. Inside, there's a public bar with pool and darts available, and a separate children's room which doubles as a function room. In addition there are seven letting bedrooms available.

The local Hunt meets at the White Horse which is why there are lots of hunting trophies displayed around the inn. An inglenook fireplace and old-fashioned window seats all add to the olde-worlde atmosphere. Collectors of curiosities, incidentally, will want to visit the parish church where there's a memorial to a young boy who was "killed by icicle" in 1776.

during this period suffered devastating fires. Tiverton's conflagration occurred in 1731, but one happy outcome of the disaster was the building of **St George's Church,** by common consent the finest Georgian church in the county, furnished with elegant period ceilings and galleries.

A quay on the south-eastern edge of Tiverton marks the western end of the Grand Western Canal which was built in the early 1800s with the idea of linking the River Exe to Bridgewater and the Bristol Channel. It was never fully completed and finally closed in 1920. But in recent years, an attractive stretch from Tiverton quay to the Somerset border has been restored and provides a pleasant easy walk.

About 4 miles north of Tiverton, on a minor road off the A396 is **Knightshayes Court** (National Trust), a striking Victorian Gothic house designed by William Burges and now the home of the Heathcoat-Amory family. The interior displays an opulent combination of medieval romanticism and lavish decoration, and the 20 hectares of gardens provide a dazzling show of colour throughout spring, summer and autumn.

Knightshayes Court is open from Easter to October, but closed on Fridays.

BAMPTON
21 miles N of Exeter on the B3190/B3227

In medieval times Bampton was quite an important centre of the wool trade but it's now best known for its annual **Exmoor Pony Sale,** held in late October. Throughout the rest of the year, though, it's a wonderfully peaceful place with some handsome Georgian cottages and houses, set beside the River Batherm, a tributary of the Exe. To the north of the village, a tree-crowned motte marks the site of Bampton Castle. Bampton's parish church of St Michael and All Angels is popular with collectors of unusual memorials. A stone on the west side of the tower replicates a memorial of 1776 which records the strange death of the parish clerk's son who was apparently killed by a falling icicle. The inscription is remarkably insensitive and reads:

> *Bless my I I I I I I (eyes),*
> *Here he lies,*
> *In a sad pickle,*
> *Killed by an icicle.*

2 | East Devon and the Heritage Coast

Coastline, Beer

No less a traveller than Daniel Defoe considered the landscape of East Devon the finest in the world. Acres of rich farmland are watered by the rivers Axe, Otter and Madford, and narrow, winding lanes lead to villages that are as picturesque and interesting as any in England. Steep-sided hills rise towards the coastline where a string of elegant Regency resorts remind the visitor that this part of the coast was one of the earliest to be developed to satisfy the early-19th century craze for sea bathing.

For the purposes of this chapter, East Devon covers the area east of the M5 up to the borders of Dorset and Somerset. Bounded by the rolling Blackdown Hills to the north, and Lyme Bay to the south, much of the countryside here is designated as of outstanding natural beauty. The best, and for much of the route, the *only* landward way to explore the glorious East Devon coastline is to follow the South West Coast Path, part of the 600-mile South West Peninsula Coast Path which starts at Minehead in Somerset and ends at Shell Bay in Dorset.

Although comprising only a small part of the county, the area boasts one of Devon's finest churches, at Ottery St Mary; outstanding landscaped gardens at Bicton Park near Budleigh Salterton; and the extraordinary man-made feature of the Beer Quarry Caves. Cadhay Manor near Ottery St Mary, a masterpiece of English domestic architecture, is one of the few remaining Tudor mansions in the county, and the austere Loughwood Meeting House near Dalwood is believed to be the oldest surviving Baptist chapel in England.

East Devon's most famous son is undoubtedly Sir Walter Raleigh who was born at Hayes Barton near Yettington in 1552 and apparently never lost his soft Devon burr - a regional accent regarded then by 16th century London sophisticates as uncouth and much mocked by Sir Walter's enemies at the court of Elizabeth I. The Raleighs' family pew can still be seen in Yettington parish church. The famous picture by Sir John Everett Millais of *The Boyhood of Raleigh* was painted on the beach at Budleigh Salterton with the artist using his two sons and a local ferryman as the models.

EAST DEVON AND THE HERITAGE COAST

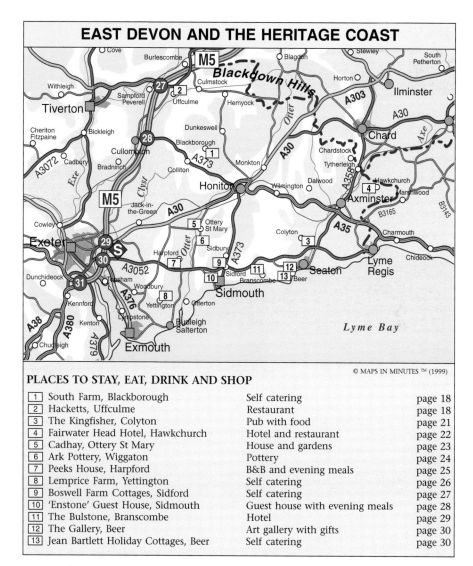

© MAPS IN MINUTES ™ (1999)

PLACES TO STAY, EAT, DRINK AND SHOP

1	South Farm, Blackborough	Self catering	page 18
2	Hacketts, Uffculme	Restaurant	page 18
3	The Kingfisher, Colyton	Pub with food	page 21
4	Fairwater Head Hotel, Hawkchurch	Hotel and restaurant	page 22
5	Cadhay, Ottery St Mary	House and gardens	page 23
6	Ark Pottery, Wiggaton	Pottery	page 24
7	Peeks House, Harpford	B&B and evening meals	page 25
8	Lemprice Farm, Yettington	Self catering	page 26
9	Boswell Farm Cottages, Sidford	Self catering	page 27
10	'Enstone' Guest House, Sidmouth	Guest house with evening meals	page 28
11	The Bulstone, Branscombe	Hotel	page 29
12	The Gallery, Beer	Art gallery with gifts	page 30
13	Jean Bartlett Holiday Cottages, Beer	Self catering	page 30

HONITON

Honiton is the "capital" of east Devon, a delightful little town in the valley of the River Otter and the "gateway to the far southwest". It was once a major stopping place on the Fosse Way, the great Roman road that struck diagonally across England from Lincoln to Exeter. Honiton's position on the main traffic artery to Devon and Cornwall brought it considerable prosperity, and its broad, ribbon-like High Street, almost two miles long, testifies to the town's busy past. By the 1960s, this "busyness" had deteriorated into appalling traffic congestion during the holiday season. Fortunately, the construction of a by-pass in the 1970s allowed Honiton to resume its true character as an attractive market town.

Surrounded by sheep pastures, Honiton was the first town in Devon to manufacture serge cloth, but the town became much better known for a more delicate material, Honiton lace. Lace-making was introduced to east Devon by Flemish immigrants who arrived

SOUTH FARM

Blackborough, Cullompton, Devon EX15 2JE Tel: 01823 681078 Fax: 01823 680483
e-mail: chapmans@southfarm.co.uk website: www.southfarm.co.uk

Set in 40 picturesque acres of the Blackdown Hills, South Farm is a delightful place in which to enjoy a self-catering holiday. The 5 comfortable cottages are surrounded by woodland and rolling farmland with uplifting views that extend as far as Exmoor. Cattle and sheep graze the land and the farm's owners, Sue and Barry Chapman, also keep chickens, goats and Vietnamese pot-bellied pigs. The amenities provided at South Farm are quite exceptional. There are 4 well-stocked fishing lakes, one third to two thirds of an acre each, stocked with carp (to double figures), roach to 3.5 pounds, tench, chub and perch. Guests can also take advantage of the all weather tennis court and if it dares to rain there's a games barn with badminton, table tennis, barbecue, wood-burning stove and space! The

really energetic will love the Health Studio with its exercise machines, spa and sauna, and there's also a 40 x 20ft outdoor pool which is heated during the summer months.

Originally farm buildings, the five holiday cottages are set in a courtyard, each in a position of peace and tranquillity. Comfortable and well-equipped, each cottage has a television, microwave, shower and bath. Outside, there's a patio table and chairs from which to enjoy the view and barbecues are available. The Chapmans believe that South Farm is a very special place and make every effort to ensure that their guests feel the same!

HACKETTS,

7 High Street, Uffculme, Devon EX15 3AB
Tel: 01884 841663

A large village of attractive Georgian and Victorian houses, Uffculme lies in the valley of the River Culm and was once an important centre for the wool trade. Just to the west of the village, the early-19th century Coldharbour Mill has been converted into a Working Wool Museum where visitors can follow the whole process of manufacturing wool and worsted. The village boasts another visitor attraction in the form of **Hacketts Restaurant**, located on the corner of the High Street. It's the creation of Vicky Hackett, a young and enthusiastic lady with a dedication to providing imaginative, wholesome and appetising food for her customers. Vicky describes her cuisine as traditional English with Continental

"twists". So among the main dishes you'll find both Rump Steak and a vegetarian Spaghetti with roasted peppers and olives in a cream & basil sauce.

Formerly a shop, the restaurant has two rooms, both of them attractively decorated with lovely prints and photographs of local scenes. Crisp linen tablecloths and quality crystal add to the charm. There's also a small lounge area for pre-dinner drinks and for studying the extremely well-chosen wine list. Hacketts is open for morning coffee (10.30-12 noon, Tuesday to Friday); lunch (12 noon-14.00, Tuesday to Saturday; from 12.30 on Sunday); and for dinner (19.00- last orders 20.30, Wednesday to Saturday). Private dining and outside catering are also available.

here during the early years of the reign of Elizabeth I. It wasn't long before anyone who could afford this new costly material was displaying it lavishly as a signal of their wealth and status. By the end of the 17th century, some 5000 people were engaged in the lace-making industry, most of them working from their own homes making fine "bone" lace by hand. Children as young as five were sent to "lace schools" where they received a rudimentary education in the three Rs of Reading, (W)Riting, and (A)Rithmetic, and a far more intensive (and commercially rewarding to their employers) instruction in the skills of lace-making. Almost wiped out by the arrival of machine-made lace in the late 1700s, the industry was given a new lease of life when Queen Victoria insisted upon Honiton lace for her wedding dress and created a new fashion for lace that persisted throughout the 19th century. The traditional material is still made on a small scale in the town and can be found on sale in local shops, and on display in **Allhallows Museum**. This part-15th century building served as a school for some 300 years but is now an interesting local museum housing a unique collection of traditional lace and also, during the season, giving daily demonstrations of lace making.

Allhallows Schoolroom was one of the few old buildings to survive a series of devastating fires in the mid-1700s. However, that wholesale destruction had the fortunate result that the new buildings were gracious Georgian residences and Honiton still retains the pleasant, unhurried atmosphere of a prosperous 18th century coaching town.

Another building which escaped the flames unscathed was **Marwood House** in the High Street. It was built in 1619 by the second son of Thomas Marwood, one of Queen Elizabeth's many physicians. Thomas achieved great celebrity when he managed to cure the Earl of Essex after all others had failed. (He received his Devonshire estate as a reward). Thomas was equally successful in preserving his own health, living to the extraordinary age of 105.

Some buildings on the outskirts of the town are worth a mention. **St Margaret's Hospital**, to the west, was founded in the middle ages as a refuge for lepers who were denied entry to the town itself. Later, in the 16th century, this attractive thatched building was reconstructed as an almshouse.

To the east, an early-19th century toll house known as **Copper Castle** can be seen. The castellated building still retains its original iron toll gates. And just a little further east, on Honiton Hill, stands the massive folly of the **Bishop's Tower**, erected in 1842 and once part of Bishop Edward Copplestone's house.

AROUND HONITON

To the north of Honiton lies an irregular diamond-shaped area of countryside whose northern edge is bounded by the M5 and the Somerset border. This area of gently undulating farmland tends to be overlooked by visitors, yet it contains some delightful rural settlements and isolated farms. Unlike the rolling hills which characterise much of the rest of Devon, here the landscape is a high, flat-topped plateau which is sliced into long fingers by a series of south-flowing rivers. On the northern edge of Honiton lies the National Trust-owned **Dumpdon Hill**, an 850ft high steep-sided outcrop which is crowned by a sizeable late-Iron Age fort. Both the walk to the summit and the views over the Otter Valley are breathtaking.

BLACKBOROUGH
10 miles NW of Honiton off the A373

Most of the villages in this corner of East Devon nestle in the valley bottoms, but Blackborough is an exception, standing high on a ridge of the Blackdown Hills. It's a comparatively new settlement which sprang up when whetstone mining flourished here for a period in the early 1800s. R.D. Blackmore's novel *Perlycross* presents a vivid picture of life in these makeshift mining camps where the amenities of a comfortable life were few and far between.

UFFCULME
13 miles NW of Honiton off the A38

In medieval times, the charming little village of Uffculme, set beside the River Culm, was an important centre for the wool trade. Profits from this booming business helped build the impressive parish church of St Mary around 1450 and to install its splendid rood screen, believed to be the longest in Devon. **Coldharbour Mill**, to the west of the village, is one of the few surviving reminders of the county's industrial wool trade. It closed down in 1981 but has since been converted into a Working Wool Museum where visitors can watch the whole process of woollen and worsted manufacture, wander around the carpenter's workshop, a weaver's cottage and the dye room. On most Bank Holidays, the massive 300 horsepower engine in the boiler house is "steamed up" - a spectacular site. Conducted tours are available and the complex also includes a Mill Shop and a waterside restaurant.

CULMSTOCK
14 miles NW of Honiton on the B3391

Lovers of R.D. Blackmore's novel *Lorna Doone* will be particularly interested in Culmstock since it was here that the author lived as a boy during the years that his father was the Vicar. One of his playmates in the village was Frederick Temple, another bright boy, and the two friends both went on to Blundell's School at Tiverton where they shared lodgings. Blackmore was to become one of the most successful novelists of his time; Temple entered the church and after several years as Headmaster of Rugby School reached the pinnacle of his profession as Archbishop of Canterbury.

In the centre of the village stands Culmstock's parish church with its famous yew tree growing from the top of the tower. The tree has been growing there for more than 200 years and, despite the fact that its only nourishment is the lime content of the mortar in which it is set, the trunk has now achieved a girth of 18 inches. It's believed that the seed was probably carried up in the mortar used to repair the tower when its spire was demolished in 1776. The church's more traditional kind of treasures include a magnificently embroidered cope of the late 1400s, now preserved in a glass case; a remarkable 14th century tomb rediscovered during restoration in the 19th century; and a richly-coloured memorial window designed by Burne-Jones.

About 3 miles east of Culmstock is **Hemyock Castle**, built around 1380. Four turrets, a curtain wall, a moat with mallard and moorhen in residence, and a dungeon are all that remains of the Hidon family's sturdy manor house, but it is a peaceful and evocative place. The castle stands behind the church in beautiful grounds and, since it lies close to the head of the lovely Culm valley, is very popular as a picnic spot. Opening times are variable, but are normally weekend and Bank Holiday afternoons in the season, and also Tuesday and Thursday afternoons during July and August.

DUNKESWELL
5 miles N of Honiton on minor road off the A30

From Hemyock Castle, a pleasant country lane leads past **Dunkeswell Abbey**, of which only the 15th century gatehouse survives, the rest of the site now occupied by a Victorian church of no great charm. A couple of miles further and the road climbs up the hillside to Dunkeswell itself. This little village lies in the heart of the Blackdown Plateau and its main claim to fame is a 900-year-old Norman font in St Nicholas' Church on which is carved a rather crude depiction of an elephant, the earliest known representation of this animal in England. Almost certainly the stonemason had never seen such a beast, but he made almost as good a fist of it as he did with his satirical carvings of a bishop and a doctor. The font was originally located in Dunkeswell Abbey, a Cistercian foundation whose ruins stand a couple of miles north of the village.

DALWOOD
6 miles E of Honiton on minor road off the A35

By some administrative freak, until 1842 the little village of Dalwood, despite being completely surrounded by Devon, was actually part of Dorset. It's other main claim to fame is as the home of the **Loughwood Meeting House**, one of the earliest surviving Baptist chapels in the country. When the chapel was built in the 1650s, the site was hidden by dense woodland, for the Baptists were a persecuted sect who could only congregate in out of the way locations. Under its quaint thatched roof, this charming little building contains a simple whitewashed interior with early 18th century pulpits and pews. The chapel was in use until 1833, then languished for many years until it was acquired by the National Trust in 1969. It is now open all year round with admission by voluntary donation.

About 3 miles south of Dalwood is another National Trust property, **Shute Barton**, an exceptional example of a medieval manor house which dates from the 1380s. Only two wings of the original building have survived, but they include some remarkably impressive features such as the Great Hall with its massive beamed ceiling, and the ancient kitchen with a huge range capable of roasting an ox whole. Entry is by way of a Tudor gatehouse. Shute Barton was owned by the Pole family, a local dynasty which is commemorated by some grand monuments in **St Michael's Church**, amongst them an overbearing memorial to Sir William Pole which depicts the Master of the Household to Queen Anne standing on a pedestal dressed in full regalia. More appealing is the 19th century sculptured panel, seven feet high and framed in alabaster, which shows Margaret Pole greeting her three little daughters at the gates of heaven.

COLYTON
7 miles SE of Honiton off the A3052

Those alighting from the **Seaton Tram** at Colyton will find an ancient and very appealing small town of narrow winding streets and interesting stone houses.

Throughout its long history, Colyton has been an important agricultural and commercial centre with its own corn mill, tannery, sawmill and iron foundry.

Many of the older buildings are grouped around the part-Norman **Church of St Andrew**, a striking building with an unusual 15th century octagonal lantern tower, and a Saxon cross brilliantly reconstructed after its broken fragments were retrieved from the tower where they had been used as building material. Nearby is the Vicarage of 1529, and the Old Church House, a part-medieval building enlarged in 1612 and used as a Grammar School until 1928.

Look out also for the **Great House** which was built on the road to Colyford by a wealthy Elizabethan merchant. Half a mile to the north of Colyton, **Colcombe Castle** contains some exceptional 16th and 17th century remains, including an impressive kitchen hearth.

AXMINSTER
10 miles E of Honiton on the A35/A358

This little town grew up around the junction of two important Roman roads, the Fosse and

THE KINGFISHER,
Dolphin Street, Colyton, Devon EX24 6NA
Tel: 01297 552476

Located in the heart of Colyton, a peaceful town just a short distance from the coast, **The Kingfisher** is a relaxing and friendly family-run public house. A warm and hospitable welcome is guaranteed from owners Graeme and Cherry and their son Iain. Father and son run the 'front of house' while Cherry oversees the excellent food. The interior boasts traditional features such as low-beamed ceilings and exposed walls, all adding to the cosy and welcoming ambience. The menu offers a wealth of options from sandwiches and salads to steaks, chicken, seafood and a range of daily specials. Food is served daily from midday to 1.45pm and from 7 to 9.30pm. A Free House, The Kingfisher offers a choice of 4 real ales from local brewers as well as a good selection of wines and spirits.

This cheerful one-time coaching inn dates back to the 16th century when it was known as The Globe. One of its early landlords took part in the Battle of Sedgemoor in 1685 and later escaped from Exeter Gaol. In 2000, the inn hosted a Rebellion Day with groups in period costumes re-enacted scenes from that uprising against James II. Graeme hopes that this will become an annual event. A more frequent activity at the inn is skittles - The Kingfisher boasts no fewer than 8 skittles teams!

FAIRWATER HEAD COUNTRY HOUSE HOTEL

Hawkchurch, Devon EX13 5TX
Tel: 01297 678349
Fax: 01297 678459

Set in glorious open countryside 'where Dorset meets Devon', the Fairwater Head Country House Hotel exudes peace and tranquillity. Approached down leafy lanes, the impressive Edwardian house stands in gardens that have been awarded the accolade of being one of the ten best hotel gardens in England. From springtime onwards the grounds are a succession of bloom, with some interesting trees and shrubs. The terrace is a sun trap and there are garden seats in sheltered corners where you can relax and breathe in the pure Devon air.

The drawing room is provided with a plentiful supply of interesting books and periodicals or you can settle down in the Garden Lounge and enjoy the wonderful views across the Axe Valley. Great

attention is paid to the cuisine on offer at Fairwater. The dinner menu offers a wide choice of table d'hôte and à la carte dishes, tailored for both conservative and more adventurous tastes. The table d'hôte menu, comprising 4 courses, is changed daily to ensure your appetite never wanes and all menus make the most of local fare. Special diets or vegetarian dishes receive the same care in preparation. No wonder Fairwater has received a red rosette from the AA for culinary excellence. Wine, too, is a Fairwater speciality and the well-balanced wine list has earned an Ashley Courtenay wine cellar award.

Naturally, the light and airy bedrooms include every facility you would expect - even fresh Devon milk for your tea or coffee. All rooms have a full en suite bathroom, complete with bath and thermostatic shower, with the exception of 1 single room which has a large shower in place of a bath. There are 4 ground floor rooms in the main building and just across the driveway lies the Garden Wing whose particularly restful rooms enjoy great popularity.

Fairwater is surrounded by idyllic walking and riding country, with many footpaths and bridleways. Wild flowers and wildlife abound in this part of deepest Devon. The picturesque village of Hawkchurch - 'the village of roses', is a leisurely 15-minute stroll away, whilst from the ancient hill fort of Lamberts Castle, about 1.5 miles down the lane, the view extends across 5 counties on a clear day. Many sporting opportunities exist nearby and include golf at Lyme Regis (just 6 miles distant) with reduced green fees for Fairwater residents, horse riding for all abilities, clay pigeon shooting, tennis in the village and deep-sea or trout fishing. Yours hosts will gladly furnish you with more choices of destination than the length of your holiday could possible enable you to visit!

the Icknield, and was important in medieval times for its Minster beside the River Axe. Its name has entered the language as the synonym for a very superior kind of floor-covering which first appeared in the early 1750s. Wandering around London's Cheapside market, an Axminster weaver named Thomas Whitty was astonished to see a huge Turkish carpet, 12 yards long and 8 yards wide. Returning to the sleepy little market town where he was born, Thomas spent months puzzling over the mechanics of producing such a seamless piece of work. By 1755 he had solved the problem, and on Midsummer's Day that year the first of these luxurious carpets was revealed to the world. The time and labour involved was so prodigious that the completion of each carpet was celebrated by a procession to St Mary's Church and a ringing peal of bells. Ironically, one distinguished purchaser of an Axminster carpet was the Sultan of Turkey who in 1800 paid the colossal sum of £1000 for a particularly fine specimen. But the inordinately high labour costs involved in producing such exquisite hand-tufted carpets crippled Whitty's company. In 1835, their

looms were sold to a factory at Wilton. That was the end of Axminster's pre-eminence in the market for top-quality carpets, but echoes of those glorious years still reverberate. St Mary's Church must be the only house of worship in Christendom whose floor is covered with a richly-woven carpet, and a new factory in Woodmead Road is now busy making 20th century Axminster carpets. Visitors are welcome.

OTTERY ST MARY
7m SW of Honiton on the B3177

The glory of Ottery St Mary is its magnificent 14th century **Church of St Mary.** From the outside, St Mary's looks part mini-Cathedral, part Oxford college. Both impressions are justified since, when Bishop Grandisson commissioned the building in 1337, he stipulated that it should be modelled on his own cathedral at Exeter. He also wanted it to be *"a sanctuary for piety and learning"*, so accommodation for 40 scholars was provided.

The interior is just as striking. The church's medieval treasures include a brilliantly-coloured altar screen, canopied tombs, and a

CADHAY,

Ottery St Mary, Devon EX11 1QT
Tel/Fax: 01404 812432
e-mail: cadhay@eastdevon.net
www.eastdevon.net/cadhay

"John Haydon, esquire, sometime bencher of Lincoln's Inn, builded at Cadhay a fair new house and enlarged his demesnes". So wrote Risdon in his Survey of Devon, published in 1620. In fact the main part of the present house was built around 1550 and it remains in all essentials unchanged. Approached by an avenue of limes, Cadhay stands in a pleasant listed garden and looks out over the original medieval fish-ponds which may well have been used by the Warden and Canons of the lovely Collegiate Church of St Mary of Ottery just a mile or so distant.

When John Haydon built his impressive mansion he retained the Great Hall of an earlier building on the site and its fine timber roof, built between 1420-1470, is still in place. In the early 1600s, Haydon's great nephew, Robert Haydon, added an Elizabethan Long Gallery thus forming a unique and attractive courtyard. It's known as the Court of Sovereigns because of the four statues of Henry VIII, Edward VI, Mary and Elizabeth which stand over the doors. Robert Haydon had married Joan, the eldest daughter of Sir Amias Poulett and interestingly the present owners of Cadhay, the William-Powletts are also descended from Sir Amias. You may well find one of them taking you on the conducted tour of the house. Cadhay and its gardens are open to the public on the Spring and Late Autumn Bank Holiday Sunday and Monday, then each Tuesday, Wednesday and Thursday during July and August.

Collegiate Church, Ottery St Mary

14th century astronomical clock showing the moon and the planets which still functions with its original machinery.

Ottery's Vicar during the mid-18th century was the Rev. John Coleridge whose 13th child became the celebrated poet, Samuel Taylor Coleridge. The family home near the church has since been demolished but in one of his poems Samuel recalls

"my sweet birth-place, and the old church-tower Whose bells, the poor man's only music, rang From morn to evening, all the hot Fair-day".

A bronze plaque in the churchyard wall honours Ottery's most famous son. It shows his profile, menaced by the albatross that features in his best-known poem, *The Ancient Mariner.*

It's a delight to wander around the narrow, twisting lanes that lead up from the River Otter, admiring the fine Georgian buildings amongst which is an old wool manufactory by the riverside, a dignified example of early industrial architecture. An especially interesting time to visit Ottery is on the Saturday closest to November 5th. The town's Guy Fawkes celebrations include a time-honoured, and rather alarming, tradition of rolling barrels of flaming tar through the narrow streets.

ARK POTTERY,

Higher Barnes, Wiggaton,
Ottery St Mary EX11 1PY
Tel/Fax: 01404 812628

Situated in a rural hamlet of picturesque cottages, **Ark Pottery** operates from an attractive former dairy building adjacent to the potters' 16th century Devon longhouse. This is a studio with a difference: though small, it maintains an approachable and friendly atmosphere. The Pottery has now been established for more than a quarter of a century. Its two founders, the artist/potters Vaughan and

Angela Glanville, endeavour to offer the unusual, designing and making a wide variety of ceramics both serious and amusing.

Open throughout the year, visitors can browse in the pottery shop, watch demonstrations or have a go on the wheel. Commissions are welcomed, and work ranges from indoor and outdoor sculpture through studio pottery to a range of animal figures. There are sometimes exhibitions of sculpture, photography and other artwork. The site, formerly a farm, offers tranquillity, free entrance and parking.

THE EAST DEVON HERITAGE COAST

Three river valleys, those of the Axe, the Sid and the Otter, cut through the hills of east Devon to meet the sea at Lyme Bay. They provide the only openings in the magnificent 20-mile long stretch of rugged cliffs and rocky beaches. Virtually the only settlements to be found along the seaboard are those which developed around the mouths of those rivers: Seaton, Sidmouth and Budleigh Salterton. The intervening cliffs discouraged human habitation and even today the only way to explore most of this part of the coast is on foot along the magnificent **South West Coast Path.** For centuries these little towns subsisted on fishing and farming until the early 1800s when the Prince Regent's fad for sea bathing brought an influx of comparatively affluent visitors in search of healthy relaxation. Their numbers were augmented by others whose accustomed European travels had been rendered impossible by Napoleon's domination of the Continent. Between them, they transformed these modest little towns into fashionable resorts, imbuing them with an indefinable "gentility" which still lives on in the elegant villas, peaceful gardens and wide promenades. We begin this exploration of the Heritage Coast at the most westerly of these civilized retreats, Budleigh Salterton.

BUDLEIGH SALTERTON
12 miles SE of Exeter, on the B3178

With its trim Victorian villas, broad promenade and a spotlessly clean beach flanked by 500ft high red sandstone cliffs, Budleigh Salterton retains its 19th century atmosphere of a genteel resort. Victorian

PEEKS HOUSE,

Harpford, Sidmouth, Devon EX10 0NH
Tel/Fax: 01395 567664 e-mail: peekshouse@FSBDial.co.uk

Harpford village nestles between the Otter River and Harpford Woods, an area popular with walkers, and the East Devon Way passes through the hamlet. Peeks House is an elegant Regency Grade II listed house, although parts of it are probably 16*th* century, and with its modern comforts, and warm and friendly atmosphere, it provides a perfect base for a relaxed holiday in this lovely part of the county. Your hosts, Fiona and Brian Rees, enjoy a well-earned reputation for excellent service and wonderful hospitality as a glance through the Visitors Book confirms. Their guests have the use of a comfortable, attractively furnished lounge and the 4 bedrooms have a 4-diamond rating. All the bedrooms are centrally heated, have a proper bathroom, i.e. one with a full size bath with a thermostatic shower above, and are equipped with easy chairs, remote control colour TV, radio alarm, hair dryer and drinks-making facilities. Double and twin rooms are available. Peeks House has a residential drinks

licence, serves dinner by prior arrangement and other amenities include a pay phone and private parking. Please note that the house has no facilities for children, pets or smokers.

Harpford village itself is noted for its 12th century church whose one-time Vicar, the Rev. Augustus Toplady, wrote the hymn Rock of Ages. Visitor attractions nearby include a riverside walk, Killerton House with its beautiful 18th century gardens, the 1000-year-old little town of Ottery St Mary, Bicton Gardens with its 63 acres of historic gardens, and the City of Exeter, renowned for its Norman cathedral.

tourists "of the better sort" noted with approval that the two-mile long beach was of pink shingle rather than sand. (Sand, apparently, attracted the rowdier kind of holiday-maker). The steeply-shelving beach was another deterrent, and the sea here is still a place for paddling rather than swimming.

One famous Victorian visitor was the celebrated artist Sir John Everett Millais who stayed during the summer of 1870 in the curiously-shaped house called **The Octagon**. It was beside the beach here that he painted his most famous picture *The Boyhood of Raleigh*, using his two sons and a local ferryman as the models.

The name Budleigh Salterton derives from the salt pans at the mouth of the River Otter which brought great prosperity to the town during the Middle Ages. The little port was then busy with ships loading salt and wool, but by 1450 the estuary had silted up and the salt pans flooded.

HARPFORD
7 miles N of Budleigh Salterton off the A3052

Attractively located on the east bank of the River Otter with wooded hills behind, Harpford has a 13th century church with an impressive tower and, in its churchyard, a memorial cross to the Rev. Augustus Toplady who was vicar of Harpford for a couple of

years in the mid-1700s. In 1775 Augustus wrote the hymn *Rock of Ages, cleft for me*, which has proved to be one of the most durable contributions to English hymnody.

If you cross the footbridge over the river here and follow the path for about a couple of miles you will come to **Aylesbeare Common**, an R.S.P.B. sanctuary which is also one of the best stretches of heathland in the area. Bird watchers may be lucky enough to spot a Dartford Warbler, Stonechats, or Tree Pipits, and even hear the strange song of the Nightjar.

YETTINGTON
3 miles NW of Budleigh Salterton off the B3178

Just to the south of the village of Yettington is **Hayes Barton**, a fine E-shaped Tudor house in which Sir Walter Raleigh was born in 1552. The Raleighs' family pew can still be seen in All Saints' Church, dated 1537 and carved with their (now sadly defaced) coat of arms. The church also contains a series of more than fifty 16th century bench-ends which were carved by local artisans into weird and imaginative depictions of their various trades.

A mile or so in the other direction is **Bicton Park**, best known for its landscaped gardens which were laid out in the 1730s by Henry Rolle to a plan by André Le Nôtre, the designer of Versailles. There is also a formal

LEMPRICE FARM,

Yettington, Budleigh Salterton,
Devon EX9 7BW
Tel: 01395 567037 Fax: 01393 569585

Lemprice Farm is situated in the beautiful Otter Valley, close to sea and moor. The hamlet of Yettington is adjacent to Woodbury Common, in an Area of Outstanding Natural Beauty. The setting of the Cottage is peaceful and idyllic, with a small lake and paddocks in front and open countryside beyond. Surrounding villages have a good choice of pubs, often specialising in fresh fish dishes. Many villages and farms have

Saxon origins and are a delight to explore. Sir Walter Raleigh was born on the neighbouring farm.

The Cottage is part of a National Award Winning barn conversion. An upside down house with 2 double bedrooms, very large sitting room, exposed beams and a small enclosed garden. The views are wonderful. The farmstead is home to many interesting birds, including a resident pair of rare Barn Owls, Tawny and Little Owls, kingfishers and nightjars. Badger and deer visit the lake at night. There's excellent birdwatching with hides from the Otter and Exe estuaries nearby. Bring binoculars!

Italian garden, a remarkable palm house known as **The Dome**, a world-renowned collection of pine trees, and a lake complete with an extraordinary summer house, **The Hermitage**. Its outside walls are covered with thousands of tiny wooden shingles, each one individually pinned on so they look like the scales of an enormous fish. Inside, the floors are made from deer's knucklebones. The Hermitage was built by Lady Louise Rolle in 1839 as an exotic summer-house; any occupation during the winter would have been highly inadvisable since the chimney was made of oak.

OTTERTON
3 miles NE of Budleigh Salterton off the B3178

This delightful village has a charming mix of traditional cob and thatch cottages, along with other buildings constructed in the distinctive local red sandstone, amongst them the tower of St Michael's parish church. Nearby stands a manor house which was built in the 11th century as a small priory belonging to Mont St Michel in Normandy. It is now divided into private apartments.

The Domesday Book recorded a mill on the River Otter here, almost certainly on the site of the present **Otterton Mill**. This handsome, part-medieval building was restored to working order in the 1970s by Desna Greenhow, a teacher of Medieval Archaeology, and visitors can now buy packs of flour ground by the same methods that were in use long before the compilers of the Domesday Book passed through the village. The site also includes a craft centre, shop and restaurant.

An interesting feature of this village of white thatched cottages is the little stream that runs down Fore Street. At the bottom of the hill, this beck joins the River Otter, which at this point has only a couple of miles to go before it enters the sea near Budleigh Salterton. There's a lovely riverside walk in that direction, and if you go northwards the path stretches even further, to Ottery St Mary some nine or ten miles distant.

SIDBURY
6 miles S of Honiton, on the A375

St Peter & St Giles' church at Sidbury boasts the unique amenity of a Powder Room, although in this case the room over the porch contained not cosmetics, but gunpowder which was stored there by the military during the fearful days when Napoleon was expected to land in England at any moment. The church is also notable for its Saxon crypt, rediscovered during restoration in 1898 - a rough-walled room just nine feet by ten located under the chancel floor. Other treasures include a remarkable 500-year-old font with a square iron lock intended to protect the holy water in the basin from witches, and a number of curious carvings on the Norman tower.

Above the village to the southwest stands **Sidbury Castle**, not a castle at all but the site of a hilltop Iron Age fort from which there are some spellbinding views of the coastline extending from Portland Bill to Berry Head.

SIDFORD
7 miles S of Honiton on the A375

As the name suggests, Sidford stands beside a narrow stretch of the River Sid - one of England's shortest rivers. Rising from spring-fed waters to the east of Ottery St Mary, the

BOSWELL FARM COTTAGES

Sidford, nr Sidmouth, Devon EX10 0PP
Tel/Fax: 01395 514162

Boswell Farm Cottages have all been lovingly converted from former farm buildings at this working farm nestling beside the Snod Brook (Snod incidentally is a medieval word meaning 'pretty'!). They enjoy breathtaking views over this Area of Outstanding Natural Beauty and each cottage has a private garden with its own garden furniture. Many of the original features have been retained and add to the charm of these beautifully furnished and well-equipped holiday cottages.

'ENSTONE' GUEST HOUSE,

Lennox Avenue, Sidmouth, Devon EX10 8TX
Tel: 01395 514444

Bright and appealing with its whitewashed walls and pink brick facings, 'Enstone' Guest House looks immediately inviting. It stands in its own grounds which extend to the bank of the River Sid and include a children's play area and attractive features such as the sun patio and the arched walkway to the riverside. Not surprisingly the garden won an award in 1999 for its carefully thought out design and colourful display. The proprietors, Suzanne and Kurt Osswald, provide a warm, friendly atmosphere in which guests can relax in homely surroundings. Kurt is the cook, noted for his generous breakfasts and his 4-course evening meal which can cater for vegetarian and other dietary requirements with advance notice. Meals are taken in the dining room overlooking the garden.

There's a spacious and comfortable residents' lounge with colour television, and all the non-smoking bedrooms are light and pleasant and tastefully decorated, with comfortable beds, central heating, electric fires, and close to bathroom and toilet facilities. 'Enstone' is quietly situated at the end of a residential cul de sac, yet it's only a few minutes level walk to Sidmouth's Regency town centre with its floral displays, clean beaches, esplanade and bus route. The Norman Lockyer Observatory and famous Donkey Sanctuary are both close by, while the historic city of Exeter is just a 30 minute drive away.

Sid tumbles and twists down a narrow valley for a mere four miles or so before spilling into Lyme Bay at Sidmouth. The suburbs of Sidmouth now flank a couple of miles of the valley of the River Sid but Sidford still stands apart at the end of a half mile cul-de-sac off the main road.

SIDMOUTH
8 miles S of Honiton off the A3052

Sidmouth's success, like that of many other English resorts, had much to do with Napoleon Bonaparte. Barred from the Continent and their favoured resorts by the Emperor's conquest of Europe, the leisure class classes were forced to find diversion and entertainment within their own island fortress. At the same time, sea bathing had suddenly become fashionable so these years were a boom time for the south coast, even as far west as Sidmouth which until then had been a poverty-stricken village dependent on fishing.

Sidmouth's spectacular position at the mouth of the River Sid, flanked by dramatic red cliffs soaring to over 500ft and with a broad pebbly beach, assured the village's popularity with the newcomers. A grand Esplanade was constructed, lined with handsome Georgian houses, and between 1800 and 1820 Sidmouth's population doubled as the aristocratic and well-to-do built substantial "cottages" in and around the town. Many of these have since been converted into impressive hotels such as the Beach House, painted strawberry pink and white, and the Royal Glen which in the early 19th century was the residence of the royal Duke of Kent. The Duke came here in 1819 in an attempt to escape his numerous creditors, and it was here that his infant daughter, Princess Victoria, later Queen Victoria, saw the sea for the first time.

The Duke had retired to Sidmouth to escape his many creditors and, attempting to evade their attentions, he had his mail directed to Salisbury. Each week he would ride there to collect his letters but in Sidmouth itself he couldn't conceal his delight in his young daughter. He would push Victoria in a little carriage along the mile-long Regency Esplanade, stopping passers-by

Coastline at Sidmouth

to tell them to look carefully at the little girl - "for one day she would be their Queen". Half a century later, his daughter presented a stained-glass window to Sidmouth parish church in dutiful memory of her father.

A stroll around the town reveals a wealth of attractive Georgian and early-Victorian buildings. Amazingly for such a small town, Sidmouth boasts nearly 500 listed buildings. Curiously, it was the Victorians who let the town down. Despite being the wealthiest nation in the world at that time, with vast resources at its command, its architects seemed incapable of creating architecturally interesting churches and the two 19th century Houses of the Lord they built in Sidmouth display a lamentable lack of inspiration. So ignore them, but it's worth seeking out the curious structure known as the **Old Chancel**, a glorious hotch-potch of styles using bits and pieces salvaged from the old parish church and from just about anywhere elsewhere, amongst them a priceless window of medieval stained glass.

Also well worth a visit is **Sidmouth Museum**, near the sea-front, which provides a vivid presentation of the Victorian resort, along with such curiosities as an albatross's swollen foot once used as a tobacco pouch. There's also an interesting collection of local prints, a costume gallery and a display of fine lace.

One of the most striking exhibits in the museum is the "Long Picture" by Hubert

THE BULSTONE,

Higher Bulstone, Branscombe, Devon EX12 3BL
Tel/Fax: 01297 680446

Anyone with young children will know how difficult it is to find a suitable holiday hotel. The Bulstone, parts of which date back to the 16th century, is specifically designed and equipped for such families, providing all the facilities they need to maintain their family routines and ensuring that Mother gets a holiday too! A brilliant idea. The hotel is located in the lovely Old World village of Branscombe where badgers outnumber people. Set in over 3 acres and surrounded by fields, The Bulstone offers comfortable accommodation in attractive, well-appointed bedrooms which have been carefully designed to be practicable and safe for those with very young children. Each family unit or suite has a Master Bedroom, an adjoining children's room and bathroom.

The hotel has a Playroom equipped with toys, games and books for all ages and, outside, a play area with swings, climbing frame and other toys.

The Bulstone's owners, Judith and Kevin Monaghan, have been assiduous in providing everything a family could wish for. There's a kitchen with laundry facilities, a separate sitting room where adults only can relax in front of a log fire, another separate Television Lounge, and a licensed bar. Families eat breakfast together but tea is for children only. It's always a cooked meal with alternatives for those who do not want the dish of the day. Adults dine later.

THE GALLERY,

Fore Street, Beer, Devon EX12 3JB
Tel: 01297 20153

Located in the main street of this enchanting little fishing town, **The Gallery** offers an outstanding range of original paintings and prints. Dora Grigg first started her gallery as part of a restaurant in the town but in 1971 moved to the present premises which date back to 1700. A member of the Fine Art Guild, Dora stocks a wide variety of paintings and prints by well-known artists like David Shepherd and Lawrence Coulson but also a large selection of works by up and coming local artists such as Andrew Coates, George Horne and Paul Butler.

Dora always make sure that she has the latest selection of David Shepherd

prints in stock. Also very popular are paintings of the local area. In addition, The Gallery offers a wide choice of fine china, glass, silverware and quality cards. A short walk from The Gallery is the picturesque cove set between the high white chalk cliffs of Beer Head and Seaton Hole that has made the town itself a popular subject for artists over many years. Traditional fishing boats drawn up on the pebble beach have provided many painters with a natural focus for their attractive seascapes.

JEAN BARTLETT COTTAGE HOLIDAYS

The Old Dairy, 7 Fore Street, Beer, Devon EX12 3JA
Tel: 01297 23221 Fax: 01297 23303

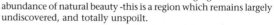

Located on the beautiful East Devon Heritage Coast in the charming fishing village of Beer, **Jean Bartlett Cottage Holidays** offers a carefully chosen selection of quality self-catering accommodation to suit all tastes and pockets. This family run agency, established since 1980, is owned and staffed by friendly 'locals' who know each property inside and out and are always happy to share their local

knowledge. Medieval manor houses, thatched country cottages, beachside apartments and working farmhouses, each with a style and personality of its own, are available to accommodate from 1 to 20 guests. Properties are selected for their quality, style and location and are all regularly inspected, lovingly cared-for and well equipped for a comfortable self-catering holiday.

This tranquil part of the world has a magical charm which once discovered, is rarely forgotten. Experience the unique spirit of East Devon and West Dorset - hidden coves with clear waters, rolling countryside with ever-changing colours and dramatic cliffs which offer challenging walks and an abundance of natural beauty -this is a region which remains largely undiscovered, and totally unspoilt.

Jean Bartlett Cottage Holidays provides accommodation throughout the year and the team will be happy to help you choose a dream holiday property. Whether you want cliff top walks in Autumn sunshine, Springtime bike rides with colourful hedgerows, deckchair dreams on a Summers day or a Winter warming log fire - there is something for everyone to discover here.

Your dream is just a telephone call away – let us make your holiday easy!

Cornish which is some 8ft (2.4 metres) long and depicts the whole of Sidmouth seafront as it was around 1814.

Demure though it remains, Sidmouth undergoes a transformation in the first week of August each year when it plays host to the International Folklore, Dance and Song Festival, a cosmopolitan event which attracts a remarkable variety of Morris Dancers, Folk Singers and even Clog Dancers from around the world.

Beer Shore

BRANSCOMBE
7 miles E of Sidmouth on minor road off the A3052

The coastal scenery near Branscombe is some of the finest in the south west with great towers of chalk rising from overgrown landslips. The village is a scattering of farmhouses and cottages with an interesting National Trust property within its boundaries - **Branscombe Manor Mill, Old Bakery and Forge**. Regular demonstrations are held at the Manor Mill which is still in working order. The water-powered mill provided flour for the adjacent bakery which, until 1987, was the last traditional bakery operating in Devon. Its vintage baking equipment has been preserved and the rest of the building is now a tea-room. The Forge is still working and the blacksmith's ironwork is on sale to visitors.

BEER
11 miles E of Sidmouth on the B3174

Set between the high white chalk cliffs of Beer Head and Seaton Hole, this picturesque fishing village is best known for the superb white freestone which has been quarried here since Roman times. Much prized for carving, the results can be seen in countless Devon churches, and most notably in the cathedrals at Exeter, Winchester, and St Paul's, as well as at the Tower of London and in Westminster Abbey. Conducted tours around the vast, man-made complex of the **Beer Quarry Caves** leave visitors astonished at the sheer grandeur of the lofty halls, vaulted roofs and

massive supporting pillars of natural stone. Not surprisingly, this complex underground network recommended itself to smugglers, amongst them the notorious Jack Rattenbury who was a native of Beer and published his *Memoirs of a Smuggler* in 1837.

SEATON
6 miles E of Sidmouth on the B3172

Set around the mouth of the River Axe, with red cliffs on one side and white cliffs on the other, Seaton was once a quite significant port. By the 16th century, however, the estuary had filled up with stones and pebbles, and it wasn't until moneyed Victorians came and built their villas (and one of the first concrete bridges in the world, in 1877) that Seaton was accorded a new lease of life. The self-confident architecture of those times gives the little town an attractive appearance which is enhanced by its well-maintained public parks and gardens.

From Seaton, an attractive way of travelling along the Axe Valley is on the **Seaton Tramway**, whose colourful open-topped tramcars trundle through an area famous for its bird life to the villages of Colyford and Colyton. The three mile route follows the course of the River Axe which is noted for its abundant wild bird life. Really dedicated tram fans, after a short lesson, are even permitted to take over the driver's seat.

3 The "English Riviera"

If you think Torbay's claim to be "The English Riviera" is a mite presumptuous, just take a look at all those palm trees. You see them everywhere here: not just in public parks and expensively maintained hotel gardens, but also giving a Mediterranean character to town house gardens, and even growing wild. They have become a symbol of the area's identity, blazoned on tourism leaflets, brochures, T-shirts, shop fronts, key-rings and hats.

The first specimen palm trees arrived in Britain in the 1820s and it was soon discovered that this sub-tropical species took kindly to the genial climate of South Devon. Today, there are literally thousands of them raising their spiky tufted heads above the more familiar foliage of English gardens. To the uninitiated, one palm tree may look much like another, but experts will point out that although the most common variety growing here is Cordyline Australis (imported from New Zealand), there are also Mediterranean Fan Palms, Trachycarpus Fortunei from the Chusan Islands in the East China Sea, and Date Palms from the Canary Islands. The oldest palm tree on record in the area is now over 80 years old and more than 40ft high.

The Mediterranean similarities don't end there. Torquay, like Rome, is set on seven hills and the red-tiled roofs of its Italianate villas, set amongst dark green trees, would look equally at home in some Adriatic resort. The resemblance is so close that in one film in the Roger Moore television series, *The Saint,* a budget-conscious producer made Torquay double for Monte Carlo.

The Torbay area has two striking houses open to the public. Oldway

Brixham Harbour

Mansion in Paignton was built by the sewing-machine tycoon Isaac Singer in 1874 and exuberantly extended by his son Paris. Much older is Torre Abbey in Torquay, founded in 1195 but largely rebuilt between 1700 and 1750. As well as all the expected resort attractions, Torbay also offers visitors an outstanding Zoo at Paignton, a remarkable natural feature at Kent's Cavern in Torquay, and for steam railway fans a wonderful 7-mile journey along the coast from Paignton to Kingswear.

In this chapter we traverse the Land of the Palm Trees, tracing a route southwards from the south bank of the River Exe, at Dawlish, to the northern bank of the River Dart.

THE "ENGLISH RIVIERA"

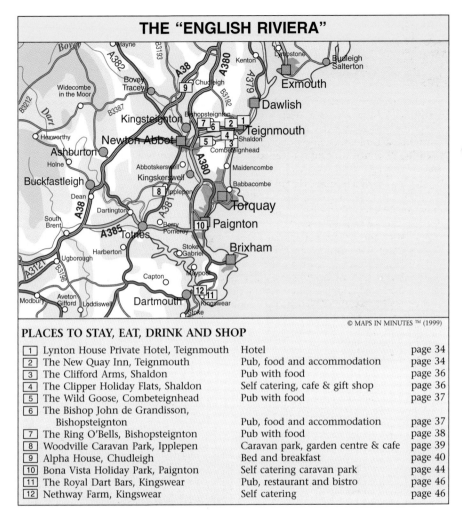

© MAPS IN MINUTES ™ (1999)

PLACES TO STAY, EAT, DRINK AND SHOP

1	Lynton House Private Hotel, Teignmouth	Hotel	page 34
2	The New Quay Inn, Teignmouth	Pub, food and accommodation	page 34
3	The Clifford Arms, Shaldon	Pub with food	page 36
4	The Clipper Holiday Flats, Shaldon	Self catering, cafe & gift shop	page 36
5	The Wild Goose, Combeteignhead	Pub with food	page 37
6	The Bishop John de Grandisson, Bishopsteignton	Pub, food and accommodation	page 37
7	The Ring O'Bells, Bishopsteignton	Pub with food	page 38
8	Woodville Caravan Park, Ipplepen	Caravan park, garden centre & cafe	page 39
9	Alpha House, Chudleigh	Bed and breakfast	page 40
10	Bona Vista Holiday Park, Paignton	Self catering caravan park	page 44
11	The Royal Dart Bars, Kingswear	Pub, restaurant and bistro	page 46
12	Nethway Farm, Kingswear	Self catering	page 46

DAWLISH

This pretty seaside resort, which boasts one of the safest beaches in England, has the unusual feature of a main railway line separating the town from its sea front. The result is, in fact, much more appealing than it sounds. For one thing, the railway keeps motor traffic away from the beachside, and for another, the low granite viaduct which carries the track has weathered attractively in the century and a half since it was built. The arches under which beach-goers pass create a kind of formal entrance to the beach and the Victorian station has become a visitor attraction in its own right.

By the time Brunel's railway arrived here in 1846, Dawlish was already well-known as a fashionable resort. John Keats, with his convalescent brother, Tom, had visited the town in 1818. The great poet was inspired to pen the less-than-immortal lines:

Over the hill and over the Dale
And over the bourne to Dawlish
Where Gingerbread wives have a scanty sale
And gingerbread nuts are smallish.

Other distinguished visitors included Jane Austen, (one of whose characters cannot understand how one could live anywhere else in Devon but here), and Charles Dickens, who, in his novel of the same name has Nicholas Nickleby born at a farm nearby. All

LYNTON HOUSE PRIVATE HOTEL,

Sea Front, Teignmouth, South Devon TQ14 8BL
Tel: 01626 774349

Occupying an ideal position overlooking the sea to the front
and the River Teign to the rear, **Lynton House Private Hotel** is a
strikingly elegant building with an interesting history. The house
is part of Powderham Terrace, an impressive example of Victorian
architecture erected in the 1860s by the Courtenay family, Earls
of Devon. Lynton House has been a hotel since at least 1930
and during World War II served as a social club for American
servicemen. Gill and Les Morris have owned the hotel for 19
years and offer visitors a very warm welcome.

Guests can relax in the elegant lounge bar, where huge
windows frame a grand view, and enjoy fine food in the spacious

dining room. Gill
and Les make every
effort to ensure that
meal-times are a
pleasure with only
the best of West
Country produce
used in the tasty home-cooked meals. The hotel has 12
guest bedrooms, all en suite, attractively decorated and
with most of them enjoying beautiful sea or river views.
For guests with mobility problems, there is a stair lift to
the first floor bedrooms.

THE NEW QUAY INN,

New Quay Street, Teignmouth, Devon TQ14 8DA
Tel: 01626774145

As the name suggests, **The New Quay Inn** stands
by the quayside, a magnificent position
commanding an ever-changing panorama of boat
traffic on the River Teign. Quayside picnic tables
provide an ideal vantage point. The building itself
is an impressive 3-storeyed, Georgian-style
structure with a rather grand pillared portal. It
once housed the Newfoundland Fishery Mission
before being converted into a hotel. Today's mine
hosts are John and Anne Mathews, a lively and

friendly couple who make every customer feel instantly welcome. John is a Cornishman through and

through. He and his forefathers used to live on the
dramatic island ofSt Michael's Mount, offMarazion in
Cornwall. John and Anne offer their customers good
food, quality ales and lashings of atmosphere. On Friday
and Saturday nights there's live music to enjoy, and
during the season an additional night is added. The New
Quay Inn's menu offers wholesome tavern food -steaks,
seafood and poultry dishes along with an All Day
Breakfast, light snacks, vegetarian and children's choices,
and sandwiches. The inn has 9 guest bedrooms, with a
choice of double, twin and single rooms available. A
hearty breakfast is included in the tariff which,
unusually, is constant throughout the year.

town, by landscaping the stream into a series of shallow waterfalls and surrounding it with attractive gardens like The Lawn. Until Regency times, The Lawn had been a swamp populated by herons, kingfishers and otters. Then in 1808, the developer John Manning filled in the marshy land with earth removed during the construction of Queen Street. Today, both The Lawn and Queen Street still retain the elegance of those early-19th century days.

A couple of miles north of the town is **Dawlish Warren**, a mile-long sand spit which almost blocks the mouth of the River Exe. There's a golf course here and also a 55-acre Nature Reserve, home to more than 450 species of flowering plants. For one of them, the Jersey lily, this is its only habitat in mainland England. Guided tours of the Reserve, led by the Warden, are available during the season.

Railway enthusiasts will want to travel a couple of miles further to the village of Starcross to see the last surviving relic of Isambard Kingdom Brunel's **Atmospheric Railway**. The great engineer had intended that the stretch of railway between Exeter and Totnes should be powered by a revolutionary new system. The train would be attached to a third rail which in fact was a long vacuum chamber, drawing the carriages along by the effects of air pressure. His visionary plan involved the building of ten great Italianate engine houses at three mile intervals along the line. Sadly, the project was a failure, partly for financial reasons, but also because the leather seals on the vacuum pipe were quickly eaten away by the combined forces of rain, salt and hungry rats. The exhibition at Starcross displays a working model, using vacuum cleaners to represent the pumping houses, and volunteers are even propelled up and down the track to demonstrate the viability of the original idea.

Brunel had to fall back on conventional steam engines but the route he engineered from Exeter to Newton Abbot is one of the most scenic in the country, following first the western side of the Exe estuary, then hugging the seaboard from Dawlish Warren to Teignmouth before turning inland along the north bank of the River Teign.

AROUND DAWLISH

TEIGNMOUTH
3 miles SW of Dawlish on the A381 & A379

Teignmouth has something of a split personality. On the coastal side is the popular holiday resort with its 2 miles of sandy beaches, a splendid promenade almost as long, and a pier. There's also a 25ft high lighthouse which serves no apparent purpose apart from looking rather fetching. The residential area contains much fine Regency and Georgian building. Particularly noteworthy are the **Church of St James** with its striking octagonal tower of 1820, and the former **Assembly Rooms**, a dignified colonnaded building which now houses the Riviera Cinema. Teignmouth's Georgian past is recalled on Wednesdays during the season when local people dress up in 18th century costume.

On the river side of the town is the working port, approached by the narrowest of channels. The currents here are so fast and powerful that no ship enters the harbour without a Trinity House pilot on board. **The Quay** was built in 1821 with granite from the

Teignmouth Harbour

THE CLIFFORD ARMS,

34 Fore Street, Shaldon,
Devon TQ14 0DE
Tel: 01626 872311

From the outside, the **Clifford Arms** has a Mediterranean look with its gleaming white walls, astonishing floral displays and spiky palm trees. No wonder the inn is often featured as a "photo opportunity". But just step inside this handsome Georgian building and you couldn't be anywhere else but in a traditional English hostelry with lots of low, dark beams, cosy settles and old-fashioned lamps. A free house, the Clifford Arms is owned and run by Hilary and Gary Twydell who have been in the hospitality business for some 20 years but only arrived here in the spring of 2000. They offer an extensive à la carte and bar menu, supplemented by daily specials listed on the blackboard. Food is served every day from noon until 2pm, and again from 6.30pm to 9.30pm, except on Mondays out of season. Patrons can complement their meal with a selection of real ales, (a selection which has earned the inn an entry in the *Good Beer Guide*), plus a wide choice of lagers, cider and stout. If the sun is shining, you can enjoy your refreshments in the beer garden, and this child-friendly inn also provides a special children's room. And for grown-ups there's live entertainment on the first Thursday of each month, (more frequently during the winter), when all kinds of music are featured.

THE CLIPPER HOLIDAY FLATS,

Shaldon, South Devon TQ14 0DL
Tel: 01626 872477

Located at the mouth of the River Teign and looking across to Teignmouth, Shaldon is a handsome village with some attractive Regency houses in Fore Street and along Marine Drive. As well as the road link, a regular passenger ferry makes the short crossing to Teignmouth and south from Shaldon runs a magnificent stretch of the South Devon Coast Path. The

Clipper Holiday Flats occupy a prime position in the village, overlooking the busy little harbour with its colourful craft. The owners, Diana and Paddy McMahon have been welcoming guests here for almost 30 years and, not surprisingly, many of them are repeat visitors. There are 3 flats, all self contained, fully equipped and accommodating

up to 4 people. Each flat has a kitchen, lounge (with either 'fold-to-the-wall bed, or double bed-settee), twin bedroom and bathroom/toilet. Electricity is supplied by £1 coin meter and if you don't want to bring your own linen, you can hire it. Children are welcome, pets too by arrangement, and there is one dedicated parking space for each flat. The McMahons also provide two other convenient amenities: - a popular café serving wholesome food, and a gift shop with a varied array of souvenirs and gifts.

THE WILD GOOSE,

Combeteignhead, Newton Abbot, Devon TQ12 4RA
Tel: 01626 872241

Located at the head of a long valley running down to the River Teign, Combeteignhead is a charming village with an ancient church and hostelry standing side by side in the time-honoured manner of English villages. The pub is **The Wild Goose** which started life in the reign of Charles I as the homestead of a small farm known as Holman's. This is probably the reason why it was called the Country House Inn when it became a pub in about 1840. The name was changed to The Wild Goose in recent times but one bar window with the old title has survived. This outstanding hostelry is owned and run by Jerry and Kate English, a lively and friendly couple who have been in the hospitality business for some 25 years but feel that in The Wild Goose they have found their ideal pub. Children and dogs are welcome here, and there's plenty of

entertainment for the grown-ups - pool, darts, a cricket team, a traditional jazz night on Mondays, and quiz nights. Devotees of real ales will be delighted to learn that the inn was CAMRA's Pub of the Year in 1996 and that there's always a choice of at least 6 real ales on draught, several of them from small local breweries. The cuisine on offer is of equally high standard, with chef Darren creating an extensive menu of appetising, home cooked food with local delicacies such as fresh Brixham fish featuring wherever possible. Another attraction at The Wild Goose is the lovely walled garden which lies in a sunny and sheltered position beneath the 14th century tower of the ancient village church.

THE BISHOP JOHN DE GRANDISSON,

Clanage Street, Bishopsteignton, Devon TQ14 9QS
Tel: 01626 775285

Set in the heart of this attractive village, the **Bishop John de Grandisson** takes its name from the 14th century Bishop of Exeter who was responsible for building the extraordinary nave of Exeter Cathedral. The bishop knew Bishopsteignton well because he also enlarged the ancient bishop's palace on the outskirts of the village. Sadly, very little remains of that once glorious building but at least visitors can drink a toast to the great medieval builder at the welcoming old hostelry named in his honour. Your hosts, Mark and Anna, arrived here in the spring of 2000 and now offer their customers a fine selection of real ales (at realistic prices), and good pub food. Anna is in charge of the kitchen and her menu provides a choice of appetising home cooked dishes, supplemented by a wide selection of daily

specials. Food is available every lunchtime and evening, except Monday evening (unless it's a Bank Holiday). Children are welcome, there's a lovely beer garden, a games room and ample parking. About once a month, usually at the weekend, Mark and Anna arrange live entertainment for their customers - please ring for details. The inn also has 4 guest bedrooms, well-equipped and available at a static price throughout the year, which provide an excellent base for exploring the glorious Torbay area and the Dartmoor National Park.

quarries on Haytor Down. This durable stone was in great demand at the time. Amongst the many buildings constructed in Haytor granite were London Bridge, (the one now relocated to Lake Tahoe in California), and the British Museum. Teignmouth's main export nowadays is potter's clay, extracted from pits beside the River Teign, but boat building also continues, albeit on a small scale.

SHALDON
4 miles SW of Dawlish on the A379

Set on the southern bank of the Teign estuary, Shaldon's Marine Parade provides a grand viewpoint for watching the busy traffic sailing in and out of the river. A goodly number of Regency houses add architectural dignity to the town, a reminder of the era when affluent Londoners, unable to holiday in a Europe dominated by Napoleon, began to discover the gentle charms of south-western England. A more recent attraction for visitors is the **Shaldon Wildlife Trust's** breeding centre for rare small mammals, reptiles and exotic birds, just to the north of the town.

COMBETEIGNHEAD
6 miles SW of Dawlish off the A380 or A379

Standing across the river from Bishopsteignton, Combeteignhead is a charming village which John Keats came to know well when he was staying with his consumptive brother Tom at nearby Teignmouth in 1818. In a letter to his family he often enclosed scraps of "happy doggerel" like this:

Here all the summer I could stay,
For there's Bishop's Teign
And King's Teign
And Coomb at the clear Teign head -
Where close by the stream
You may have your cream
All spread upon Barley bread.

BISHOPSTEIGNTON
5 miles SW of Dawlish off the A381

This sizeable village overlooking the estuary of the River Teign is noted for its church which contains some of the finest Norman work in the county. There's a doorway carved

THE RING O'BELLS,

Fore Street, Bishopsteignton, Teignmouth, Devon TQ14 9QP
Tel: 01626 775468

Bishopstainton is a sizeable village with some pleasant Regency-style houses, a church with an extremely fine Norman doorway, and glorious views across the estuary of the River Teign. The village also boasts a notable pub, the **Ring O'Bells** which dates back to at least 1600 and could well be much older. It was originally a beer-house with a cottage next door that once housed the Liberal Club before both were transmuted into the present delightful hostelry.

The attractive interior with its ancient beams, stone walls and interesting local memorabilia dotted around the walls has a wonderfully olde-worlde atmosphere. Mine hosts, Brian and Jan Ainsworth, have been here since 1993 although their experience in the hospitality business stretches back nearly 20 years.

Open every lunchtime and evening, and all day on Friday and Saturday, the inn serves a full range of quality food daily - except on Thursdays when only basket meals are available. Sunday lunch is especially popular and booking is essential. This lively tavern hosts a fun quiz on Tuesday evenings, a music quiz on Fridays, and on Saturday evenings there's live entertainment, usually a soloist, from 9pm.

with 15 beak-heads, bunches of grapes, birds and a man with a sword. Equally impressive is the 900-year-old tympanum in the blocked south door which depicts the Adoration of the Magi.

NEWTON ABBOT

From Teignmouth, the A381 runs inland beside the river to Newton Abbot, an ancient market town which took on a quite different character in the 1850s when the Great Western Railway made it the centre of its locomotive and carriage repair works. Neat terraces of artisans' houses were built on the steep hillsides to the south; the more well-to-do lived a little further to the north in Italianate villas around Devon Square and Courtenay Park.

The town's greatest moment of glory was on November 5th, 1688 when William, Prince of Orange, "the glorious defender of the Protestant religion and the liberties of England" was first proclaimed King as William III. This climactic moment of the "Glorious Revolution" took place in front of St Leonard's Church of which only the medieval tower now remains. The new King had landed at Brixham and was on his way to London. Stopping off in Newton Abbot, he stayed at the handsome Jacobean manor, **Forde House**, which is now used as offices by the District Council.

On the western edge of the town stands **Bradley Manor** (NT), a notable example of medieval domestic architecture. Most of it dates from around 1420 and includes a chapel, Solar, Great Hall and porch. By the mid-1750s this quaint style of architecture was decidedly out of fashion and the building became a farmhouse - with poultry occupying the chapel.

AROUND NEWTON ABBOT

IPPLEPEN
5 miles S of Newton Abbot off the A381

The name of this large village is Celtic - Ippela's hill - and a mile or so to the north-west, crowning an extinct volcano, is the site

WOODVILLE CARAVAN PARK,

Totnes Road, Ipplepen, Newton Abbot, Devon TQ12 5TN
Tel: 01803 812240 Fax: 01803 813984 or 814072
e-mail: woodvillepark@lineone.net
website: caravan-sitefinder.co.uk/sthwest/devon/woodville.html

Barbara, a regular visitor to **Woodville Caravan Park** was so impressed with the site that she was inspired to poetry:

Just had another holiday
At Woodville Park, in Devon
It's such a pretty 'van site
And the nearest thing to Heaven.

Other visitors to this beautifully landscaped 3.5 acre site share her sentiments. Quiet and secluded, Woodville provides a perfect location for mature Caravanners looking for a peaceful and relaxing holiday at a site which is ideally situated for exploring the whole of South Devon. (Please note that Woodville is not suitable for children as ball games,

cycling, etc. are not allowed). The site offers panoramic views of Dartmoor and, since it faces southwest, takes maximum advantage of the summer sun. Each of the 25 spacious "all-weather" pitches is provided with electric hook-ups and is situated around a central lawned area where you'll also find the Pergola Bar-B-Q, a popular venue for friends to get together over a sizzling sausage! Another up-to-date amenity is the modern, spotlessly clean toilet and shower block which provides free hot water and has facilities for the less able. There's a boules/petanque pitch on site, an 18-hole golf course and driving range directly opposite, and right next door Fermoys Garden Centre sells everything from a litre of milk to a swimming pool and also has one of the most popular coffee shops in the area.

of Denbury fort, "the fort of the men of Devon". In Ipplepen itself, the most striking building is the 14th century church with its massive tower and, inside, some fine stained glass and a beautifully carved pulpit.

About 3 miles southeast of Ipplepen, **Compton Castle** (NT) dates back to the 1300s and in Elizabethan times was the home of Sir Humphrey Gilbert, Walter Raleigh's half brother and the coloniser of Newfoundland in 1583. Complete with battlements, towers and portcullis, the castle also boasts an impressive Great Hall, a solar and an ancient kitchen.

ABBOTSKERSWELL
2 miles SW of Newton Abbot, off the A381

A couple of miles south-west of Newton Abbot, the attractive village of Abbotskerswell lies peacefully just off the A381. Its lovely old **Church of St Mary the Virgin** still bears the scars of its ransacking by Henry VIII's Commissioners at the time of the Dissolution, and outside stands an Elizabethan lych-gate, believed to be the oldest in the country. When the lych-gate was built its purpose was to provide a sheltered resting place for coffins while awaiting the burial service.

At the time of the Domesday Book, the village was owned by the Abbot of Horton, in Dorset, which explains the first part of its name. The "Kerswell" part refers to watercress, a popular item in the medieval diet which grew here in water from a freshwater spring.

CHUDLEIGH
7 miles N of Newton Abbot off the A38

Activists who oppose the building of new roads will find little sympathy in this former coaching town on what used to be the main thoroughfare between Exeter and Plymouth. By the 1960s, the volume of traffic had reached unbearable levels, especially during the holiday season. Mercifully, the dual carriageway A38 now bypasses the little town and it is once again possible to enjoy Chudleigh's 14th century church, containing some fine memorials to the Courtenay family, and its former Grammar School nearby which was founded in 1668. (It is now a private house). It was at the coaching inn

ALPHA HOUSE,

11 Fore Street, Chudleigh, Newton Abbot, Devon TQ13 0HX
Tel: 01626 852691

Not many bed & breakfast establishments have a letter signed by Winston Churchill displayed in the hallway. **Alpha House** does. This attractive old building, parts of which date back some 400 years, was used a hospital during World War I and Churchill, as Minister for War, wrote to thank the then owners. Today, Alpha House is the home of Jean Smith who has lived here since 1987 and has been welcoming bed and breakfast guests for most of that time. Jean is fascinated by the history of the house. It once belonged to the church and later to the famous Bishop Lacy who also owned 16 other adjacent properties. But for modern day visitors perhaps the most intriguing feature of Alpha House is its hidden garden, an unexpected and huge expanse at the rear of the house. Beautifully tended, the garden is open to the public one day a year as part of the Millennium Gardens scheme. Residents, of course, can enjoy it throughout the year as well as a choice of 3 quality, double en suite rooms, all of which have 4-poster beds and tea/coffee-making facilities. Jean serves a hearty Devonshire breakfast complete with home made bread, home laid eggs and tomatoes from her greenhouse. Chudleigh is an ideal base for exploring South Devon - the Torbay beaches are only half an hour drive away, the lovely scenery of the Dartmoor National Park is on the very doorstep, and the historic city of Exeter with its shops, restaurants and riverside interests is a mere 6 miles away.

here that William of Orange stayed after his landing at Torbay. From one of the its windows, the new King addressed the good people of Chudleigh. His English was so bad however they were unable to understand what he was saying. They cheered him anyway. At the bottom of Clifford Street the old town mill has been imaginatively converted into the **Wheel Craft Workshop Centre**. Visitors climb up through the floors of the mill to see craft workshops and crafts for sale alongside the mill machinery. The most imposing feature of the mill is its huge waterwheel which has been meticulously restored.

Clifford Street is named after Sir Thomas Clifford, Lord Treasurer to Charles II and a member of the king's notorious Cabal, a secretive inner Cabinet. As was the custom then, Sir Thomas used his official position to amass a considerable fortune. This was later put to good use by his grandson who employed Robert Adam and Capability Brown to design **Ugbrooke House and Park**, a couple of miles southwest of Chudleigh and well worth visiting.

TORBAY

The most extensive conurbation in Devon, Torbay includes the three major towns of Torquay, Paignton and Brixham, strung around the deep indentation of Tor Bay. The excellent beaches and leisure facilities here have made it the county's busiest resort area, with a host of indoor and outdoor attractions on offer. Torquay is the more sophisticated of the three, with elegant gardens, excellent shops and a varied nightlife. Paignton prides

Elberry Cove, Torbay

itself as being "unbeatable for family fun", and Brixham is a completely enchanting fishing town where life revolves around its busy harbour.

TORQUAY

In Victorian times, Torquay liked to be known as "The English Naples", a genteel resort of shimmering white villas set amongst dark green trees and spread, like Rome, across seven hills. It was indisputably the West of England's premier resort with imposing hotels like the Imperial and the Grand catering for "people of condition" from across Europe. At one time, the town could boast more royal visitors to the square mile than any other resort in the world. Edward VII came here on the royal yacht *Britannia* and anchored in the bay. Each evening he would be discreetly ferried across to a bay beneath the Imperial Hotel and then conducted to the first floor suite where his mistress, Lily Langtry, was waiting.

The town's oldest building is **Torre Abbey**, founded in 1195 but largely remodelled as a Georgian mansion by the Cary family between 1700 and 1750. Within its grounds stand the Abbey ruins and the Spanish Barn, a medieval tithe barn so named because 397

Torre Abbey, Torquay

prisoners from the Spanish Armada were detained here in 1588. Torre Abbey was sold to Torbay Council in 1930 and, together with its extensive gardens, has been open to the public ever since. The principal reception rooms now house fine collections of

Agatha Christie Memorial Room, Torre Abbey

paintings (mostly Victorian, and including Holman Hunt's *The Children's Holiday*), silver, porcelain and glass. A suite of rooms at the Abbey is also reserved for civic receptions by the Mayor of Torbay. One of its most popular attractions is the **Agatha Christie Memorial Room** in the Abbot's Tower, containing fascinating memorabilia loaned by her daughter. Dame Agatha was born in Torquay in 1890 and the town has created an **Agatha Christie Mile** which guides visitors to places of interest that she knew as a girl and young woman growing up in the town.

Torquay Museum also has an interesting exhibition of photographs recording her life, as well as a pictorial record of Torquay over the last 150 years, and displays chronicling the social and natural history of the area. Amongst the Museum's other treasures are many items discovered at **Kents Cavern**, an astonishing complex of caves regarded as "one of the most important archaeological sites in Britain". Excavations in the 1820s

Cockington Church

revealed an remarkable collection of animal bones - the remains of mammoths, sabre-toothed tigers, grizzly bears, bison, and cave lions. These bones proved to be the dining-room debris of cave dwellers who lived here some 30,000 years ago, the oldest known residents of Europe. The caves are open daily, all year, offering guided tours, a sound and light show, a gift shop and refreshment room.

Just a mile or so from the town centre is **Cockington Village**, a phenomenally picturesque rural oasis of thatched cottages, a working forge, and the Drum Inn designed by Sir Edward Lutyens and completed in 1930. From the village there's a pleasant walk through the park to **Cockington Court**, now a Craft Centre and Gallery. Partly Tudor, this stately old manor was for almost three centuries the home of the Mallock family. In the 1930s they formed a trust to preserve "entire and unchanged the ancient amenities and character of the place, and in developing its surroundings to do nothing which may not rather enhance than diminish its attractiveness". The Trust has been

Torquay Harbour

Thatcher Rock, Torquay

spectacularly successful in carrying out their wishes.

About a mile north of Torquay is another village but this village is one-twelfth life size. **Babbacombe Model Village** contains some 400 models, many with sound and animation. Created by Tom Dobbins, a large number of the beautifully crafted models have been given entertaining names, "Shortback & Sydes", the gents hairdresser, for example, "Walter Wall Carpets" and "Jim Nastik's Health Farm". The site also contains some delightful gardens, including a collection of more than 500 types of dwarf conifer, a 1000ft model railway, an ornamental lake stocked with koi carp and much more.

AROUND TORQUAY

PAIGNTON
3 miles SW of Torquay, on the A379

Today, Torquay merges imperceptibly into Paignton, but in early Victorian times Paignton was just a small farming village, about half a mile inland, noted for its cider and its "very large and sweet flatpole cabbages". The town's two superb sandy

beaches, ideal for families with young children, were to change all that. A pier and promenade add to the town's appeal, and throughout the summer season there's a packed programme of specials events, including a Children's Festival in August, funfairs and various firework displays.

The most interesting building in Paignton is undoubtedly **Oldway Mansion**, built in 1874 for Isaac Singer, the millionaire sewing-machine manufacturer. Isaac died the following year and it was his son, Paris, who gave the great mansion its present exuberant form. Paris added a south side mimicking a music pavilion in the grounds of Versailles, a hallway modelled on the Versailles Hall of Mirrors, and a sumptuous ballroom where his mistress Isadora Duncan would display the new, fluid kind of dance she had created based on classical mythology. Paris Singer sold the mansion to Paignton Borough Council in 1946 and it is now used as a Civic Centre, but many of the splendid rooms (and the extensive gardens) are open to the public free of charge and guided tours are available.

An experience not to be missed in Paignton is a trip on the **Paignton and Dartmouth Steam Railway**, a seven mile journey along

Oldway Mansion, Paignton

The Harbour, Paignton

the lovely Torbay coast and through the wooded slopes bordering the Dart estuary to Kingswear where travellers board a ferry for the ten-minute crossing to Dartmouth. The locomotives and rolling stock all bear the proud chocolate and gold livery of the Great Western Railway, and on certain services you can wine and dine in Pullman style luxury in the "Riviera Belle Dining Train". During the peak season, trains leave every 45 minutes or so; for full details of services telephone 01803 555872.

Another major attraction in the town is **Paignton Zoo**, set in 75 acres of attractive botanical gardens and home to some 300 species of world animals. A registered charity dedicated to protecting the global wildlife heritage, the Zoo is particularly concerned with endangered species such as the Asiatic lions and Sumatran tigers which are now provided with their own forest habitat area, and orang utans and gorillas who roam freely on large outdoor islands, free from cages. The route of the Jungle Express miniature railway provides good views of these and many other animals.

Located on Goodrington Sands, **Quaywest** claims to be Britain's "biggest, best, wildest and wettest waterpark", with the hottest, highest and hairiest water slides in the country. Other amusements include go-karts, bumper boats, and crazy golf and the site also offers a choice of bars, restaurants and cafés.

BRIXHAM

9 miles S of Torquay, on the A3022

In the 18th century, Brixham was the most profitable fishing port in Britain and fishing is still the most important activity in this engaging little town, although the trawlers now have to pick their way between flotillas

BONA VISTA HOLIDAY PARK,

Totnes Road, Paignton, South Devon TQ4 7PZ
Tel: 01803 551971

Located in the heart of Torbay, **Bona Vista Holiday Park** is a small and homely holiday park nestling in rolling hills. The site is run by Mr and Mrs Hill, the resident proprietors who have been entertaining guests since 1986 - many of their visitors returning year after year. Bona Vista boasts some 13 caravans and 3 flats, laid out on a 1-acre site which includes a children's play area. All car parking is together at the front, leaving the park quiet and traffic free. The caravans are fully connected to mains services, with no charges made for gas or electricity. All caravans have flush toilets, colour TVs and fridges, with showers and fires available in all. They are fully equipped with crockery, cutlery and cooking utensils - all you need to bring is your own linen. Other amenities on the site include laundry facilities, further toilets and showers, and a payphone. The park is located just a few hundred yards from the local bus stop which serves the Plymouth to Torquay route, with scheduled stops at Paignton Zoo and the charming old town of Totnes. Special rates for 2 people in a 2-bedroom 6 berth. Dogs welcome.

of yachts and tour boats. On the quay there are stalls selling freshly caught seafood and around the harbour a maze of narrow streets where you'll find a host of small shops, tea rooms and galleries. From the busy harbour, there are regular passenger ferries to Torquay.

It was at Brixham that the Prince of Orange landed in 1688 to claim the British throne as William III. And in 1815, all eyes were focussed on the *Bellerophon*, anchored in the bay. On board was Napoleon Bonaparte, getting his only close look at England before transferring to the *Northumberland* and sailing off to his final exile on St Helena.

Brixham has another claim to fame because of its 19th century vicar of All Saints' Church, Henry Francis Lyte. During his last illness, in 1847, the Rev. Lyte composed what is perhaps the best known and best loved English hymn - *Abide with me*.

Brixham's lighthouse has been called "the highest and lowest lighthouse in Britain". The structure is only 15ft high, but beneath it

Berry Head, Brixham

is a 200ft high cliff rising at the most easterly point of Berry Head. The lighthouse stands within **Berry Head Country Park** which is noted for its incredible views (on a good day as far as Portland Bill, 46 miles away), its rare plants, (like the white rock-rose), and its colonies of sea birds such as fulmars and kittiwakes nesting in the cliffs. The Park also boasts the largest breeding colony of guillemots along the entire Channel coast. A video camera has been installed on the cliffs to relay live close-up pictures of the guillemots and other seabirds.

MAYPOOL
8 miles S of Torquay off the A3022

A narrow country lane off the A3022 passes through the village of **Galmpton** and just over a mile further comes to a fork in the road. If you turn right here you will come to the passenger ferry across the River Dart to the pretty yachting village of **Dittisham**. Nearby is **Greenway House**, the home of Dame Agatha Christie for the last thirty years of her life. Her daughter now lives there and the house is not open to the public, but the gardens are open on the last Thursday in

Brixham Harbour

THE ROYAL DART BARS,

The Square, Kingswear, Devon TQ6 0AA
Tel: 01803 752213

The **Royal Dart Bars** occupy one of the grandest riverside locations in England. It looks across the River Dart to the lovely town of Dartmouth with the passenger and vehicle ferry terminals at the rear of the inn. Running alongside is the preserved steam railway which provides regular services from Kingswear through spectacularly scenic countryside to Paignton. A building has stood on the Royal Dart's site for many years. It was once owned by the Royal Dart Yacht Club, became a hotel and was purchased by the Great

Western Railway but has always been known as the Royal Dart since the 1860s. Ray and Sue bought the premises in August 2000 and quickly established a solid reputation for serving excellent food and quality ales. Downstairs is the bistro area serving appetising bar snacks where children are welcome. The upstairs restaurant, (closed on Mondays), overlooks the River Dart and has seating for 40 inside and a further 10 on the balcony. On Friday evenings a pianist entertains - booking at weekends is strongly recommended. The Royal Dart always has 4 real ales on tap - London Pride and Bass, along with 2 other rotating guest ales.

NETHWAY FARM,

Kingswear, nr Dartmouth, South Devon TQ6 0EE
Tel/Fax: 01803 752477

Just a mile inland from the beach and sea at Man Sands, **Nethway Farm** offers 5 self-catering cottages in a gloriously secluded rural situation on a 47-acre working farm. Imaginatively formed within a charming group of barns, they are set in landscaped shared gardens. An indoor heated swimming pool and a sauna have been created in a separate building, and a further barn offers facilities for table tennis, pool, 'fun' netball and badminton. There's a well-equipped children's play area, an 'Under 7s' playroom, and children are welcome to help feed the animals. The taste of

rural life at Nethway continues with walks through the fields - and the chance to enjoy the farm's

own eggs and fresh seasonal fruit. The cottages themselves have been meticulously converted, with careful use of traditional stone and slate. All are tastefully furnished and decorated throughout and comprehensively equipped, and all have their own patios with furniture. The cottages stand in an Area of Outstanding Natural Beauty and since they are available all year round (including Christmas) visitors can enjoy this region in the quieter off-season months when it is especially beautiful.

April and the first Thursday in May, from 2pm to 6pm, in aid of the National Gardens Scheme.

KINGSWEAR
11 miles S of Torquay off the A379

Kingswear sits on the steeply rising east bank of the River Dart, looking across to the picturesque panorama of Dartmouth stretched across the hillside on the opposite bank. The town is the terminus for the Paignton and Kingswear steam railway and passengers then join the ferry for the 5 minute crossing to Dartmouth. There's also a vehicle ferry. Above the town stand the impressive remains of Kingswear Castle which is now owned by the Landmark Trust and has been converted to holiday flats. Together with its twin across the river, Dartmouth Castle, the fortresses guarded the wide estuary of the Dart and as an additional deterrent to invaders, a huge chain was dragged across from Dartmouth to stop enemies sailing up the river.

About 3 miles to the east of Kingswear, **Coleton Fishacre** (NT) is a delightful coastal garden basking in a mild climate which is ideal for growing exotic trees and shrubs. The garden was created between 1925 and 1940 by Lady Dorothy D'Oyly Carte (of Gilbert and Sullivan fame) who introduced a wonderfully imaginative variety of plants. The 20-acre site, protected by a deep combe, contains formal gardens, wooded areas with wild flowers, tranquil pools and secret paths weaving in and out of glades.

4 Plymouth and the South Hams

With around a quarter of a million inhabitants, Plymouth is the largest centre of population in the south west peninsula but its development has been comparatively recent. It wasn't until the end of the 12th century that the harbour was recognised as having any potential as a military and commercial port and it wasn't until the 1500s that it was established as the main base for the English fleet guarding the western channel against a seaborne attack from Spain.

Much of the city was grievously damaged during World War II but most of the historic Barbican area survived along with Plymouth Hoe, forever identified in the national consciousness as the place where Sir Francis Drake nonchalantly completed his game of bowls before setting off to harry the Spanish Armada.

An important commercial centre, Plymouth also boasts one of the county's great stately homes, Saltram House, which occupies a grand site overlooking the River Plym and has some sumptuous interior decoration by Robert Adam.

To the east of Plymouth lies the South Ham - *"The frutefullest part of all Devonshire"* according to one old writer. This favoured tract of land lying south of Dartmoor, bounded by the River Dart to the east and the River Erme to the west. *Coastline, Bolt Head*
The climate is exceptionally mild, the soil fertile and the pastures well watered. But the rivers that run off Dartmoor to the sea, slicing north-south through the area, created burdensome barriers to communications until fairly recent times. This comparative isolation kept the region unspoilt but also kept it poor.

There are few towns of any size - only Totnes and Kingsbridge really qualify, along with the wonderfully picturesque ports of Dartmouth and Salcombe. For the rest, the South Hams is a charmed landscape of drowsy villages linked by narrow country lanes running between high banks on which wildflowers flourish: thanks to an enlightened County Council in the 50s and 60s the verges were never assaulted with massive quantities of herbicides as in *Salcombe Harbour* other areas.

PLYMOUTH AND THE SOUTH HAMS

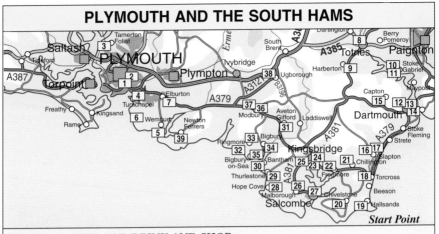

MAYFLOWER GUEST HOUSE,

209 Citadel Road East, The Hoe, Plymouth PL1 2JF
Tel: 01752 667496 Fax: 01752 202727
e-mail: info@mayflowerguesthouse.co.uk
website: www.mayflowerguesthouse.co.uk

Only 300 yards from the historic Barbican and opposite the Hoe Park, **The Mayflower Guest House** offers visitors not only a great location but also great food, great prices and a welcoming, homely atmosphere. The spacious building dates back more than a century and the owners, Dick and Angela Dickerson, who arrived here in March 2000, have beautifully decorated and furnished it throughout.

Altogether, they have been in the hospitality business for more than 14 years so they have a pretty good understanding of their customers' needs and their guest house has a very warm and welcoming atmosphere. Commended by the English Tourist Board, the Mayflower has 9 guest bedrooms, 8 of them with en suite facilities. Three of the rooms are family rooms and one of them, a twin en suite, is located on the ground floor - convenient for those guests who find difficulty with stairs. All the rooms have central

heating, colour TV and tea/coffee-making facilities, and no-smoking rooms are available. A hearty English breakfast is included in the Mayflower's tariff, with alternative choices available for vegetarians.

Guests are provided with their own house keys: hair dryers, ironing facilities and a pay phone are also available. The Mayflower is open all year round, children are welcome, most major credit cards are accepted and, an important amenity for a city centre location, car parking can be arranged through the guest house. The tariff varies according to the time of year but there are special prices for longer stays.

The Dickersons know the city and the surrounding area very well and will be happy to advise you on the many visitor attractions within easy reach of the guest house. Plymouth itself offers visitors a wide choice of entertainment and activities, and is the major shopping centre for south and west Devon. The city's oldest area, the Barbican, has a large number of restaurants and pubs as well as an enterprising small theatre. Just outside the city, overlooking the estuary of the River Plym, is Saltram House, built in the 1760s for the Parker family. It has a sumptuous interior designed by Robert Adam and the treasures on show include some fine family portraits of the Parkers by Sir Joshua Reynolds and some outstanding furniture crafted by Thomas Chippendale.

PLYMOUTH

Perhaps the best way of getting to know this historic city is to approach **Plymouth Hoe** on foot from the main shopping area, along the now-pedestrianised Armada Way. It was on the Hoe on Friday, July 19th, 1588, that one of the most iconic moments in English history took place. Commander of the Fleet, and erstwhile pirate, Sir Francis Drake was playing bowls here when he was informed of the approach of the Spanish Armada. With true British phlegm, Sir Francis completed his game before boarding *The Golden Hind* and sailing off to harass the Spanish fleet. A statue of Sir Francis, striking a splendidly belligerent pose and looking proudly to the horizon, stands on the Hoe which is still an open space, combining the functions of promenade, public park and parade ground.

Just offshore, the striking shape of **Drake's Island** rises like Alcatraz from the deep swirling waters at the mouth of the River Tamar. In its time, this stark fortified islet has been used as a gunpowder repository, (it is said to be riddled with underground tunnels where the powder was stored), a prison, and a youth adventure centre.

View from The Hoe, Plymouth

Two miles from the Hoe, Plymouth's remarkable **Breakwater** protects the Sound from the destructive effects of the prevailing south-westerly winds. Built by prisoners between 1812 and 1840, this massive mile-long construction required around four million tons of limestone. The surface was finished with enormous dovetailed blocks of stone, and the structure rounded off with a lighthouse at one end.

On a clear day, it's possible to see the famous **Eddystone Lighthouse**, twelve miles out in the Channel. The present lighthouse is the fourth to be built here. The first, made of timber, was swept away in a huge storm in 1703 taking with it the man who had built the lighthouse, the ship-owner Winstanley. In 1759, a much more substantial structure of dovetailed granite blacks was built by John Smeaton. It stood for 120 years and even then it was not the lighthouse but the rocks on which it stood which began to collapse. The lighthouse was dismantled and re-erected on the Hoe where, as **Smeaton's Tower**, it is one of the city's most popular tourist attractions. From the top, there are good views of Millbay Docks,

The Hoe, Plymouth

PLATTERS,

12 The Barbican, Plymouth, Devon PL1 2LS
Tel: 01752 227262

For many The Platters are remembered as a chart-topping group from the states, but in Plymouth **Platters** is synonymous with the best seafood in town. It's a family business with a comfortable and friendly atmosphere, though most importantly, it offers first class food. Platters reputation for excellent cuisine has grown steadily during the more than twenty years since it was established by Rocky and

Celia Achilles. They are still involved in the business though their son Nicholas and daughter-in-law Julie took over the helm in 1993. That was also the year in which chef David Robinson joined the team. His extensive menu offers an excellent choice and the restaurant is renowned for its lobster, dressed crab and other imaginative fish dishes. The fish is bought fresh each day from the quayside just across the road to create mouth-watering and delicate flavours in fish cuisine. Given 24 hours notice, the restaurant will prepare any species of fish to your personal requirements.

Although fish is the speciality of the house, the menu also includes grills, omelettes, salads, giant home made burgers, vegetarian dishes and children's choices. A blackboard lists a choice of scrumptious

desserts. The restaurant is fully licensed and in addition to the short but well-chosen wine list, house wines are available by the glass, or by a half-litre or litre carafe. There's also a regular "Wines of the Month" feature which offers real quality at a very competitive price. Guests can enjoy their meal at a private table or with other diners on longer bench-type tables and seating.

Customers entering Platters are immediately struck by the impressive murals. These were created in plaster by local artist Ginger Keaton who literally throws the plaster on to the wall to create the seascapes! Platters is open every day from 11.30am to 11pm, all year round, and it's essential to book for Friday and Saturday nights, Sunday lunchtime and on Tuesdays.

The restaurant occupies a prime position in this, the oldest quarter of the city. It's close to the Mayflower Steps where the Pilgrim Fathers embarked for their historic voyage, and also near The Citadel, a massive fortification built by Charles II which is still a military base but open for guided tours during the season.

The Barbican, Plymouth

Plymouth's busy commercial port which was once busy with transatlantic passenger liners. Today, the docks handle a variety of merchant shipping, including the continental ferry services to Brittany and northern Spain. To the east, the view is dominated by **The Citadel**, a massive fortification built by Charles II, ostensibly as a defence against seaborne attack. Perhaps bearing in mind that Plymouth had resisted a four-year siege by his father's troops during the Civil War, Charles' Citadel has a number of gun ports bearing directly on the city. The Citadel is still a military base, but there are guided tours every afternoon from May to September (tel: 01752 775841).

Close by the Citadel is Plymouth's oldest quarter, the **Barbican**. Now a lively entertainment area filled with restaurants, pubs, and an innovative small theatre, it was once the main trading area for merchants exporting wool and importing wine.

Nearby are the **Mayflower Steps** where the Pilgrim Fathers boarded ship for their historic voyage to Massachusetts. The names of the Mayflower's company are listed on a board on nearby Island House, now the tourist information office. Many other emigrants were to follow in the Pilgrim Fathers' wake, with the result that there are now more than forty communities named Plymouth scattered across the English-speaking world.

A number of interesting old buildings around the Barbican have survived the ravages of time and the terrible pasting the city received during World War II. **Prysten House**, behind St Andrew's Church, is a 15th

century priest's house; the **Elizabethan House** in New Street has a rich display of Elizabethan furniture and furnishings, and the **Merchant's House** in St Andrew's Street, generally regarded as Devon's finest Jacobean building, is crammed full of interesting objects relating to Plymouth's past. A particularly fascinating exhibit in the Merchant's House is the **Park Pharmacy**, a genuine Victorian pharmacy complete with its 1864 fittings and stocked with such preparations as Ipecacuanha Wine (one to two tablespoonfuls as an emetic) and Tincture of Myrrh and Borax, "for the teeth and gums".

A recent addition to the Barbican's visitor attractions is the **National Marine Aquarium**, located on the Fish Quay. State-of-the-art techniques allow visitors to travel through the oceans of the world, dropping from mountains and rivers to the darkest depths of the Atlantic. The virtual reality tour includes encounters with brilliantly coloured fish, seahorses and even Caribbean sharks. The Aquarium is open daily from 10am to 6pm.

Locally, the Tamar estuary is known as the Hamoaze, (pronounced ham-oys), and it's well worth taking one of the boat trips that leave from the Mayflower Steps. This is

Sutton Harbour, Plymouth

Seven Stars Lane, Tamerton Foliot, Plymouth,
Devon PL5 4NN
Tel: 01752 772901

Tucked away on the northern edge of Plymouth, the old village of Tamerton Foliot is well worth seeking out to visit **The Seven Stars Inn**. It's believed to date back to medieval times when it was used as a lodging for travelling monks but has been an inn since at least the 17th century. Not surprisingly, the interior has a very olde-

worlde atmosphere with lots of beams and gleaming brass and copper items around the walls. But there's also a very elegant conservatory restaurant where your hosts, Mary and her daughter Sarah, offer a tempting choice of wholesome and appetising food with steaks and fish dishes among the specialities of the house. They host a special Steak Night on the last Wednesday of every month when the value for money prices are quite remarkable. Food is served every lunchtime and evening with bar meals, snacks and sandwiches also available. Children are welcome in the restaurant and there's also a safe beer garden and patio area.

THE NEW INN,

1 Boringdon Road, Turnchapel, Plymouth,
Devon PL9 9TB
Tel: 01752 402765

Originally three buildings - a bakery, a butcher's and a tavern, **The New Inn** occupies a lovely position looking out across Cattewater to Plymouth Hoe. The inn has been owned and run since 1992 by John and Marlene Wills, a welcoming couple with nearly 20 years experience in the hospitality business. They have an established reputation for serving quality food every evening and

lunchtimes on Friday, Saturday and Sunday. (The inn is closed Monday-Thursday lunchtimes, except for Bank Holidays). The extensive menu is displayed on a large blackboard and offers a very varied choice, including vegetarian options. Such is the popularity of the food here, it is wise to book for Saturday evenings and Sunday lunchtimes, and at all times during the season. To complement the food, there are at least 4, sometimes 6, real ales on tap along with all the usual popular beverages. Well-located for exploring Devon and Cornwall, the inn has 5 guest bedrooms, all en suite and one of them on the ground floor.

St Budeaux Church, Plymouth

certainly the best way to see Devonport Dockyard, while the ferry to Cremyll on the Cornish bank of the Tamar drops off passengers close to **Mount Edgcumbe Country Park** and the old smuggling village of Cawsand.

The blackest date in Plymouth's history is undoubtedly March 21st, 1941. On that night, the entire centre of the city was razed to the ground by the combined effects of high-explosive and incendiary bombs. More than a thousand people were killed; another 5000 injured. After the war, the renowned town planner Sir Patrick Abercrombie was commissioned to design a completely new town centre. Much of the rebuilding was carried out in the 1950s, which was not British architecture's Golden Age, but almost half a century later the scheme has acquired something of a period charm.

The new city has some excellent facilities, including a first-rate **Museum and Art Gallery,** near Drake Circus, the **Theatre Royal** with its two auditoria in Royal Parade, the **Arts Centre** in Looe Street, and the

Saltram House, Plymouth

Pavilions complex of concert hall, leisure pool and skating rink at the foot of Western Approach.

On the southern outskirts of Plymouth stands one of Devon's grandest mansions, **Saltram House** (National Trust). Built during the reign of George II for the Parker family, this sumptuous house occupies a splendid site overlooking the Plym estuary. In the 1760s Robert Adam was called in, at enormous expense, to decorate the dining room and "double cube" saloon, which he accomplished with his usual panache. There are portraits of the Parkers by the locally born artist Sir Joshua Reynolds, and amongst the fine furniture, a magnificent four-poster bed by Thomas Chippendale. Other attractions include the great kitchen with its fascinating assortment of period kitchenware, an orangery in the gardens, and the former chapel, now a gallery displaying the work of West Country artists. Saltram House which, incidentally, starred in the film of Jane Austen's *Sense and Sensibility* as Norland House, is open from April to October - for precise times telephone 01752 336546.

AROUND PLYMOUTH

TAMERTON FOLIOT
4 miles NW of Plymouth on the B3373

Set on a hillside overlooking a large creek that runs into the River Tamar, Tamerton Foliot was the birthplace of Gilbert Foliot who was to hold the position of Bishop of London for 25 years, from 1153 to 1188. He was an arch-adversary of Thomas à Becket who excommunicated him, a punishment overturned by the Pope. The village has a 15th century church with some outstanding monuments to the local landowners, the Copleston, Gorges and Radcliffe families, and an interesting Tudor pulpit with linen fold panelling.

TURNCHAPEL
3 mile SE of Plymouth on minor road off the A379

Enjoying views across Cattewater to Plymouth, the village of Turnchapel is strung along the waterside. The village was declared a Conservation Area in 1977 and, with its two pubs, church and waterfront, a pleasant place to wander around. Nearby, there are ex-RAF Catalina flying boats to wonder at; and from Mountbatten Peninsula grand vistas open up over to Plymouth Hoe and Drake's Island. Incidentally, it was at RAF Mountbatten that Lawrence of Arabia served as a humble aircraftman for several years.

A short distance to the south is a stretch of coastline known as **Abraham's Garden**. The story goes that, during the fearful plague of 1665, a number of Spanish slaves were buried here. In their memory, the shrubbery always remains green, even in winter.

CHURCHWOOD VALLEY,

Wembury Bay, Plymouth, South Devon PL9 0DZ
Tel: 01752 862382 Fax: 01752 863274
e-mail: churchwoodvalley @btinternet.com

If "getting away from it all" is the most important part of your holiday, then **Churchwood Valley** will be your idea of paradise. Set in a beautiful, natural wooded valley running down to the sea at Wembury Bay, the top quality timber cabins here are built to an extremely high standard with many large windows or patio doors to give visitors great views, while their location ensures privacy. Churchwood is packed with wildlife from badgers and foxes to squirrels and many species of birds. Each cabin is fully equipped with everything for holiday use, apart from linen, and each has its own private patio area complete with garden furniture and barbecue if required. The 76-acre site, which includes beaches and a rocky foreshore is beautifully landscaped. In recognition of "the exceptional achievements it has made to protect and enhance the natural environment", Churchwood Valley has won the David Bellamy Conservation Award at Gold standard five years running. Additional amenities at Churchwood Valley include a launderette and a licensed shop that sells everything from buckets and spades to shampoo and charcoal.

BOVISAND LODGE ESTATE,

Bovisand, Plymouth, Devon PL9 0AA
Tel: 01752 403554 Fax: 01752 482646
e-mail: blodge@netcomuk.co.uk
website: www.bovisand.com

Occupying a beautiful location in 25 acres of rolling Devon countryside, the **Bovisand Lodge Estate** offers visitors a good choice of holiday accommodation. In the Lodge itself, which was once used as a base by the two engineers who built the Plymouth Breakwater, John Rennie and Joseph Whidbey, a wing of the house is being converted into 3 new self-catering apartments, each of which can accommodate 4 people.

Nearby, standing in its own grounds in a sunny wooded valley is Bovisand Lodge Cottage, a charming 3-bedroomed property which was formerly the home of the Estate's owners, John and Rita Hart. In 1958 Johns parents opened a caravan park in the valley that leads down to Plymouth Sound.

Most of the caravans here are privately owned but there are 12 caravans available to rent. All of them are either new or less than 3 years old, 12 feet wide, and fully equipped with just about every amenity you can think of. The site has a spacious indoor heated swimming pool complex which includes a launderette and is surrounded by a sun terrace. There's also a small children's Play Park with swings and ropes. The nearby beach is very safe for bathing and at low tide a large expanse of sand with rock pools is exposed, a wonderful place for children to search for crabs and shrimps.

WEMBURY

7m SE of Plymouth, on minor road off the A379

Wembury church makes a dramatic landmark as it stands isolated on the edge of the cliff, and the coastal path here provides spectacular views of the Yealm estuary to the east, and Plymouth Sound to the west. The path is occasionally closed to walkers when the firing range is in use, so look out for the red warning flags. **The Great Mew Stone** stands a mile offshore in Wembury Bay. This lonely islet was inhabited until the 1830s when its last residents, the part-time smuggler Sam Wakeham and his family, gave up the unequal struggle to make a living here. The Mew Stone is now the home of seabirds who surely can't take kindly to its use from time to time by the HMS Cambridge gunnery school on Wembury Point.

ELBURTON

4 miles E of Plymouth off the A379

Located on the very edge of the South Hams, Elburton was once a separate village but is now effectively a suburb of Plymstock and a popular residential centre for commuters into Plymouth who only have to travel a few miles in the other direction to find themselves in the soft, rolling hills of the South Hams.

THE SOUTH HAMS

The South Hams coastline presents enormous variety with some of the most spectacular cliff scenery in Devon running from the Erme to Start Point; and in contrast a long, low-lying stretch of beach extending north towards Dartmouth. No fewer than ten South Hams beaches won awards in 1997, with Blackpool Sands near Dartmouth achieving "Resort" status for its excellent facilities.

Inland, the landscape is one of deep valleys and broad, wooded hills. The area is bounded to the north by the dual carriageway A38 but away from this main thoroughfare, the area is celebrated for its winding lanes running between steep high banks with profuse displays of wild flowers and plants.

The area has been known as the South Hams, the "homesteads south of Dartmoor", since Saxon times, but one town here claims a history stretching much further back in time.

TOTNES

9 miles S of Newton Abbot on the A381/A385

We begin our exploration of the South Hams at Totnes, a town which proudly claims to be the second oldest borough in England. Totnes sent its first Member of Parliament to London in 1295, and elected the first of its 630-odd Mayors in 1359.

THE ELBURTON HOTEL,

221 Elburton Road, Elburton, Plymouth,
Devon PL9 8HX
Tel: 01752 403213

Located on the A379 Kingsbridge road, about 2 miles from Plymouth city centre, **The Elburton Hotel** is an impressive Victorian building with some interesting stained glass windows. When Dave and Christine Colmer took over here in 1998, this handsome property was in a parlous state and about to close. They have completely refurbished and redecorated the inn and re-introduced a food service every lunchtime and evening. There are more than 40 different choices on the menu, including some excellent vegetarian dishes and a children's selection. (Please note that bookings can be made for the evenings). The inn offers a wide choice of beverages, including real ales and wine by the glass, and in good weather you can enjoy your drinks in the patio area. Darts, dominoes and pool are available, and if you are visiting on a Monday evening, feel free to take part in the regular quiz that starts at 9pm.

Totnes Castle

This captivating little town also claims a much more ancient heritage. According to tradition it was founded by an Ancient Trojan named Brutus around 1200BC. The grandfather of Aeneas, the hero of Virgil's epic poem *The Aeneid*, Brutus sailed up the River Dart, gazed at the fair prospect around him and decided to found the first town in this new country which would take its name, Britain, from his own. The **Brutus Stone**, set in the pavement of the main shopping street, Fore Street, commemorates this stirring incident when both the town and a nation were born. Well, it *could* be true!

In fact, the first recorded evidence of this town, set on a hill above the highest navigable point on the River Dart, doesn't appear until the mid-10th century when King Edgar established a mint at Totnes. The Saxons already had a castle of sorts here, but the impressive remains of **Totnes Castle** are Norman, built between the 1100s and early 1300s. Towering over the town, it is generally reckoned to be the best-preserved motte and bailey castle in Devon.

A substantial section of Totnes' medieval town wall has also survived. The superb **East Gate**, which straddles the steep main street is part of that wall, and although grievously damaged by fire in 1990 has been meticulously restored. Just a little way down the hill from East Gate is the charming **Guildhall** of 1553, a remarkable little building with a granite colonnade overarching the pavement. The Guildhall houses both the Council Chamber (which is still in use) and the gloomy underground Town Gaol (which, happily, is not).

Almost opposite the Guildhall is another magnificent Elizabethan building, currently occupied by Barclays Bank. It was built in 1585 for Nicholas Ball who had made his fortune from the local pilchard fishery. When he died, his wife Anne married Sir Thomas Bodley and it was the profit from pilchards that funded the world-famous Bodleian Library at Oxford University.

The town's Elizabethan heritage really comes alive if you are visiting on a Tuesday morning in summer. You will find yourself stepping into a pageant of Elizabethan colour, for this is when the people of Totnes array themselves in crisp, white ruffs and velvet gowns for a charity market which over the years has raised thousands of pounds for good causes.

The parish church of Totnes is **St Mary's**. It was entirely rebuilt in the 15th century when the town's cloth industry was booming - at that time a business second in importance only to Exeter's. The church's most glorious possession is a stone rood-screen delicately carved in stone from the quarry at Beer.

Close by at 70, Fore Street is the **Totnes Museum**, housed in an attractive half-timbered Elizabethan building whose upper floors overhang the street. One of the fascinating exhibits here honours a distinguished son of Totnes, Charles Babbage (1791-1871), whose "Analytical Machine" is now universally acknowledged as the forerunner of our ever-present computer. The Museum display records Babbage's doomed, but inspiring, struggle to perfect such a calculator using only mechanical rather than electronic elements.

A little further up the hill, in High Street, the **Butterwalk** and **Poultrywalk** are two appealingly picturesque covered shopping arcades whose upper storeys rest on pillars of granite, timber or cast iron.

In recent years, Totnes has claimed for itself the title of "Natural Health Capital of the West Country". In 1989 the first Natural Health Centre in Britain selected Totnes as its base and in subsequent years other practitioners have also arrived, offering a huge range of alternative medicine therapies. In alphabetical order they include acupuncture, the Alexander technique for those suffering from eye problems, aromatherapy, chiropractic, homoeopathy, genuine non-sexual massage, osteopathy and reflexology. Visitors will also find specialist shops stocked

The Guildhall, Totnes

with natural medicines, organic food, aromatherapy products, relaxation tapes and books on spiritual healing. Other craft and antique shops, and a Bear Shop with more than a thousand Teddy Bears in residence all add to the town's appeal.

For centuries, Totnes was a busy river port and down by Totnes Bridge, an elegant stone structure of 1828, the quay was lined with warehouses, some of which have survived and been converted into highly desirable flats. Nearby, on the Plains, stands a granite obelisk to the famous explorer William Wills, a native of Totnes who perished from starvation when attempting to re-cross the Australian desert with Robert Burke in 1861.

Also at the riverside, at Steamer Quay, is the **Totnes Motor Museum** which houses an unusual collection of vintage, sports and racing cars spanning 80 years. Many are still regularly raced in vintage competitions all over Europe by the enthusiastic family which owns the collection.

One excursion from Totnes not to be missed is the breathtakingly beautiful river trip to Dartmouth, seven miles downstream. This stretch of the river has been called the "English Rhine" and the comparison is not at all fanciful. The river here runs well away from roads, making it an ideal location for seeing wading-birds, herons, cormorants, and even seals. During the summer, there are frequent departures from the quay by Totnes bridge.

Another memorable journey from Totnes is by steam train along the 7-mile stretch of the

Primrose Line which runs through the glorious scenery of the Dart Valley to Buckfastleigh. Most of the locomotives and carriages are genuine Great Western Railway stock, and are painted in the G.W.R.'s famous chocolate and cream livery. For details of services, call 01364 642338.

Even that list of Totnes attractions isn't exhaustive. Anyone interested in photography will want to visit **Bowden House Photographic Museum**, a mile or so southwest of the town, which contains a vast collection of photographs, photographic bygones, vintage and classic cameras, all housed in a grand Tudor and Queen Anne mansion. Bowden House also claims to be seriously haunted. Visitors frequently authenticate sightings of spectral monks, of gentlefolk in 18th century costume, and of a pathetic figure known as "Little Alice". Needless to say, the Halloween Night candlelit tours of the house are extremely popular.

BERRY POMEROY
2 miles E of Totnes off the A385 or A381

For the last 1000 years this small village has been owned by just two families. The de la Pomerais dynasty arrived with William the Conqueror and held the land for almost 500 years. In the early 1300s they built **Berry Pomeroy Castle** in a superb position on a wooded promontory above the Gatcombe Brook. Substantial remains of the castle still stand, including sections of the curtain wall and the 14th century gatehouse. In 1548 the Pomeroys, as they were now known, sold the estate to Sir Edward Seymour whose sister, Jane, had been the third wife of Henry VIII. Sir Edward built a 3-storey Tudor mansion within the medieval fortifications but this too is now a shell. Although the castle is still owned by Sir Edward's descendant, the Duke of Somerset, it is administered by English Heritage and open to the public daily during the season. In the village itself, St Mary's Church contains some interesting monuments to the Pomeroys and Seymours, as well as an outstanding rood screen.

FOALES LEIGH FARM,

Harberton, Totnes, Devon TQ9 7SS
Tel/Fax: 01803 862365

Occupying a delightful position in peaceful, unspoilt countryside **Foales Leigh** is a delightful 16th century farmhouse in a traditional courtyard setting which has been owned by the Chudley family for more than a century. Carol and Ted Chudley are the current owners and they have been welcoming bed & breakfast guests for many years. The comfortable accommodation comprises 3 guest bedrooms, (1 double, 1 twin, 1 family), all en suite, spacious and very comfortable, some with power showers and all equipped with TV, central heating and beverage tray. Guests have the use of a large oak-beamed lounge and a delicious Aga-cooked breakfast is included in the tariff, served with lots of home produce such as eggs and locally-made sausages. The house stands on 300 acres of a mixed beef and sheep farm, and despite the rural location is within easy reach of the South Hams beaches, the Dartmoor National Park and attractive old towns such as Totnes. Please note that Foales Leigh is a non-smoking establishment and that dogs are not accepted.

CHURCH HOUSE INN,

Harberton, nr Totnes, Devon TQ9 7SF
Tel: 01803 863707

Just a couple of miles southwest of Totnes, off the A381, is Harberton where those two traditional centres of English village life, church and inn, sit comfortably almost side by side. Harberton's house of God and its hostelry have been closely linked for almost 900 years. St Andrew's Church is famous for its amazing, fantastically carved 15th century altar screen: **The Church House Inn** is equally renowned for its wonderfully atmospheric interior and its exceptionally good food and drink. The inn was originally built to house the masons working on the church around 1100 AD. Harberton was then almost as important a place as Totnes - a major centre for church administration. The inn became the Chantry House for the monks, the civil servants of their time, and what is now the bar comprised their Great Hall, chapel and workshop where they would congregate for a glass of wine. In 1327 the Abbot handed the property over to the poor of the parish and it was not until 1950 that it passed out of the Church's hands altogether. During restoration work ancient plaster was removed to reveal massive beams of fluted mellow oak and a fine medieval screen. Other treasures discovered then, and still in place, were a Tudor window frame and a latticed window containing priceless panes of 13th century hand-made glass. The inn's ecclesiastical connections are enhanced even more by the old pews from redundant churches which provide some of the seating.

David and Jennifer Wright have been the custodians of this unique hostelry for more than ten years. (They also look after the oldest public house in Totnes, the Kingsbridge Inn). Jennifer has ensured that the food and drink served at the Church House Inn lives up to its magnificent setting by providing a wide choice of beautifully-prepared food. The extensive menu ranges from Cordon Bleu specialities to a humble sandwich, from charcoal-grilled steaks to vegetarian dishes. In addition 3 double bedrooms are now available for bed and breakfast accommodation. If you find yourself anywhere near Totnes, do go that extra mile or two and seek out the Church House Inn.

DARTINGTON
2 miles NW of Totnes on the A384

When Leonard and Dorothy Elmhirst bought **Dartington Hall** and its estate in 1925 the superb Great Hall had stood roofless for more than a century. The buildings surrounding the two large quadrangles laid out in the 1390s by John Holand, Earl of Exeter, were being used as stables, cow houses and hay lofts. The Elmhirsts were idealists and since Dorothy (née Whitney) was one of the richest American women of her time, they possessed the resources to put their ideals into practice. They restored the Hall, re-opened it as a progressive school, and set about reviving the local rural economy in line with the ideology of the Indian philosopher, Rabindranath Tagore. The Elmhirsts were closely involved in the creation of the famed Dartington Glass. Sadly, long after their deaths, their school closed in 1995 as a consequence of financial problems and a pornography scandal. But the Headmaster's house, a classic Modernist building of the early 1930s which has now been converted into an art gallery, is open to the public. Visitors are welcome here and also to wander around the 26 acre gardens surrounding the Hall. There is no charge for entry to the quadrangle and Great Hall, but donations for its upkeep are welcomed. Guided tours are available by appointment.

Dartington Hall hosts more than a hundred music performances each year during its International Summer School, a season which attracts musicians and artistes of the highest calibre from all over the world. All year round, even more visitors are attracted to the **Dartington Cider Press Centre**, a huge gallery on the edge of the estate which displays a vast range of craft products - anything from a delicate hand-made Christmas or birthday card to a beautifully modelled item of pottery.

HARBERTON
3 miles SW of Totnes off the A381

This delightful village is regarded as absolutely typical of the South Hams. It lies cradled in a fold of the hills with the striking 78ft high tower of its Perpendicular church rising high above the cottages and houses.

THE RED SLIPPER,

Stoke Gabriel, Devon TQ9 6RU
Tel/Fax: 01803 782315
e-mail: clive@redslipper.co.uk
website: www.redslipper.co.uk

The Red Slipper, set in the heart of the picturesque village of Stoke Gabriel with its quiet tangle of quaint cottages leading down to the River Dart, offers comfortable en suite accommodation in delightful surroundings. The rooms are either double or twin bedded and have tea and coffee making facilities, colour TVs and alarm clock radios. Most rooms are on

the ground floor and have level access from the visitor's car park at the front of the building. No smoking is allowed in the bedrooms or dining room. Guests enjoy a choice of a full English or continental breakfast, and evening meals are available most evenings if booked in advance. Wherever possible the Red Slipper's owners, Clive and Pam Wigfall, use produce from the local area which abounds in excellent variety and taste. Polite pets and children are also welcome. Stoke Gabriel is ideally situated for visiting the local area which has so many different places and attractions to see - from the bleak yet beautiful landscape of Dartmoor to secluded sandy beaches along the coast, you are spoilt for choice whatever the time of year. At the Red Slipper guests are assured of a warm welcome and the Wigfalls endeavour to make your stay a comfortable experience so that you can enjoy the tranquillity and beauty of the South Hams area of Devon.

Inside the church there's an outstanding example of a 15th century wooden screen and one of the last remaining medieval stone pulpits to be found in Devon. An ancient inn stands beside the church and at the heart of the village there's still a working dairy farm.

STOKE GABRIEL
4 miles SE of Totnes off the A385

A charming village of narrow lanes and alleys, Stoke Gabriel stands on a hillside above a tidal spur of the River Dart. A weir was built across the neck of the creek in Edwardian times and this traps the water at low tide, giving the village a pleasant lakeside atmosphere. The part-13th century church of St Gabriel has a restored late-medieval pulpit and a truncated screen with some good wainscot paintings. In the churchyard are the rather forlorn remains of an oak tree reputed to be more than 1500 years old. To the west of the village, a lane leads to the riverside hamlet of Duncannon where, by general consent, the River Dart is at its most lovely.

DARTMOUTH & START BAY

Near the eastern boundary of the South Hams flows the enchanting River Dart, surely one of the loveliest of English rivers. Rising in the great blanket bog of the moor, the Dart flows for 46 miles and together with its tributaries

drains the greater part of Dartmoor. Queen Victoria called the Dart the "English Rhine", perhaps thinking of the twin castles of Dartmouth and Kingswear that guard its estuary. It was her ancestor, Alfred the Great who developed Dartmouth as a strategic base and the town's long connection with the senior service is reflected in the presence here of the Royal Naval College. The spectacular harbour is still busy with naval vessels, pleasure boats and ferries, and particularly colourful during the June **Carnival** and the **Dartmouth Regatta** in late August.

The most picturesque approach to the town is to drive to Kingswear and then take one of the two car ferries for the ten minute trip across the river. Parking space in Dartmouth is severely restricted and it is strongly recommended that you make use of the Park & Ride facility located just outside the town on the A3122.

DARTMOUTH
14 miles SE of Totnes on the A3122

For centuries, this entrancing little town clinging to the sides of a precipitous hill was one of England's principal ports. During the 1100s, Crusaders on both the Second and Third Crusades mustered here, and from here they set sail. In its sheltered harbour, Elizabeth's men o'war lay in wait to pick off the stragglers from the Spanish Armada. Millions of casks of French and Spanish wine have been offloaded onto its narrow quays. And in 1620, the *Mayflower* put in here for a

HIGHER WELL FARM & HOLIDAY PARK,
Waddeton Road, Stoke Gabriel, Totnes,
Devon TQ9 6RN
Tel: 01803 782289

Higher Well Farm is a secluded holiday park just under a mile from the riverside village of Stoke Gabriel and is surrounded by lovely Devonshire countryside. Yet it is not far from Torbay and South Devon's many towns and attractions. The farm has been in the same family for 75 years with John and Liz Ball being the third generation to run it. It is still a working farm with cattle, sheep and horses on about 120 acres. The holiday business has grown gradually over the past 30 years. There are 18 holiday caravans to let, including some all-electric ones new in 2000. In a separate area there is accommodation for 80 tourers, motor homes or tents. In this area a new toilet block is being opened in 2001: it will include family rooms, a disabled room and a dishwashing area. Other amenities include a small shop which has a free facility for freezing ice packs, electric hook-ups and a pay phone.

The Old Front, Dartmouth

embarked later became the major location for the BBC-TV series, *The Onedin Line,* and was also seen in the feature film *Sense and Sensibility* starring Emma Thompson and Hugh Grant.

Geoffrey Chaucer visited the town in 1373 in his capacity as Inspector of Customs and is believed to have modelled the Shipman in his *Canterbury Tales* on the character of the then Mayor of Dartmouth, John Hawley. Hawley was an enterprising merchant and seafarer who was also responsible for building **Dartmouth Castle** (English Heritage). Dramatically sited, it guards the entrance to the Dart estuary and was one of the first castles specifically designed to make effective use of artillery. In case the Castle should prove to be an inadequate deterrent, in times of danger a heavy chain was strung across the harbour to Kingswear

few days for repairs before hoisting sail on August 20th for Plymouth and then on to the New World where the pilgrims arrived three months later. The quay from which they

GUNFIELD HOTEL,

Castle Road, Dartmouth, Devon TQ6 0JN
Tel: 01803 834571 Fax: 01803 834772
e-mail: enquiry@gunfield.co.uk
website: www.gunfield.co.uk

The Dart is one of England's loveliest rivers and patrons of the **Gunfield Hotel** can enjoy spectacular views of the Dart estuary and out to sea. Many a pleasant hour can be spent watching the yachts, fishing boats, sailing dinghies and ocean cruisers criss-crossing the river. It was a yachtsman, the Hon. H. Hare, who built a villa on this superb site in 1842. Much enlarged, the house became a hotel just over a hundred years later and since 1998 has been owned and run by Mike and Lucy Swash.

Their guests can enjoy a whole range of water-based activities, from water-skiing to wave blasting or wildlife cruises in either the hotel's RIB or its luxury sports boat. If you have your own boat, just moor up to the deep water trots or pontoon. This outstanding boasts a delightful waterside restaurant offering a delicious and modestly priced menu with an international flavour. Guests can dine inside or outside on the upper terrace, or on the wooden waterside deck where barbecues take place in summer. The bar also commands grand views of the river as do all of the 10 guest bedrooms, eight of which are en suite.

Guests can relax in the beautiful gardens surrounding the hotel or, if they are feeling more active, follow the Heritage coastal footpath which runs literally past the door, take a short boat or car journey to Blue Flag beaches such as Blackpool Sands, while for golf devotees the hotel offers privileged green fees at the Dartmouth Golf and Country Club championship course.

KENDRICKS,

29 Fairfax Place, Dartmouth, Devon TQ6 9AB
Tel: 01803 832328

One of several ancient buildings to be found in Dartmouth, **Kendricks** catches the eye with its colourful frontage which displays the coats of arms of several famous Dartmouth families. The property was built on land reclaimed from the estuary in the 1580s. Kendricks retains many interesting architectural features including the splendid oak panelling dated 1585 in the first floor lounge.

In February 2000 the premises were purchased by Bob and Georgia Kendrick who completely refurbished it and opened as a Californian-style restaurant offering a good choice of Lite Bites and Appetisers, burgers, salads, pizzas and main courses that include steaks, fish, poultry and vegetarian dishes. A feature of Kendricks is home-made food with interesting and imaginative specials served everyday in ample portions. There's a good wine list supplemented by a monthly guest wine.

This popular restaurant is open all year, except for two weeks in January, and booking is recommended especially during the season.

THE SHIP IN DOCK,

Ridge Hill, Dartmouth, Devon TQ6 9PE
Tel: 01803 835916

Only a couple of hundred yards from the quayside, **The Ship in Dock** inn is also close to Newcomen Lodge where Dartmouth's most famous son, Thomas Newcomen, once lived. A handsome, white-painted building the inn was built in 1656, (just a few years before Newcomen was born), and partly rebuilt in 1871. No-one is quite sure how the pub gained its name but with the quayside so close it seems very appropriate.

Mine hosts, Geoff and Beverley Hicksmoran, have been here since 1997 but their experience in the hospitality business all around the country goes back some 25 years. The Ship in Dock is open all day, every day for ale, including Courage Best and a rotating guest ale, which can be enjoyed in the olde worlde bar or lounge. (Please note that children are not admitted). Food is available every evening from 7pm until 9.30pm. Choices are listed on the blackboard and the wide variety of dishes includes locally caught fresh fish as the speciality of the house. If you are planning to stay in this delightful town, the Ship in Dock has 5 attractive guest bedrooms, all doubles and all en suite.

Quayside, Dartmouth

Castle on the opposite bank. (Kingswear Castle is now owned by the Landmark Trust and available for holiday rentals).

There's a striking monumental brass to John Hawley and his two wives in the **Church of St Saviour's**, a part 14th century building against whose wall ships used to tie up before the New Quay was constructed in the late 1500s. Nearby is the **Custom House**, a handsome building of 1739 which has some fine internal plasterwork ceilings.

Also worth seeking out are **The Butterwalk**, a delightful timber-framed arcade dating from 1640 in which the **Dartmouth Museum** occupies the ground floor, and the working steam pumping engine built to a revolutionary design by Thomas Newcomen, the celebrated inventor, who was born in Dartmouth in 1663.

Two other buildings in Dartmouth should be mentioned. One is the railway station, possibly the only one in the world which has never seen a train. It was built by the Great Western Railway as the terminus of their line from Torbay and passengers were ferried across to Kingswear where the railway actually ended. The station is now a restaurant. The other building, which is inescapable, is the **Britannia Royal Naval College** (guided tours during the season). This sprawling red and white building, built between 1899 and 1905, dominates the northern part of the town as you leave by the A379 towards Kingsbridge.

BROWNS FARM HOLIDAY COTTAGES,

Browns Farm, Capton, Dittisham,
South Devon TQ6 0JE
Tel/Fax: 01803 712556

Hidden away in the hamlet of Capton, **Browns Farm Holiday Cottages** offer an outstanding choice of characterful cottages set in wonderfully tranquil surroundings but within easy reach of Dartmouth and the South Devon coast. There are delightful walks nearby and children can wander freely and safely. They can also enjoy the field with its swings, climbing frame, stream and pond.

Browns Farm is owned and run by Carol and Laurie Fraenkel. Laurie is a local builder and he has converted the old stone farm buildings to form 4 holiday cottages. Each of the cottages is very different since the Fraenkels sought to retain the character of each original building even if this meant accommodating a tree in the middle of one of them! The cottages are equipped to a very high standard - the Tourist Board awarded them a 4-Key Highly Commended rating - and they all have full oil-fired central heating. Each cottage has its own separate access, parking and garden or sitting-out area. The cottages sleep 4, 6, 9 or 10 people and two of them have Grade II Accessible disabled access. Well-behaved dogs are welcome.

CAPTON
4 miles NW of Dartmouth off the A3122

The term "In Deepest Devon" could well have been coined especially for Capton. It's tucked away in the hills to the northwest of Dartmouth, well off the beaten track. But excavations in the 1980s revealed that the nearby hilltop was occupied in neolithic times. The remains of a chambered tomb were discovered along with a number of artefacts dating from palaeolithic to medieval times.

STOKE FLEMING
3 miles S of Dartmouth, on the A379

Stoke Fleming is one of the most delightful villages in the South Hams, perched high on the cliffs 300ft above Start Bay and with a prominent church that has served generations of mariners as a reassuring landmark. Inside is a brass of 1351 which is reckoned to be one of the oldest in Devon and another which commemorates the great-grandfather of the celebrated engineer, Thomas Newcomen. Less than a mile from the village are the misleadingly-named **Blackpool Sands**, a broad crescent of sandy beach overhung by Monterey pines, which boasts a Blue Flag Award for its safe and healthy bathing.

SLAPTON
6 miles S of Dartmouth off the A379

To the south of Stoke Fleming, the A379 runs for 2.5 miles along the top of a remarkable

World War 2 Memorial, Slapton Sands

sand and shingle bank which divides the salt water of Start Bay from the fresh water of Slapton Ley, the largest natural lake in Devon. Continually replenished by three small rivers, this shallow body of water is a designated Nature Reserve and home to large numbers of freshwater fish, insects, water-loving plants and native and migrating birds. The **Slapton Ley Field Study Centre**, located in Slapton village, has leaflets detailing the delightful circular nature trails through this fascinating Site of Special Scientific Interest.

Normally, the 4-mile stretch of sand and shingle beach on the seaward side of Slapton is too extensive to ever become crowded but back in 1943 things were very different. The

OLD WALLS,
Slapton, Kingsbridge, Devon TQ7 2QN
Tel: 01548 580516

Located only half a mile from the beach and Slapton Ley, **Old Walls** is a handsome Grade II listed Georgian house which has been the home of Valerie Mercer for more than 40 years. For the last 25 or so years she has been welcoming bed and breakfast guests to this lovely old house. There's a delightful garden and a south facing veranda where guests can sit and enjoy both the garden and the countryside views beyond. The 3 guest bedrooms are centrally heated and comfortably furnished, and equipped with television and tea/coffee-making facilities. There's an en suite family room, another family room, and a twin with private bathroom. Breakfast is served in the oldest part of the house, probably part of the 16th century cottage which was here before Old Walls was built in 1720. Breakfast times are flexible and there's a choice of full English, vegetarian cooked or continental breakfast - fresh local produce is used wherever possible. Almost every kind of country activity is within easy reach - fishing, riding, sailing, windsurfing, golf, tennis, walking, bird watching, or you might just prefer to relax somewhere along the glorious 3-mile stretch of Slapton Sands.

beach had been selected by the Allied Commanders for a "dress rehearsal" of the impending D-Day invasion of Normandy. The area was swarming with troops and because live ammunition was being used in the training exercise, all the local people were evacuated, more than 3,000 of them from seven coastal villages. An obelisk on the beach near Slapton, presented by the U.S.

Army authorities to the people of the South Hams, commemorates this hugely disruptive event in their lives.

TORCROSS
8 miles S of Dartmouth on the A379

Those D-Day preparations are also recalled at Torcross where a Sherman tank recovered

THE TOWER INN,

Church Road, Slapton, South Devon TQ7 2PN Tel: 01548 580216
e-mail: towerinn@slapton.org website: www.slapton.org

The most striking feature of this picturesque village is the tower of the Collegiate Chantry of St Mary, founded in 1373 by Sir Guy de Brian, standard bearer to King Edward III. At the foot of this interesting ancient monument is the delightful **Tower Inn**, built around 1347 as cottages to house the men working on the chantry. It seems likely that the Tower Inn began as the College's guesthouse where

alms and hospitality were dispensed.Today, the pub offers a warm welcome to visitors from all around the world. The inn is approached down a narrow lane leading into a small courtyard car park. Step through the porch into a low-ceilinged rustic bar with beams and pillars, scrubbed oak tables, church pew seating, log fires and flagstone floors.

The owners, Josh and Nicola Acfield, offer freshly prepared and interesting food and an exciting range of traditional beers together with a good selection of Old and New World wines. If you'd like to stay in this charming village, there are 3 double rooms available, all en suite, in a self-contained wing of the Tower Inn where guests have the freedom to come and go as they please.

COVE HOUSE,

Torcross, nr Kingsbridge, South Devon TQ7 2TH
Tel/Fax: 01548 580350

Occupying one of the most beautiful settings in South Devon, **Cove House** offers holiday-makers the best of both worlds - it's by the sea and also in the country. It stands on the coast, in a sheltered bay, with a backdrop of scenic rolling hills and a patchwork of field rising to Dartmoor in the north. The house is yards away from its own private beach, ideal for all types of watersports. The accommodation at Cove House has a 2-Crown Commended recommendation from the English Tourist Board and the 11 bedrooms all have en suite facilities and television. John and Judy Chittenden are the owners of this small and friendly guest house, and they welcome all the family - including dogs. They have two whippets of their own which always enjoy company! John and Judy set their guests up for the day with a full English breakfast with all the trimmings. The house is within easy reach of Devon's main attractions or you can just laze about on the beach, go fishing or walk along the Coastal Path which goes past the front door.

TROUT'S,

South Hallsands, nr Kingsbridge, South Devon TQ7 2EY
Tel/Fax: 01548 511296
e-mail: troutshallsands@netscapeonline.co.uk
websites: www.troutsholidaysco.uk www.selfcateringdevon.com

Beautifully situated and commanding a magnificent panorama of Start Bay, Start Lighthouse and the rolling hills of South Devon, **Trout's** offers an outstanding choice of holiday accommodation, whether in

apartments or in the adjacent cottage. Originally built in 1923 and extended over the years, the complex stands in 7 acres of grounds, surrounded by delightful gardens.

Within the grounds are an all weather tennis court, a 9-hole putting green, a golf practice net, a heated swimming pool and an adventure playground. There's also a games room in the barn with table tennis, pool, darts, table football and a special area for younger children. An especially popular amenity is Trout's Servery - place your order before 4pm and your meal will be served either in the Conservatory restaurant or in the comfort of your own accommodation.

All the apartments and the cottage enjoy spectacular views of the sea and countryside. They are well furnished and equipped to a high standard, and even provided with books and games to suit everybody.

SOUTH ALLINGTON HOUSE,

Chivelstone, Kingsbridge, South Devon TQ7 2NB
Tel: 01548 511272 Fax: 01548 511421
e-mail: barbara@sthallingtonbnb.demon.co.uk
website: www.sthallingtonbnb.demon.co.uk

Offering a choice of bed & breakfast or self-catering accommodation, **South Allington House** is a grand, Georgian-style house built between 1826-30 and set in beautiful grounds. The quiet hamlet of Chivelstone is ideally situated for the beach and wonderfully scenic coastal walks, and provides the opportunity to view birds and animals in their natural habitat. Bed & breakfast guests stay in the main house where 9 rooms are available, (5 en suite, two en suite and with 4-poster beds, and two with private facilities). All rooms have tea/coffee-making facilities, colour television and hairdryer.

There's a visitors' television lounge and guests are free to use the grounds during the day and your hosts, Edward and Barbara Baker, can provide bowls, croquet and coarse fishing for your entertainment. For those who prefer self-catering, the east wing of the house, The Laurels, provides home comforts in relaxing surroundings for up to 4 people, Also available are The Coach House, which sleeps 7, and Coachman's Lodge, which sleeps six. Both are former outbuildings which have been tastefully modernised to a high standard, each has it own garden with outdoor furniture, barbecue - and attractive views across the grounds.

from the sea in 1984 is on display in the car park. While the exercises were in progress, an enemy E-boat attacked the landing forces and more than 600 Allied servicemen lost their lives. Beside the tank are memorial tablets to the men who died during this little-publicised military tragedy, and to the many who later perished on the Normandy beaches.

BEESANDS
9 miles S of Dartmouth off the A379

Beesands lies little more than a mile due south of Torcross and can easily be reached on foot along the coast path. By car, a four mile detour is required. If you don't want to walk, it's well worth negotiating the narrow Devon lanes to reach this tiny hamlet, just a single row of old cottages lining the foreshore of Start Bay. Less than a hundred years ago, Beesands was a busy little fishing village. There are photographs from the 1920s showing fishermen who have drawn their boats laden with lobster, crab and mullet up the beach virtually to their cottage doors. Sadly, the fishing fleet is no longer operating but the mile-long shingle beach is as appealing as ever and has qualified for the coveted yellow and blue flag of the grudgingly granted "Seaside Award". This accolade is only bestowed on beaches which have met 28 different European standards, covering everything from safety and tidiness to provision of facilities for the disabled and the purity of the water.

HALLSANDS
11 miles S of Dartmouth off the A379

South of Beesands, the only way to follow the coastline is by a well-trodden footpath. It's part of the **South Devon Coast Path** and the route takes you through the ruined village of Hallsands which was almost completely demolished by a violent storm in January 1917. Another mile or so further brings you to the lighthouse at **Start Point**, built in 1836, and open to visitors from Monday to Saturday during daylight hours. And if you want to be able to boast that you once stood at the most southerly point in Devon, continue along the Coast Path for about five miles to **Prawle Point**, an ancient lookout site where today there is a Coastguard Station.

CHIVELSTONE
13 miles SW of Dartmouth off the A379

Even in Devon it would be hard to find anywhere further away from the madding crowd than Chivelstone, an unassuming village hidden away in a maze of country lanes in the extreme southwest of the county and well worth seeking out. It's the tranquil rural surroundings that make Chivelstone so appealing but the village also has a fine parish church, the only one in England dedicated to the 4th century pope, St Sylvester. Historically, Sylvester is a misty figure but an old tradition claims that his saintly ministrations cured the Roman emperor, Constantine, of leprosy. Chivelstone church was built at a time (the 15th century) when

THE OPEN ARMS,

Chillington, Kingsbridge, Devon TQ7 2LD
Tel: 01548 581171

About halfway between Kingsbridge and the sea, Chillington is a typical South Hams village, complete with an inviting traditional hostelry, **The Open Arms**. As the name suggests, you'll find a warm welcome here from mine hosts, Jed and Nicki, the chef Pat, and the friendly staff, Lucy, Duncan, John and Sarah. A free house, the inn offers a wide choice of quality ales, including 4 real ales and local draught cider. Quality food is available every

lunchtime and evening: choose from the regular menu or from the specials chalked up on the ancient beams, (the building is some 250 years old). There's an extensive choice, with home made Steak & Kidney Pudding and steaks the specialities of the house. Such is the popularity of the food served here that it's definitely wise to book ahead for weekends in the season. Children are welcome at The Open Arms and there's a no smoking area. In good weather, customers can enjoy their refreshments on the spacious terrace where you can sit and admire the enchanting view across the valley.

THE GLOBE INN,

Frogmore, nr Kingsbridge, Devon TQ7 2NR
Tel/Fax: 01548 531351 e-mail: horsley@theglobeinn.co.uk

The pretty village of Frogmore is not only well placed for magnificent scenery, uncrowded beaches and historic towns and villages, but is also the home of **The Globe Inn**. Overlooking Frogmore Creek, this picturesque 18th century coastal inn provides wonderful, traditional English hospitality tailored to the needs of the 21st century family. Perhaps this seems a little strange when visitors first meet landlords John and Lynda Horsley who come from Australia. They have certainly not only embraced English inn keeping with style and enthusiasm but they are also a welcoming and personable couple who greet everyone as friends.

The inn has 2 bars - the sportsman's with its flagstone floor, pool table and darts, and the lounge bar with its open fire and nautical memorabilia. Both are well stocked with a good range of real ales and farmhouse ciders. Food too is important here so, as well as the extensive menu of bar snacks and meals, there's an ever-changing menu served in the inn's candlelit restaurant. From traditional pub fare to the more exotic there is something

to suit every taste and pocket. Locally caught seafood appears on the list of house specialities as does a variety of other delicious dishes, including Barbary duck and Chicken Stilton. Whilst providing excellent food and drink in relaxed and comfortable surroundings, the Globe Inn also offers visitors a choice of accommodation that is ideal for families and those wishing to explore the South Devon coast. (Please note that The Globe Inn is closed on Monday lunchtimes during the winter).

SHIP TO SHORE RESTAURANT,

45 Church Street, Kingsbridge,
Devon TQ7 1BT
Tel: 01548 854076 Fax: 01548 857890

For quality dining in smart, attractive surroundings the place to make for in Kingsbridge is the **Ship to Shore Restaurant** in Church Street, a licensed restaurant which also offers accommodation. It's owned and run by the Stanton family who moved to the South Hams from Shropshire where Roger was a farmer and his wife Rosamund ran a specialist china shop.

Their son Richard is a fully trained chef and his regularly changing menus offer an excellent choice of dishes based on fresh local meat, fish and garden produce. Everything is prepared on the premises and served in the stylish 30-seater restaurant with its crisp white tablecloths and flowers on every table. In addition to the main dining room, there's a separate area for small parties. The restaurant has its own car park at the rear and if you are planning to stay in this pleasing corner of the county, Ship To Shore has a double room and a twin room, both en suite, which are available all year round for bed & breakfast guests.

this disfiguring disease was still common in England: it seems likely the parishioners hoped that by dedicating their church to him, St Sylvester would protect them from the ravages of a deeply feared illness which, once contracted, imposed total social exclusion on its innocent victims.

CHILLINGTON
9 miles SW of Dartmouth on the A379

A few minutes drive northwards from Chivelstone will bring you to Chillington on the A379. In Saxon times Chillington was part of a Royal estate.

FROGMORE
12 miles SW of Dartmouth off the A379

Frogmore is a small cluster of houses, rather more than a hamlet but you couldn't really call it a village, which stands at the neck of Frogmore Creek, a 2-mile long waterway which flows into the Kingsbridge estuary. It enjoys an attractive setting and also has a pub, The Globe Inn, that is well worth stopping off for (see panel opposite).

KINGSBRIDGE
15 miles SW of Dartmouth on the A381

About four miles beyond Chillington, the A379 skirts what is officially known as **Kingsbridge Estuary,** although strictly speaking it is not an estuary at all, (no river runs into it), but a ria, or drowned valley.

Kingsbridge Harbour

Whatever you call it though, this broad expanse of water provides an attractive setting for this busy little town, an agreeable spot in which to spend an hour or two

THE BLUE DOLPHIN BISTRO,

10 Mill Street, Kingsbridge, South Devon TQ7 1ED
Tel: 01548 852243
website: www.members.tripod.com/BlueDolphinBistro

For quality food served in stylish surroundings, the place to make for in Kingsbridge is the **Blue Dolphin Bistro** in Mill Street. It's just a two minute walk from the car park on the quay, housed in a building which was originally two cottages dating back to the 16th century.

The extensive menu at the Blue Dolphin poses some difficult choices. Amongst the starters, for example, how do you decide between the freshly made soup of the day, the grilled goat's cheese served on a bed of endive with a raspberry vinaigrette, the home made Potted Salcombe Crab, or any of the other half a dozen options? Even more difficult to choose from are the main courses on offer -

an appetising array of steak, poultry, fish, pasta and vegetarian dishes. In addition to the regular menu, a selection of locally caught fish is featured daily, dependent on season and availability. And then there are the wonderful puddings. Amongst them you'll find Fruit Pavlova, Lemon Tart, Crème Brûlée, Steamed Pudding of the Day and a Cheese Board selection of local, regional and Continental cheeses served with crackers and celery. To complement your meal, the Blue Dolphin offers an extensive wine list and also features two Wines of the Month - two different wines selected from interesting and unusual sources.

strolling along the quayside or through the narrow alleys off Fore Street bearing such graphic names as Squeezebelly Passage.

In Fore Street is St Edmund's parish church, mostly 13th century, and well known for the rather cynical verse inscribed on the gravestone of Roger Phillips who died in 1798:

Here lie I at the chancel door
Here lie I because I'm poor
The further in the more you pay
Here lie I as warm as they.

Nearby is **The Shambles**, an Elizabethan market arcade whose late-18th century upper floor is supported on six sturdy granite pillars. Above the church, the former Kingsbridge Grammar School, founded in 1670, now houses the **Cookworthy Museum of Rural Life**, named after William Cookworthy who was born at Kingsbridge in 1705. Working as an apothecary at Plymouth, William encountered traders from the Far East who had brought back porcelain from China. English pottery makers despaired of ever producing such delicate cups and plates, but Cookworthy identified the basic ingredient of porcelain as kaolin, huge deposits of which lay in the hills just north of Plymouth. Ever since then, the more common name for kaolin has been China clay.

During the season, a popular excursion from Kingsbridge is the river cruise to Salcombe. Coastal cruises and private charter boats are also available.

JUST JULIE'S,

17 Fore Street, Kingsbridge, Devon TQ7 1PG
Tel: 01548 852283

On the placard outside **Just Julie's** in Fore Street there's a slogan that says it all: *"The Smile Will Cost You Nothing!"* Just Julie's is indeed a friendly place and the owner, Julie Solomon, has a dazzling smile that would brighten up the gloomiest day. Julie has been running this welcoming restaurant since 1994 and its reputation for good food at value for money prices is now firmly established. A typical menu might include "Summer Sizzlers", crab or seafood salads, ploughman's and some wonderfully delicious desserts based on locally made ice cream. Service in the split-level restaurant is courteous, efficient and of course comes with that "smile that costs nothing". In addition to running this popular restaurant, Julie has somehow managed to find time for other ventures - a trip in a hot air balloon for example, and she has recently taken her first flying lesson in a light aircraft.

HIGHER REW,

Malborough, Kingsbridge, Devon TQ7 3DW
Tel: 01548 842681 Fax: 01548 843681
website: www.HigherRew.co.uk

Located only a mile from South Sands, **Higher Rew Camping and Caravanning** is a family run park in an area of outstanding natural beauty. Soar Mill, a sandy cove, is within walking distance and several other sandy beaches are within easy reach by car. The camp site was established in the late 1950s by John and Valerie Squire and is now run by their two sons, Ian and Malcolm along with Malcolm's wife Sue. Over the years, the site's amenities have been constantly improved and Higher Rew now offers an outstanding range of facilities. The park of 5 acres is gently sloping but terraced to provide level pitches, over 50 of which have electric hook-ups and views across the valley. There are ladies' and gentlemen's toilet blocks, meticulously clean and equipped with showers with thermostatically controlled temperature. The Play Barn has table tennis, skittle alley and a pool table with swings and a slide etc. for younger children. The 160 acres of surrounding ground provides plenty of space for everyone. The Shop/Reception is well stocked, with newspapers available to order, and other amenities include a fully equipped Laundry Room, pay phone and ice pack freezing facilities.

MALBOROUGH
3 miles S of Kingsbridge on the A381

For anyone travelling this corner of the South Hams, the lofty spire of Malborough's 15th century church is a recurrent landmark. It's a broach spire, rising straight out of the low tower. Inside, the church is wonderfully light, so much so that the splendid arcades built in Beer stone seem to glow.

About half a mile to the east of Malborough, just off the A381, is an outstanding example of a medieval farmhouse. **Yarde** is a Grade I listed manor farm with an Elizabethan bakery and a Queen Anne farmhouse. This is a privately owned working farm but Yarde can be visited on Sunday afternoons from Easter to the end of September, and by groups at any time by arrangement.

SALCOMBE
7 miles S of Kingsbridge, on the A381

Standing at the mouth of the Kingsbridge "Estuary'", the captivating town of Salcombe enjoys one of the most beautiful natural

Salcombe Harbour

THE YEOMAN'S COUNTRY HOUSE,

Collaton, Salcombe, South Devon TQ7 3DJ
Tel: 01548 560085 Fax: 01548 562070
e-mail: yeomans.house@easicom.com
website: www.yeomanshouse.co.uk

A traditional Devon longhouse, built of stone and with a thatched roof, The Yeoman's Country House looks as pretty as a picture. Dating back to 1680 and now a Grade II listed building, this outstanding B&B enjoys a peaceful and spectacular location, hidden away at the head of its own lush 19 acre valley of fields, cider

orchards and springs - in summer the scent of fresh flowers from its English cottage garden fills every room.

Another pleasant aroma to be savoured is the smell of baking bread which the owners, Mark and Greg, bake fresh every morning. They also make their own muesli and preserves, and all other produce is organic, free range, local and seasonal whenever possible. Breakfast, (traditional English or continental), is served in the delightful dining room with its stone inglenook fireplace and polished oak floor and candlelit dinner parties here are available by arrangement. Each of the en suite bedrooms is individually decorated, has wonderful views, lavender scented linens, TV and tea tray with home made biscuits, together with many thoughtful touches that make country living so enjoyable. For that special occasion, a four-poster en suite room is available and the house can also be booked for luxurious house parties, accommodating up to 8 guests.

Salcombe Coastline

settings in the country. Sheltered from the prevailing west winds by steep hills, it also basks in one of the mildest micro-climates in England. In the terraced gardens rising from the water's edge, it's not unusual to see mimosa, palms, and even orange and lemon trees bearing fruit. The peaceful gardens at **Overbecks** (National Trust), overlooking Salcombe Bar, have an almost Mediterranean character.

Like other small South Devon ports, Salcombe developed its own special area of trading. Whilst Dartmouth specialised in French and Spanish wine, at Salcombe high-sailed clippers arrived carrying the first fruits of the pineapple harvest from the West Indies, and oranges from the Azores. That traffic has ceased, but pleasure craft throng the harbour and a small fishing fleet still operates from **Batson Creek**, a picturesque location where the fish quay is piled high with lobster creels. The town's seafaring history is interestingly evoked in the **Salcombe Maritime & Local History Museum** in the old Customs House on the quay.

THE COTTAGE HOTEL,

Hope Cove, Kingsbridge, South Devon TQ7 3HJ
Tel: 01548 561555 Fax: 01548 561455
e-mail: info@hopecove.com
website: www.hopecove.com

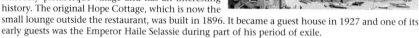

Enjoying superb views of the sea and coastline, **The Cottage Hotel** occupies a magnificent position in this famously picturesque village and has an interesting history. The original Hope Cottage, which is now the small lounge outside the restaurant, was built in 1896. It became a guest house in 1927 and one of its early guests was the Emperor Haile Selassie during part of his period of exile.

The Ireland family arrived here in 1973 and have been providing outstanding hospitality ever since, with a style of service you probably thought had disappeared for ever. The Irelands have established the restaurant's excellent reputation for food and wine, so much so that it's advisable to book ahead. Specialities include locally caught crab and lobster dishes, and the hotel's own pastry chef creates some irresistible desserts. Drinks can be enjoyed in the intimate Herzogin Cecilie cabin, built entirely from the timbers of the famous windjammer wrecked along the coast over 50 years ago, or on the sun terrace with its glorious views of Bolt Tail and the sea.

The Cove Room has a full size table tennis table and games equipment for youngsters, and a tots' play area is set aside in the garden. This peaceful and relaxing hotel has 35 guest bedrooms, 25 of which have sea views - many with balconies, and if you are travelling with young children cots and high chairs, a baby listening service and a laundry are all available. Dogs too are welcome and are allowed on a lead everywhere except the restaurant - and they can be catered for too!

The coastline to the south and west of Salcombe, some of the most magnificent in Britain, is now largely owned by the National Trust. Great slanting slabs of gneiss and schist

Hope Cove

tower above the sea, making the Clifton walk here both literally and metaphorically breathtaking. At **Bolt Head,** the rock forms a jagged promontory protruding onto the western approaches to the Kingsbridge estuary, and further west, the spectacular cliffs between Bolt Head and **Bolt Tail** are interrupted by a steep descent at Soar Mill Cove. After rounding Bolt Tail, the footpath drops down to the sheltered sandy beach of Hope Cove.

HOPE COVE
6 miles SW of Kingsbridge off the A381

There are two Hopes here: Outer Hope, which is more modern and so gets less attention, and Inner Hope which must be one of the most photographed villages in the country. A picturesque huddle of thatched cottages around a tiny cobbled square, Inner Hope once thrived on pilchard fishing but nowadays only a few fishermen still operate from here, bringing in small catches of lobster and crab.

THURLESTONE
5 miles SW of Kingsbridge off the A381

One of the most attractive coastal villages, Thurlestone can boast not just one, but two beaches, separated by a headland. Both beaches are recommended, especially the one to the south with its view of the pierced, or "thyrled", stone, the offshore rock from which the settlement gets its name and which was specifically mentioned in a charter

BEACON POINT HOTEL,

Thurlestone Sands, nr Salcombe, South Devon TQ7 3JY
Tel: 01548 561207

Standing on cliffs overlooking Thurlestone Sands and enjoying magnificent and uninterrupted views over Bigbury Bay to Burgh Island, **Beacon Point Hotel** is a small, family-run licensed hotel where John and Sandra Litchfield extend a very warm welcome to all the family - including dogs! Non-smoking throughout, Beacon Point offers a choice of 8 rooms, a comfortable TV lounge and a relaxing and friendly Bar Lounge with a superb view. There are en suite rooms on both the ground and first floors, some rooms have showers in addition to wash basins, and all have tea/coffee-making facilities. The Litchfields offer a varied and interesting menu, beginning the day with a substantial English breakfast. A 4-course dinner is served every evening and to make the best of your day, packed lunches can be provided. This beautiful rural part of South Devon has plenty to keep the visitor occupied. There are spectacular walks along the South West Coast Path and rural bridleways, award-winning sandy beaches, golf and water sports, two sports centres and an all weather leisure park - all within a short drive.

THE SLOOP INN,

Bantham, nr Kingsbridge, South
Devon TQ7 3AJ
Tel: 01548 560489/560215
Fax: 01548 561940

Situated in the 'olde worlde'
village of Bantham where the
Avon estuary meets the sea, **The
Sloop Inn** offers a rare
opportunity to relax, away from
it all, in this beautiful corner of
the unspoilt South Hams. Dating
back to the 16th century, the inn
has had long associations with
local smugglers - indeed, it was
once owned by John Whiddon, one of the most notorious smugglers and wreckers in the South
Hams.

The Sloop is renowned for its extensive menu of fresh fish and shellfish, local meats and home
made sweets. To accompany your meal, there's a fine range of draught and bottled beers, lagers and
ciders, along with an excellent, quality wine list. The inn makes it an ideal base for a family holiday.
Nearby Bantham beach, just a 5 minute walk over the sand dunes, is one of the best surfing beaches
on the south coast and has also been awarded a 'Rural Clean Beach' flag which means that its great
sandy stretches and many rock pools make it perfect for children. The Sloop offers both bed & breakfast
and self-catering accommodation. In the inn itself there are 5 double rooms, all with en suite facilities,
2 of them family rooms. Self-catering guests are accommodated in 4 luxury cottages at the rear of the
inn. All are equipped to the highest Tourist Board standards and enjoy stunning views over Bigbury
Bay.

WAKEHAM FARM,

Aveton Gifford, Kingsbridge, South Devon TQ7 4NE
Tel: 01548 550263

Wakeham Farm stands in 22 acres of unspoilt countryside close to the village of Aveton Gifford and
just off the A379 Plymouth to Kingsbridge road. The rambling old farmhouse dating back to the 17th
century is a lovely old black and white building that seems to have grown up randomly over the ages.

At the time of writing, the owners of Wakeham Farm are completely refurbishing an annexe to
the house to provide comfortable self-catering accommodation for up to 6 people. All modern amenities
will be provided but at the same time great care is being taken to preserve as many original features as

possible, especially the magnificent
carved wood staircase which was
crafted by french prisoners during the
Napoleonic wars. The completed
annexe will be available to rent all year
round, by the week during the season,
for shorter periods out of season.
Children will be very welcome.

During the lifetime of this book, the
owners of Wakeham Farm also expect
to have modernised and refurbished
two nearby barns, each of which will
also provide accommodation for up to
6 people. The farm's location makes it
a very convenient base for exploring
the South Hams, the Dartmoor
National Park, Torbay and the historic
city of Plymouth.

of 846AD. The village itself stands on a long, flat-topped ridge above the beaches and is an attractive mixture of flower-decked cottages, old farm buildings and long-established shops and inns. The parish church of All Saints is worth a visit to see its impressive 15th century south porch, Norman font and Lady Chapel.

BANTHAM
5 miles SW of Kingsbridge off the A379 or A381

One mile to the north of Thurlestone (as the crow flies) is another fine sandy beach, at Bantham. This small village has a long history since it was a centre of early tin trading between the ancient Britons and the Gauls. By the 8th century, Anglo-Saxons were well-established here, farming the fertile soil. The sea also provided a major source of income in the form of pilchard fishing. A small armada of boats were kept busy during the boom years and the humble pilchards were cured and even exported. Bantham continued to be a busy little port until the early 1900s with sailing barges bringing coal and building stone for the surrounding area.

The village has also seen its fair share of shipwrecks. The bay has yielded some fascinating finds over the years and some of the timbers from the wrecks have been incorporated into the village houses.

AVETON GIFFORD
5 miles NW of Kingsbridge on the A379

Pronounced "Awton Jiffard", this pleasant small village, little more than one main street, had one of the oldest churches in Devon until it was almost completely destroyed by a German bomb in 1943. The modern replacement is surprisingly satisfying. The village's most famous son was born here in 1790, the son of a mason. After learning his father's trade, Robert Macey also studied as an architect. He then walked all the way to London where he successfully established himself and was responsible for designing many hospitals, factories, churches and theatres, of which the most notable were the Adelphi and the Haymarket.

At the southern end of the village, just before the three-quarter mile long medieval causeway, a lane on the right is signposted to

BAY BUNGALOWS,

Challaborough Bay,
nr Bigbury on Sea, Kingsbridge,
South Devon TQ7 4JB
Tel: 01548 810425

With Challaborough Bay a mere 250 yards walk away, **Bay Bungalows** provide an ideal location for a seaside family holiday. A glorious stretch of the South Devon Coast Path runs eastwards from here to Salcombe through some of the most dramatic scenery in the country and there are many magnificent National Trust properties within east reach, amongst them Overbecks gardens, Dartmouth Castle and Saltram House, to name just a few.

All the Bay Bungalows are detached, self-contained and fully furnished, and comprehensively equipped with telephone, colour television and video recorder. The modern kitchens all have a washer/dryer, fridge freezer, dishwasher, microwave and food mixer. The bathrooms have a bath and shower, WC and shaver point. There are two styles of bungalow. The "Bigbury" has two bedrooms and sleeps 4 plus a cot; the "Bigbury on Sea" has three bedrooms, (1 double, 1 twin and 1 triple) and can accommodate seven plus a cot. In all the bungalows, the lounge settee converts to a double bed. Each bungalow has its own car parking space alongside, an enclosed garden and sun patio with garden seating and table, and the site has children's play area. And if you want a change from self-catering, Steven Chapman, the owner of the site, also runs "Fryer Tucks". Located on the edge of Challaborough Beach, it's an excellent fish and chip shop which also serves a variety of other hot and cold food and drinks to take away.

RINGMORE VEAN,

Ringmore, Kingsbridge, Devon TQ7 4HL
Tel: 01548 810123 e-mail: contact@ringmore.com
website: www.ringmore.com

Ringmore Vean is indeed a hidden place, deep in the heart of Ringmore in the South Hams. Ringmore is a Doomsday village, a mixture of slate and thatch, with many properties dating from the mid 17th century. It has an ancient church and inn, the Journey's End, an appropriate name for Ringmore's location, at the end of the road close to the coast - a tranquil setting in which to recharge the batteries. Ringmore Vean dates from the 17th/19th centuries. It is set in a large garden and has its own unheated swimming pool available to the more hardy guest! The rooms have an en-suite shower or bathroom as well as everything necessary for a pleasant stay, including television, tea and coffee making facilities and a hairdryer. Modern amenities ensure a comfortable stay all-year-round. A hearty RV breakfast will set you up for the day.

There is much to occupy your time locally including a number of delightful walks. The lane from the house leads to the sea or to footpaths connecting with our neighbouring villages of Kingston and Bigbury on Sea. Ayrmer Cove, Ringmore's own beach accessible only on foot, is always worth a visit. In summer it is never crowded and at other times it is possible to be alone with your thoughts. Further afield, up to half an hour away, is the city of Plymouth, the market town of Totnes, the sailing mecca of Dartmouth or the wide open spaces of Dartmoor. There are many National Trust properties within easy reach. Whatever your choice you are assured of a warm welcome at Ringmore Vean. However we regret that the house is not suitable for children and we ask guests not to smoke in the house.

THE ROYAL OAK,

Bigbury, Kingsbridge, Devon TQ7 4AP
Tel: 01548 810313

Not to be confused with Bigbury-on-Sea, Bigbury village lies a couple of miles inland. Standing in the heart of the village, **The Royal Oak** is a delightful old hostelry which was originally built as fishermen's cottages and a forge. Inside, the wealth of old beams and many nooks and crannies testify to the antiquity of the building which became an inn sometime in the 1700s. Today, the Royal Oak is owned and run by Martin and Tina Uren who took over in May 2000 with the

experience of a decade or so in the hospitality business to their credit. They serve quality home-cooked food every lunchtime and evening, and customers can enjoy their meals in the bars or in the separate, non-smoking restaurant. Bass cask ale is always available, supplemented by another two guest ales. Children are welcome here and there's a safe play area for them in the spacious beer garden. The inn's 2 guest bedrooms make a good base for exploring glorious South Devon. The rooms have a separate entrance from the inn and are both en suite with a double and a single bed in each.

Bigbury. This very narrow road runs right alongside the River Avon and is very beautiful, but be warned - the river is tidal here and when the tide is in the two fords along the way are impassable.

LODDISWELL
4 miles NE of Kingsbridge off the A379

After the Norman Conquest, Loddiswell became part of the 40,000 acre estate of Judhel of Totnes, a man who with an apparently insatiable appetite for salmon. Instead of rent, he stipulated that his tenants should provide him with a certain number of the noble fish: Loddiswell's contribution was set at thirty salmon a year.

The benign climate of South Devon has encouraged several viticulturists to plant vineyards in the area. The first vines at **Loddiswell Vineyard** were planted in 1977 and since then its wines have been laden with awards from fellow wine-makers and consumer bodies. The Vineyard welcomes visitors for guided tours or walkabouts on weekday afternoons from Easter to October, and also Sunday afternoons in July and August.

BIGBURY
8 miles W of Kingsbridge on the B3392

This small village on a hilltop enjoys grand views over Bigbury Bay to Burgh Island. It has an interesting 14th century church with some fine brasses of that time. Two of them depict the daughters of Sir William Bigbury whose family had lived at Bigbury Court for some 300 years. But Sir William was killed in a duel and the Bigbury line came to an end.

BIGBURY ON SEA
9 miles W of Kingsbridge on the B3392

This popular family resort has a stretch of National Trust coastline and extensive sands. The most interesting attraction here though is **Burgh Island** which is actually only a part-time island. When the tide is out, it is possible to walk across the sandbar linking it to the mainland. At other times, visitors reach the island by a unique "Sea Tractor", specifically designed for this crossing. It can operate in 7ft of water, in all but the roughest conditions, and it's well worth timing your visit to enjoy this novel experience.

MOUNT FOLLY FARM,

Bigbury-on-Sea, nr Kingsbridge,
South Devon TQ7 4AR
Tel: 01548 810267

The South Hams offers some glorious coastal views and one of the most spectacular is to be enjoyed from **Mount Folly Farm** which overlooks Bigbury Bay and the Avon estuary and adjoins the very popular Bigbury Golf Club. There are sandy beaches within walking distance and the bay is ideal for swimming, surfing, wind surfing and fishing. Self-catering guests stay in a self-contained part of the large farmhouse which dates from the early 1900s. The accommodation sleeps up to 7 people in 3 bedrooms, 2 of them with washbasins but is also well suited and popular with couples. The comfortable lounge has a colour TV and video with bay windows overlooking the sea. There's also a well-equipped kitchen/diner, an upstairs bathroom and toilet, and also a downstairs toilet. A cot and high chair are available and baby-sitting can be arranged. Guests are welcome to walk the footpaths of this family-run working farm, or they can follow the breathtaking coastal path. The charming little town of Modbury is just 5 miles away while other places of interest within easy reach include picturesque Salcombe (11 miles), Kingsbridge (9 miles), the historic city of Plymouth (16 miles) and Dartmoor (12 miles). Contact Mrs Jane Tucker for further details.

The whole of the 28-acre island, complete with its 14th century Pilchard Inn, was bought in 1929 by the eccentric millionaire Archibald Nettlefold. He built an extravagant Art Deco hotel which attracted such visitors as Noel Coward, the Duke of Windsor and Mrs Wallis Simpson, and Agatha Christie. The "Queen of Crime" used the island as the setting for two of her novels, *Ten Little*

Niggers, (later renamed *And Then There Were None*), and *Evil Under the Sun*.

MODBURY
9 miles NW of Kingsbridge on the A379

Modbury's main street climbs steeply up the hillside, its pavement raised above street level and stepped. The many Georgian buildings

THE EXETER INN,
Church Street, Modbury, Devon PL21 0QR
Tel: 01548 830239

Standing in the main street of this charming little town, **The Exeter Inn** is as pretty as a picture with is black and white frontage smothered in hanging baskets and tubs of flowers. There's been an inn on this site since the 1300s and a building here was recorded in the Domesday Book. During the Civil War when this peaceful little town saw hand to hand fighting on the streets, the inn was the headquarters of the Royalist forces. Today, the present building is the second oldest in Modbury, only the church is more ancient. Christine Wroe took over here in 1997 when the inn had fallen on hard times but she has restored its reputation for excellent food and quality ales. The interior is very olde worlde with low ceilings, old beams and flagstone floors and, as you might expect of such an ancient building, there are plenty of ghost stories associated with it. Just ask Christine!

THE MODBURY INN,
Brownston Street, Modbury, Ivybridge, Devon PL21 0RQ
Tel: 01548 830275

Located just off the main street of this charming little town, **The Modbury Inn** is an inviting-looking hostelry with cream-coloured walls and hanging baskets of flowers. Formerly known as the Modbury Hotel, the inn dates back to the 1500s and positively exudes a welcoming old world atmosphere.

Mine hosts, Colin and Mary, offer their customers a good choice of food with fresh fish dishes a speciality. Meals are served every lunchtime and evening except on Tuesdays. There are always at least two real ales on tap, (Courage Best and Bass, with a third guest ale during the summer), as well as a wide selection of draught keg bitters, lager, cider and stout. At the rear of the inn is an attractive beer garden for those fine summer days. On Sunday evenings the inn hosts a quiz with everyone welcome to join in.

Modbury makes an ideal base for exploring the South Hams, noted for its lovely countryside and splendid beaches. The inn offers visitors a choice of guest bedrooms available all year round - a single, a double, a small family room and a family en suite room.

give this little town an air of quiet elegance and the numerous antique, craft and specialist shops add to its interest. **St George's Church** contains some impressive, if damaged, effigies of the Prideaux and Champernowne families; the **White Hart and Assembly Rooms** is 18th century, the **Exeter Inn** (see panel opposite), even older.

Road to Burgh Island

Once a coaching inn, this inviting old pub dates back to the 1500s. Modbury's Fair Week in early May is a jolly affair, though perhaps not as riotous as it was in the 19th century when it lasted for nine days and the town's ten inns stayed open from morning to night.

UGBOROUGH
12 miles NW of Kingsbridge on the A3121

This attractive village, which has regularly won awards in "Best Kept Village" competitions, has an imposing church more than 130ft long which stands on top of a substantial prehistoric earthwork. Inside, there are some exceptional features, including a rood screen with a set of 32 painted panels, an unusual monumental brass of an unknown 15th century woman, and a carved roof boss in the north aisle depicting a sow and her litter.

NEWTON FERRERS
19 miles W of Kingsbridge on the B3186

A picturesque fishing village of whitewashed cottages sloping down to the river, Newton Ferrers is beloved by artists and is also one of the south coast's most popular yachting centres. Part of the village sits beside the River Yealm (pronounced "Yam"), the rest

THE ANCHOR INN,

Lutterburn Street, Ugborough, Devon PL21 0NG
Tel: 01752 892283 Fax: 01752 690722

The Anchor Inn takes its name, not from a boat's mooring device, but from the fact that in the days of the Press Gang it was too far from Plymouth for the Navy's brutal recruiting force to reach and return within a day. So it was a haven, or anchor, for the area's young men unwilling to take the King's shilling. It's a particularly pretty village inn, with bench seating at the front, and was originally built as three cottages in the 14th century.

Inside, the inn is just as attractive and, with many of the original features still in place, such as the leaded windows, oak beams and open fireplaces, there's a wonderfully cosy and friendly atmosphere. As well as the lounge with its thatched bar, there's a charming, intimate restaurant where the ceiling beams have been decorated

with a collection of bells. Managed by Sheelagh Jeffreys on behalf of her daughter Samantha, the Anchor is well known locally for the excellent quality and range of the dishes on offer. The selection ranges from local Devon beef to ostrich, wild boar, alligator and bison, but vegetarians are also well-catered for and the wine list provides an interesting selection from around the globe. The high standard of hospitality on offer here doesn't end with the food and drink as, to the rear of the inn, there are 5 self-contained cabins which provide the perfect opportunity for a quiet, undisturbed break.

THE DOLPHIN INN,

1 Riverside Road East, Newton Ferrers, Devon PL8 1AE
Tel: 01752 872007   website: www.dolphin-inn.net

Overlooking the River Yealm, **The Dolphin Inn** is a charming cottage style riverside pub located in the heart of this idyllic village. Built in 1770, it has been an inn since 1840, a time when the name was especially appropriate since schools of bottle-nosed dolphins could still be seen in the tidal river. The interior of the pub is as enchanting as the outside, with ancient beams in the bar and restaurant and a slate floor in the bar. The owners, Sandy and Ian Dunbar-Rees offer their customers an excellent selection of food with locally caught fish the speciality of the house. There are 3 real ales on top, two of them Cornish Ales, plus the local Heron Valley cider and organic apple juice as well as all the usual popular beverages. This is a place where you will want to linger and the Dolphin has a double room, overlooking the river, which is available all year round, and there's also an adjacent self-catering cottage which sleeps four.

alongside a large creek. When the creek dries out at low tide, it is possible to walk across to Noss Mayo on the southern bank. (When the tide is in, a ferry operates, but only during the season).

5 In and Around Dartmoor

Roughly 21 miles long and 15 miles wide, the Dartmoor National Park covers an area of 365 square miles and rises to a height of more than 2000ft. Geologists believe that some 400 million years ago this volcanic tableland stood at 15,000ft above the Devonian Sea. Aeons of erosion have reduced it to a plateau of whale-backed granite ridges. The highest and most dramatic area of the moor lies to the northwest, on Okehampton Common where High Willhays and Yes Tor rise to a height of 2038ft and 2029ft respectively.

The tors are Dartmoor's most characteristic feature - great chunks of fragmented granite which have stood up to centuries of rain, wind and ice better than the less resistant rock which once surrounded them.

The moor is notorious for its abundant rainfall - an

Clapper Bridge, Dartmoor

annual average of 60 inches, twice as much as falls on Torbay, a few miles to the east. In some of the more exposed westerly fringes, an annual rainfall of 100 inches is common. In prehistoric times the climate was much drier and warmer. The moor then was dotted with settlements and this Bronze Age population left behind them a rich legacy of stone circles, menhirs, burial chambers, and single, double or even triple rows of stones. The row of 150 stones on Stall Moor above Burrator Reservoir is believed to be the longest prehistoric stone row in the world.

Buckland Abbey

Wild and untamed as it looks now, the moor has seen a considerable amount of commercial activity. Tin has been mined here since at least the 12th century as the many streamers, gullies and adits bear witness. Lead, copper, iron, and even arsenic have all been mined at some time. This activity has left the moor pitted with the scars of disused mine workings, ruined pump and smelting houses, although most of them are now softened by a cloak of bracken and heather.

We begin this exploration at Tavistock, near the moor's most westerly point, travel clockwise around the Park and then take the only road that crosses the whole of the moor from west to east. As you traverse this huge area of dome-shaped granite, the most frequently seen living creatures are the famous Dartmoor ponies which have roamed here freely since at least the 10th century.

IN AND AROUND DARTMOOR

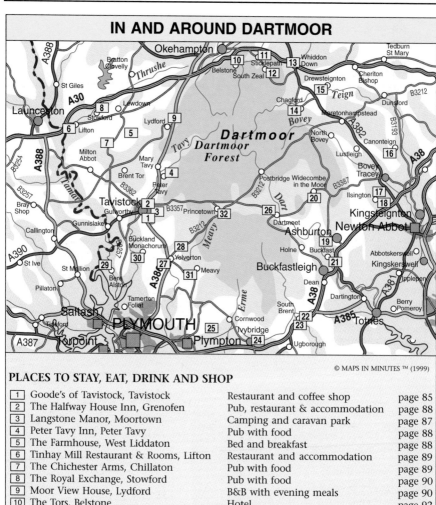

© MAPS IN MINUTES ™ (1999)

PLACES TO STAY, EAT, DRINK AND SHOP

TAVISTOCK

This handsome old town is one of Devon's four Stannary Towns. The name comes from the Latin word for tin, *stannum*, and these four towns (the others are Ashburton, Chagford and Plympton) were the only ones licensed to weigh and stamp the metal mined on the moor.

For most of its recorded history, Tavistock has had only two owners. From 974 until 1539 the town was the property of Tavistock Abbey. Then Henry VIII closed the Abbey and sold the building, along with its vast estates to John Russell whose family, as Earls and Dukes of Bedford, owned most of the town until 1911. The present town centre is essentially the creation of the Russell family, who after virtually obliterating the once-glorious Abbey, created a completely new town plan. Later, in the 1840s, Francis the 7th Duke diverted some of the profits from his copper mines to build the imposing **Guildhall** and several other civic buildings. He also remodelled the Bedford Hotel, and constructed a model estate of artisans' cottages on the western side of the town.

One of the legacies of the Abbey is the annual three-day fair, granted in 1105, which has now evolved into **Goose Fair**, a wonderful traditional street fair held on the second Wednesday in October. Tavistock was also permitted to hold a weekly market which, almost 900 years later, takes place every Friday in the Pannier Market, so named because country folk used to arrive carrying their produce in pannier bags. The Market building was another gift of the 7th Duke of Bedford; virtually unaltered since it was built in the 1850s, it's considered one of finest examples in the south west of a traditional pannier market. The town also holds an antiques and crafts market on Tuesdays, and a Victorian market on Wednesdays when many of the stallholders appear in period costume.

Incidentally, if you think the statue of Sir Francis Drake looks uncommonly like the one on Plymouth Hoe, the fact is that Tavistock's statue is the original, the one at Plymouth a copy.

GOODE'S OF TAVISTOCK,

46-47 Brook Street, Tavistock, Devon PL19 0HE
Tel: 01822 612901

Located in the heart of the town, **Goode's of Tavistock** has been offering quality food and drink to residents and visitors alike since 1957. That was when Stanley and Edna Goode established their popular coffee room and restaurant. Today their son, daughter and son-in-law continue that fine tradition. Customers can start the day at 8.30am with a hearty All Day Breakfast, or indeed with anything from a menu that offers a wide choice of dishes that ranges from steaks to salads, burgers to baps, along with jacket potatoes, vegetarian options, fish dishes and 'olde favourites' such as home cooked ham, egg and fries. There's also a Kiddie Menu and some really alluring desserts. The regular menu is supplemented by daily specials. Nothing served here comes from a freezer. The fish has been landed at Plymouth's Barbican; fruit and vegetables come from the nearby Tamar Valley. These prime ingredients are deftly prepared by chef Gary Cann who was recently voted Young Employee of the Year by the local Rotary Club. The restaurant is licensed and in good weather you can enjoy your refreshments at the pavement tables.

THE HALFWAY HOUSE INN,

Grenofen, Tavistock, Devon PL19 9ER
Tel: 01822 612960 Fax: 01822 617697

A spacious black and white building, **The Halfway House Inn** was originally built in the 16th century as eight cottages, a fact which becomes more apparent when you go upstairs where there are four guest bedrooms. The pub has an immediate feeling of warmth and friendliness with its old beamed ceilings and open log fire in the lounge bar. There's always a genuinely warm welcome from mine hosts, Peter and Maureen Jones, who have been here since 1997 but have many years experience in the hospitality business.

A major attraction at this appealing old hostelry is the quality of the food on offer. There are two separate restaurants, one smoking, one non-smoking, both offering a very extensive à la carte menu. Amongst the starters for example there's a Gratin of Mussels with Camembert or a Crab & Russian Salad; the main courses range from a hearty 10oz traditional Sirloin Steak through Monkfish Kebabs to a Baked Egg & Spinach Tartlet; and to round off your meal there's a daily selection of desserts, many of which are home-made. In addition, there's a blackboard listing daily specials and also special wine offers. Children are welcome and have their own menu. In the bar you'll find an equally wide choice of meals and snacks and for real ale lovers there's a choice of brews that includes Sharp's Doom Bar and Bass. The spacious public bar has a pool table, its own free lending library and a coal fire in the winter.

In good weather you can enjoy your refreshments in the delightful beer garden with its glorious view across the moor to Hessary Tor. The accommodation comprises 2 double en suite rooms,

individually decorated, 1 large en suite family room (very pretty, with a country theme), and a single room with excellent private facilities. A substantial breakfast is included in the tariff - either traditional English or continental. The inn has a large car park and is ideal for walkers since a nearby path takes you down to the local beauty spot of Double Waters where the River Walkham meets the River Tavy. The interesting old town of Tavistock is only 2 miles away and for anglers there's good coarse and salmon fishing in the rivers on the edge of the moors. Incidentally, the inn takes its name from its location halfway between the Barbican in Plymouth and the Market Place at Launceston in Cornwall - in stage coach days it would have been an important staging post.

AROUND TAVISTOCK

GULWORTHY
2 miles SW of Tavistock on the A390

This little village stands at the heart of an area which had a global reputation in the mid-1800s. A quarter of the world's supply of copper was being extracted from nearby mines and, much more alarming, so was 50% of its requirements for arsenic. Mining for copper hereabouts has long since been abandoned, and Gulworthy's arsenic has also gone out of fashion as an agent of murder.

A couple of miles north of Gulworthy is the tiny hamlet of Chipshop. Don't expect to be greeted with the heady aroma of hot fat. The name goes back to the days when the local squire paid his workforce in "chips" or tokens. These could only be exchanged at the shop here (which the squire also owned).

MARY TAVY
4 miles NE of Tavistock off the A386

Roughly twice the size of its east bank twin,
Mary Tavy stands in the heart of Dartmoor's former lead, tin and copper mining area. The most evocative survival of those days stands about one mile north of the village. Standing lonely on the hillside, a conspicuous feature of the landscape, **Wheal Betsy** (NT) is a restored pumping-engine house, part of the Prince Arthur Consols mine which produced lead, silver and zinc.

For lovers of Dartmoor and its history, St Mary's church is a place of pilgrimage. In its churchyard lies William Crossing, the historian of the moor, whose magisterial guide published in the early 1900s is still in print.

PETER TAVY
3 miles NE of Tavistock off the A386

The twin villages of Peter Tavy and Mary Tavy sit on opposite banks of the River Tavy, each taking its name from the patron saint of their respective parish churches. Peter Tavy is the smaller of the two and has changed little since William Crossing, the historian of Dartmoor, came here in 1909 and described "A quiet little place, with a church

Langstone Manor Caravan & Camping Park,

Moortown, Tavistock, Devon PL19 9JZ
Tel/Fax: 01822613371 e-mail: jane@langstone-manor.freeserve.co.uk
website: www.langstone-manor.co.uk

Located in a sheltered wooded valley on the favoured southwest edge of Dartmoor, with many species of mature trees creating a beautiful setting, **Langstone Manor Caravan & Camping Park** offers visitors a wide choice of quality accommodation. In addition to the 42 caravan and camping pitches there are two spacious, well-appointed cottages and two holiday flats within the Manor House. The camping pitches occupy approximately half the site, all on level, well-drained positions and the static caravan homes are all brand new 6-8 berthers with full facilities. The owners, Jane and David Kellett, who took over Langstone Manor in 1999 have provided this attractive site with top of the range facilities and it is also the proud possessor of a David Bellamy Silver Award.

A popular amenity here is the Manor House which has a comfortable lounge bar serving evening

meals. Wonderfully quiet and peaceful, the site is conveniently located only a short distance off the main road (B3357) from Tavistock to Princetown.

Langstone Manor is an ideal base for those of you who enjoy exploring the beautiful West Country with its rich diversity of attractions such as the amazing Eden Project, the Lost Gardens of Heligon and a multitude of National Trust properties. Or, if you just want to get away from it all, there is spectacular Dartmoor at the back door with 365 square miles to explore.

embosomed in trees, a chapel, a school and a small inn". Inside the impressive medieval church, there's a poignant memorial to the 5 daughters of a 17th century rector. The oldest of them was less than a year old when she died:

They breathed awhile and looked the world about,
And, like newly-lighted candles, soon went out.

BRENT TOR
5 miles N of Tavistock off the A386

One of the most striking sights in the whole of Dartmoor is the church of "**St Michael of the Rocks**" which stands atop Brent Tor, an 1100ft volcanic plug which rears up from the surrounding farmland in dramatic fashion. It's the fourth smallest complete church in England, only 15ft wide and 37ft long, with

PETER TAVY INN,

Peter Tavy, Tavistock, Devon PL19 9NN
Tel: 01822 810348 Fax: 01822 810835

The long history of the **Peter Tavy Inn** goes back to the mid-1400s when a single storey one or two-roomed thatched cottage was built to accommodate the masons working on the rebuilding of St Peter's Church. Over the years, that original building has been extended but the inn still retains an atmosphere full of charm and character - stone-flagged floors, exposed stone walls, lots of horse brasses and other vintage agricultural mementoes.

The inn is owned and run by Karen and Graeme Sim who offer their customers a warm and friendly welcome, an excellent menu, real ales and fine wines. Food is available every lunchtime and evening and the inn's professional chef offers an appetising menu with a wide range of choices - Monkfish Orly with Thai Sauce, for example, along with more traditional dishes like Roast Rack of Lamb. One of the specialities of the house is the Game Platter, an intriguing combination of ostrich, pheasant, wild boar, rabbit and venison. There's a large, no smoking room, children and dogs are welcome, there's ample parking and the inn also has a delightful beer garden at the rear.

THE FARMHOUSE,

West Liddaton, Coryton, Okehampton, Devon EX20 4AD
Tel: 01822 860445

Set in idyllic rural countryside in the beautiful Lyd Valley, **The Farmhouse** is a delightful traditional Devon farmhouse offering quality bed & breakfast accommodation. It's the home of Janet and Barry Albrighton, a welcoming couple who greet arriving guests with tea and home made cakes. Delicious home cooked evening meals based on organically grown produce are available and vegetarian food is a speciality. Breakfast is similarly satisfying - prepared with quality ingredients and served in the panelled, slate-floored sitting/dining room. The Farmhouse has two guest bedrooms. There's a spacious double room with Edwardian décor, colour TV and tea/coffee-making facilities, and a light, relaxing bathroom en suite. The second room is a large, country style twin-bedded room with its own private bathroom, well appointed and with a stunning view. Please note that The Farmhouse is a no-smoking establishment.

There's good walking all around West Liddaton, along winding lanes and woodland walks with abundant wildlife and wild flowers. Just a couple of miles away is Brentor Church, a beautiful small gaslit building perched on top of the tor, 1130ft above sea level, and Rowden Gardens where 3000 varieties of aquatic plants can be seen in and around the ponds. The celebrated beauty spot Lydford Gorge is only a little further and the wild expanses of the Dartmoor National Park stretch for miles to the east.

walls just 10ft high but 3ft thick. St Michael's was built around 1140, with additions in the 13th and 14th centuries, and constructed of stone quarried from the rock beneath it. The church is surrounded by a steep churchyard which contains a surprising number of graves considering its precarious and seemingly soilless position. Though sometimes lost in cloud, the scramble to the summit is rewarded on a clear day with magnificent views of Dartmoor, Bodmin Moor and the sea at Plymouth Sound.

LIFTON
10 miles NW of Tavistock on the A30

Standing on the banks of the River Lyd, Lifton was an important centre of the wool

trade in medieval times. But Dartmoor sheep tend to have rather coarse fleeces, because of the cold pastureland. So the good weavers of Lifton petitioned Henry VII, *"by reason of the grossness and stubbornness of their district"* to allow them to mix as much lambs' wool and flock with their wool *"as may be required to work it"*.

LEWDOWN
10 miles N of Tavistock off the A30

It's astonishing to realise that Lewdown's main street was, until the early 1990s, part of the main trunk road, the A30 from Exeter to Launceston. Fortunately, a bypass now takes that busy thoroughfare a couple of miles north of the village. Lewdon lies within the

TINHAY MILL RESTAURANT WITH ROOMS - AA ROSETTE 4 DIAMONDS

Lifton, Devon PL16 0AJ Tel/Fax: 01566 784201

Tinhay Mill Restaurant with Rooms quickly established a reputation for outstanding cuisine. Credit for the quality of food served here goes to Margaret, a gifted chef who has written and published two cookery books using Devon recipes. Tinhay Mill is owned and run by Paul and Margaret Wilson, their delightful house dates from the 1500's, it has a warm and cosy atmosphere. The bedrooms are spacious and comfortable with ensuite shower rooms. Tinhay Mill is open all year, the restaurant is open evenings,

from 7pm until 9.30pm. Both à la carte and table d'hôte menus are available. There's an excellent choice of imaginative dishes using meat, poultry, game, fish and vegetarian - the desserts are delectable. After dinner relax with one of 40 malt whiskys, a liqueur or a vintage port.

Guest reports: 18.09.2000, Helen & Allen Burton Sydney Australia - "excellent hosts, food perfect & accommodation very good"; 21.09.2000, Joan & Denis Clark Toronto - "deserving of every accolade".

Tel/Fax for a brochure, tariff and sample menu.

THE CHICHESTER ARMS,

Chillaton, Lifton, Devon PL16 0HR
Tel: 01822 860283

Hidden away in the rolling hills north of Tavistock, Chillaton is a peaceful little village with a traditional Devon pub, **The Chichester Arms**, at its heart. Originally built as three cottages in the 1700s, it became an inn around the middle of the 19th century when it was named The Carpenters Arms after the family which owned a large estate here. Mine hosts, Roy and Bridget Passmore, took over here in 1996 - their first venture in the pub trade. They quickly established a reputation

for serving good pub food and well-maintained ales. Courage Best is the regular ale with occasional guest ales plus all the popular beverages. Food is served every lunchtime and evening except Monday lunchtimes (unless it's a Bank Holiday), and Thursday evening because that's when the mobile fish and chip van visits the village. Customers are welcome to bring their fish and chips into the pub. A traditional roast is served at Sunday lunchtime when booking is strongly recommended.

THE ROYAL EXCHANGE,

Stowford, Lewdown, nr Okehampton,
Devon EX20 4BX
Tel: 01566 783494

A carved stone by the church gate testifies that the little village of Stowford is a very ancient community. In the old ogham script it bears the name of a Roman, Gunglei. The interior of the church is also worth seeing for its wagon roofs and some fine monuments to the Harris family. The reason most people seek out Stowford though is to visit **The Royal Exchange**, a charming 16th century free house with low-beamed ceilings and open log fires. The inn serves a comprehensive choice of meals and traditional ales. It offers a menu that has something for everyone, from home-cooked Steak & Kidney Pie to Hawaiian Chicken Curry, from Salmon & Broccoli Pasta to a freshly prepared sandwich. Do save yourself for one of the delectable desserts - treacle tart, perhaps, or a lemon meringue roulade, both served with delicious clotted cream. Children's portions are available for most meals and in good weather you can enjoy your meal in the spacious garden at the rear where there's also a small caravan park with standing for 5 caravans.

Your hosts at the Royal Exchange are both horse enthusiasts which explains the many sporting prints, photographs and memorabilia displayed around the inn. Linda rides to hounds and the Royal Exchange also sponsors a local point to point, the Lamerton Men's Open.

MOOR VIEW HOUSE,

Vale Down, Lydford, Devon EX20 4BB
Tel/Fax: 0182 282 0220

From the front, **Moor View House** looks out across Dartmoor; from the rear, there are stunning views across the Devon and Cornwall countryside. This substantial Victorian house was built in 1869 as a guest house and has been offering hospitality to visitors ever since. One of its regular residents in the early days was the writer Eden Phillpots, author of the long running play *A Farmer's Wife* and the song *Widecombe Fair*. Moor View is now the home of David and Wendy Sharples who have created a welcoming home with a wonderfully relaxing atmosphere. Tasteful furnishings, elegant antiques and a Victorian decorative theme make each room a pleasure to the eye, nowhere more so than the dining room with its crisp linen, sparkling crystal, bone china and gleaming silver. Wendy is the chef and her daily 4-course dinner offers a choice of traditional country-style recipes based on the finest local seasonal meat, fish and game.

The 4 en suite guest bedrooms are all beautifully furnished and decorated. The house stands in an extensive mature garden with lawns and paddock to the rear. The famous Lydford Gorge and Castle are close by, the Dartmoor National Park stretches for miles to the east, and visitor attractions such as the picture postcard village of Clovelly and the cathedral city of Exeter are within easy reach.

parish of Lewtrenchard whose rector for 43 years, from 1881 to 1924, was the Rev. Sabine Baring-Gould. He's best known as the author of the hymn *Onward, Christian Soldiers* but he was also an extraordinarily prolific writer, regularly producing two or three books a year - novels, historical works such as *Curious Myths of the Middle Ages*, and books on Devon legend and folklore. He nevertheless found time to restore St Peter's church, an operation whose most remarkable success was in creating a replica of a glorious medieval screen which his grandfather, as rector, had destroyed. The grandson found enough pieces for the replica to be made, and very impressive it is with an elaborate canopied loft decorated with paintings of 23 saints.

The Rev. Sabine scandalised Victorian society by marrying a Lancashire mill girl. But it proved to be a happy and romantic marriage and they had a huge family. The story goes that "One day, emerging from his study, the rector saw a little girl coming down the stairs. 'You do look nice, my dear, in your pretty frock' he said, vaguely recalling that a children's party was in train. 'Whose little girl are you?' 'Yours, papa', she answered, and burst into tears".

STOWFORD
10 miles N of Tavistock off the A30

An unusual feature in the churchyard of **St John's** is a stone by the gate which is carved in the Ogham script with the word "Gunglei", believed to be the name of a Roman soldier who was buried here some 1600 years ago. Inside the church are two monuments to the Harris family, John who died in 1767, and Christopher who died in 1718. The latter is curious not only for showing Christopher in the costume of a Roman warrior but also because "the figures are life-size down to the waist, and then stunted as if the sculptor had grown weary of them".

LYDFORD
10 miles N of Tavistock off the A386

In Saxon times, there were just 4 royal boroughs in Devon: Exeter, Barnstaple, Totnes and, astonishingly, Lydford which is now a pleasant small town but still occupies the same strategic position on the River Lyd

Old Stone Wall, Dartmoor

which made it so important in those days. In the 11th century, the Normans built a fortification here which was superseded a hundred years later by the present **Lydford Castle** (English Heritage - entrance free), an austere stone fortress which for generations served the independent tin miners of Dartmoor as both a court and a prison. The justice meted out here was notoriously arbitrary. William Browne of Tavistock (1590-1643) observed:

> *I oft have heard of Lydford law,*
> *How in the morn they hang and draw*
> *And sit in judgement after.*

Lydford parish is the largest in England, encompassing the whole of the Forest of Dartmoor, and for many centuries the dead were brought down from the moor along the ancient Lych Way for burial in St Petroc's churchyard. A tombstone near the porch bears a lengthy and laboriously humorous epitaph to the local watchmaker, George Routleigh, who died in 1802. The inscription includes the statement that George's life had been *Wound up in hope of being taken in hand by his Maker and of being thoroughly cleansed and repaired and set going in the world to come.*

To the southwest of the village, the valley of the River Lyd suddenly narrows to form the 1.5 mile long **Lydford Gorge** (NT), one of Devon's most spectacular natural features. Visitors can follow the riverside path to the **Devil's Cauldron**, or wander along the 2-

mile walk to the **White Lady**, a narrow 100ft high waterfall. Back in the 17th century, the then remote Lydford Gorge provided a secure refuge for a band of brigands who called themselves the Gubbinses.

Their leader was a certain Roger Rowle, (dubbed the "Robin Hood of the West"), whose exploits are recounted in Charles Kingsley's novel *Westward Ho!*

OKEHAMPTON

The old travel-writer's cliché of a "county of contrasts" can't be avoided when describing the landscape around Okehampton. To the north and west, the puckered green hills of North Devon roll away to the coast; to the south, lie the wildest stretches of Dartmoor

THE TORS,

Belstone, nr Okehampton, Devon EX20 1QZ
Tel: 01837 840689

Belstone lies just inside the Dartmoor National Park, a picturesque village 1000ft up on High Moor near Okehampton. It has a church dating back to 1260 and, adjacent to the church, is The Tors, a small and intimate family run hotel which also serves as the village inn. It has an inviting traditional atmosphere and mine hosts, Ann and Tony Cooper, have made comfort, good food and value for money their priorities. Bar meals, snacks and packed lunches are available every day and real ale devotees will be pleased to know that The Tors is CAMRA approved. The well-furnished bedrooms have either double or single beds, with hot and cold water in each room. Guests can stay on either a B&B or B&B and evening meal basis. This peaceful spot is within easy walking distance of some of the most beautiful and wild parts of Dartmoor. There are Riding and Pony Trekking Centres in the village, fishing close by and golf at Okehampton just a few miles away.

THE DEVONSHIRE INN,

Sticklepath, Okehampton,
Devon EX20 2NN
Tel: 01837 840626

Whether a pub thrives or languishes depends greatly on the personality of its landlord. So, with John Verner-Jeffries as 'mine host' it's no surprise that The Devonshire Inn is as popular as it is. John is an ex-naval officer who had travelled the world before buying what was, in 1988, a desperately run down pub in this curiously named village. He completely refurbished the inn and today this 16th century thatched building is a delight to the eye, both inside and out. Inside, ancient beamed ceilings, stone-tiled floors, horse brasses and gleaming copper pieces

reflect the inn's ancestry; messages painted on the beams demonstrate John's modern sense of humour: "10% off for Octogenarians; 20% off for Nonagenarians; £1 corkage for Telephone Yuppie Users". Most customers couldn't agree more.

The food on offer at the Devonshire Inn is simple and wholesome - pies and pasties, for example, all of them offering remarkable value for money. You can enjoy your meal in the bar, in the beer garden at the back, or at the picnic tables at the front. Dog owners will be delighted to see a prominent message by the front door of the inn proclaiming "Dogs Always Welcome" - according to John "People with dogs can be trusted". And for anyone interested in Britain's industrial heritage, the inn is right next door to the Finch Foundry, a restored working mill with three huge waterwheels.

with the great peaks of High Willhays and Yes Tor rising to more than 2000ft. At this height they are, officially, mountains but quite puny compared with their original altitude: geologists believe that at one time the surface of Dartmoor stood at 15,000ft above sea level. Countless centuries of erosion have reduced it to a plateau of whale-backed granite ridges with an average height of around 1200ft. After so many millions of years of erosion, the moor has become strewn with fragments of surface granite, or moorstone. It was because of this ready-to-use stone that Dartmoor became one of the most populous areas of early Britain, its inhabitants using the easily quarried granite to create their stone rows, circles, and burial chambers. Stone was also used to build their distinctive hut-circles of which there are more than 1500 scattered across the moor.

From Celtic times Okehampton has occupied an important position on the main route to Cornwall. Romantically sited atop a wooded hill and dominating the surrounding valley of the River Okement are the remains of **Okehampton Castle** (EH). This is the largest medieval castle in Devon and the ruins are still mightily impressive even though the castle was dismantled on the orders of Henry VIII after its owner, the Earl of Devon, was convicted of treason.

A good place to start a tour of the town is the **Museum of Dartmoor Life**, housed in a former mill with a restored water wheel outside. In the surrounding courtyard, you will also find the Dartmoor National Park Visitor Centre, craft and gift shops, and a tea-room. Amongst the town's interesting buildings are the 15th century **Chapel of Ease**, and the **Town Hall**, a striking three-

storey building erected in 1685 as a private house and converted to its current use in the 1820s. And don't miss the wonderful Victorian arcade within the shopping centre which is reminiscent of London's Burlington Arcade.

Walking on the fringes of the moor here is a delight, and for those who prefer to see the scenery from horseback, there are some excellent riding stables nearby. Golf courses, too, the one in the town having been reclaimed from the moor which makes it both a very rewarding course to play and an extremely scenic one.

AROUND OKEHAMPTON

BELSTONE
3 miles SE of Okehampton off the A30

Surrounded by the magnificent scenery of the Dartmoor National Park, Belstone is a picturesque village with a triangular village green (complete with stocks), a church dating back to the 13th century, and a splendid pub, The Tors (see panel opposite).

A path from Belstone village leads up to the ancient standing stone circle known as the **Nine Stones**, although there are actually well over a dozen of them. Local folklore asserts that these stones under Belstone Tor were formed when a group of maidens was discovered dancing on the Sabbath and turned to stone. The problem with this story is that the stone circle was in place long before the arrival of Christianity in England. It is also claimed that the mysterious stones change position when the clock strikes noon. What is certain is that the view across mid-Devon from this site is quite breathtaking.

For lovers of solitude, this is memorable country, unforgettably evoked by Sir Arthur Conan Doyle in *The Hound of the Baskervilles*. Recalling the villain's fate in that book, walkers should beware of the notorious "feather beds" - deep bogs signalled by a quaking cover of brilliant green moss.

STICKLEPATH
5 miles E of Okehampton off the A30

The little village of Sticklepath boasts one of the most interesting exhibits of industrial

Haytor, Dartmoor

POLTIMORE COUNTRY HOUSE,

South Zeal, Okehampton, Devon EX20 2PD
Tel: 01837 840209 Fax: 01837 849032

Enjoying a delightful location on the edge of the Dartmoor National Park, **Poltimore Country House** is an appealing early-19th century thatched house set in extensive gardens covering 3 acres. The house positively radiates peace and tranquillity, a perfect place to stay while exploring this lovely part of Devon. The owner, Selina Courtenay is a local girl, one of 5 sisters of a farming family, so she knows the area well and is very happy to share her 'local knowledge' with guests. Her family organises shoots in the area and also run the largest covered equestrian centre in the west. There are 7 guest bedrooms at Poltimore, all en suite and all attractively decorated in country house style, and fully equipped with TV and hospitality tray. The drawing room has 'sink into' comfy sofas where it's not at all difficult to nod off after a day absorbing the pure Devon air. Breakfast is traditional, but vegetarians and others with dietary requirements can also be catered for, given prior notice.

If you prefer self-catering, there are two attractively converted barns within the grounds, both fully furnished and equipped, and with their own outside areas. Whichever option you choose, you'll be close to the spectacular scenery of Dartmoor and with the cathedral city of Exeter only a 40-minute drive away.

DARTMOOR VIEW HOLIDAY PARK,

Whiddon Down, Okehampton,
Devon EX20 2QL
Tel: 01647 231545 Fax: 01647 231654
e-mail: anybody@dartmoorview.co.uk
website: www.dartmoorview.co.uk

To the south of Dartmoor View Holiday Park stretch the untamed acres of the Dartmoor National Park where you can walk for some 10 miles or more before seeing anywhere more populated than an occasional farmhouse or isolated cottage. If you are feeling more sociable, the lively market town of Okehampton is just 6 miles away and within an hour's drive are the coastal resorts of Exmouth, Bude, Torquay and Paignton. Families are well provided for with attractions such as Woodlands Park and the famous Paignton Zoo.

The five star **Dartmoor View Holiday Park** offers an attractive environment for visitors to the area. The Park is beautifully laid out with lots of trees and flower-beds and the many facilities on offer include a shop, off-licence, campers kitchen, children's play area with a fort, heated outdoor swimming pool, small putting green, games room and a cosy bar. There's also a heated toilet and shower block and a laundry with washing machine, tumble dryer, spin dryer and ironing facilities. Visitors can bring their own touring caravan, tent or motorhome, or hire one of the Park's quality holiday homes. All the Park's static caravans have 2 or 3 bedrooms with additional sleeping facilities in the lounge area. They are very well equipped with a fully-fitted kitchen, full bathroom with shower and flush toilet, and a gas fire and TV in the lounge.

archaeology in Devon. **The Museum of Waterpower** is housed in the Finch Foundry which from 1814 to 1960 was renowned for producing the finest sharp-edged tools in the West Country. The three massive waterwheels are now working again, driving the ancient machinery, and pounding rhythms of the steam hammer and rushing water vividly evoke that age of noisy toil.

SOUTH ZEAL
7 miles E of Okehampton off the A30

South Zeal is yet another of the many Devon villages which have good reason to be grateful for the major road-building undertakings of the 1970s. The village sits astride what used to be the main road from Exeter to Launceston and the Cornwall coast - a road which as late as 1975 was still laughably designated on maps of the time as a "Trunk (major) Road". The "Trunk Road" was actually little more than a country lane

Sunset, Dartmoor

but it was also the only route available for many thousands of holiday-makers making their way to the Cornish resorts. Today, the village is bypassed by the A30 dual carriageway.

Isolated in the middle of the broad main street stand a simple medieval market cross and St Mary's chapel, rebuilt in 1713. To the

south of the village rises the great granite hump of Dartmoor. On its flanks, for the few years between 1901-9, the villagers of South Zeal found sorely needed employment in a short-lived copper mine.

WHIDDON DOWN
8 miles E of Okehampton off the A30

About a mile south of the village stands the **Spinsters Rock**, the best surviving chambered tomb in the whole of Devon. According to legend, three spinsters erected the dolmen one morning before breakfast, an impressive feat since the capstone, supported by just three uprights 7 feet high, weighs 16 tons.

DREWSTEIGNTON
12 miles SE of Okehampton off the A30

This appealing village stands on a ridge overlooking the valley of the River Teign and the celebrated beauty spot of Fingle Bridge. Thatched cottages and a medieval church stand grouped around a square, very picturesque and much photographed. To the south of the village, Prestonbury Castle and Cranbrook Castle are not castles at all but Iron Age hilltop fortresses. **Castle Drogo**, on the other hand, looks every inch the medieval castle but in fact was built between 1911 and 1930 - the last castle to be built in England (see panel on page 97).

CHAGFORD
13 miles SE of Okehampton off the A382

An ancient settlement and Stannary town, Chagford lies in a beautiful setting between

THE GLOBE INN,

High Street, Chagford,
Devon TQ13 8AJ
Tel: 01647 433485
website: www.the-globe.org.uk

Located in the heart of this delightful village, opposite the parish church's lofty 15th century tower, **The Globe Inn** is a striking building with white-painted walls set off by colourful window boxes of flowers. A former coaching inn, its history stretches back to the 16th century and the interior, with its open log fire, exposed stonework and partly panelled walls, is full of charm and character and reflects the inn's long tradition of hospitality. Mine hosts, Andrew and Milla, took over here in the spring of 2000 and have already acquired a well-earned reputation for providing good food, quality ales and comfortable accommodation. The Country Style menu, served in both bars, is extensive and offers all the traditional favourites along with a good choice of bar snacks such as home-cooked ham, egg and chips, omelettes, ploughmans, sandwiches and jacket potatoes, as well as grills based on locally sourced meat. The blackboard lists daily specials and desserts,

and all the food is freshly cooked to order. During the season, food is available throughout the day until 9.30pm; out of season it is served from noon until 3pm, and from 6pm until 9pm. The inn itself is open all day, every day, serving a wide selection of lagers, cider and stout as well as a choice of real ales that includes Courage and Directors.

If you are thinking of staying in this lovely part of the Dartmoor National Park, the Globe has 3 quality rooms available all year round. They are all en suite, with colour TV, refrigerator and tea/coffee-making facilities. The hotel is also happy to provide picnic lunches for your days out and there are special rates for stays of 3 nights or more. Unfortunately, the accommodation is not suitable for young children and babies.

Chagford is a superb centre for touring or walking, with all the moorland beauty spots within easy reach. There's fishing on the nearby River Teign, in the Fernworthy Reservoir and in many other fine rivers; riding from local stables and golf at the magnificent 18-hole Manor House course. Famous Castle Drogo is only 3 miles away, the historic cities of Exeter and Plymouth, and the Riviera-like seaside resort of Torquay are all within easy reach, as is the spectacular north Devon coast. And of course, there are the hundred square miles of the Dartmoor National Park to explore with its rugged scenery, historic features such as the medieval Clapper Bridge, and enchanting villages like Widecombe-in-the-Moor - the celebrated destination of Uncle Tom Cobley and all.

CASTLE DROGO,

Drewsteignton, Devon EX6 6PB
Tel: 01647 433306 Fax: 01647 433186

About 10 miles east of Okehampton, on a minor road off the A382, stands one of Devon's most interesting architectural oddities, Castle Drogo - the last 'castle' to be built in England. This intriguing building was the brainchild of Julius Drewe, a founder of the Home and Colonial Stores, the Victorian equivalent of Tesco supermarkets today. The enterprise was so successful that Julius was able to retire in 1889 at the age of 33, taking with him a colossal fortune. Julius spent his early (and very comfortable) retirement researching his family ancestry. He was able to prove to his own satisfaction that one of the Drewe forebears was a Norman baron, Drogo de Teign, after whom the parish of Drewsteignton had been named in the 12th century.

Some 20 years later, by an extraordinary coincidence, the Drogo Estate at Drewsteignton arrived on the property market in 1910 and Julius snapped it up. He then commissioned the most celebrated architect of the day, Sir Edwin Lutyens,

to *"build a medieval fortress to match the grandeur of the site"* - a site that stands at more than 900ft above sea level, overlooking the wooded gorge of the River Teign and commanding superb views across Dartmoor. Lutyens was in his prime and undaunted by either his determined client or his unusual brief. His preliminary sketches envisaged a house of heroic size, but practicalities and the intervention of World War I prevailed and the size was gradually reduced by about two-thirds. Nevertheless, the granite castle, finally completed in 1930, is one of Lutyens' most remarkable works. It combines the grandeur of a medieval castle with the comfort of the

20th century and is very visitor-friendly - a great country house with a terraced formal garden, a woodland spring garden, colourful herbaceous borders and a huge circular croquet lawn where visitors are welcome to play (equipment may be hired).

Julius Drewe died having lived only a few years in his magnificent new home. He was succeeded by his son Basil and in 1974 by his grandson Anthony, who continued to live in the castle. It was Anthony Drewe and his son Christopher who gave the house and 600 acres to the National Trust in 1974 - the first twentieth century house to pass into its possession.

the pleasant wooded valley of the North Teign river and the stark grandeur of the high moor. The famous Dartmoor guide, James Perrot, lived in the town between 1854 and 1895, and is buried in St Michael's churchyard. It was he who noted that some of the farms around Chagford had no wheeled vehicles as late as 1830. On the other hand, Perrot lived to see the town install electric street lighting in 1891 making Chagford one of the first communities west of London to possess this amenity.

It was Perrot also who began the curious practice of letterbox stamp collecting. He installed the first letterbox at **Carnmere Pool** near the heart of the moor so his Victorian clients could send postcards home, stamped to prove they had been there. Today, there are hundreds of such letterboxes scattered all over Dartmoor.

In the centre of the town stands a charming octagonal building, formerly the Market House, built in 1862. Around the square are some old style family shops offering some interesting shopping and lots of atmosphere. St Michael's church, mostly 15th century, has an elaborate monument to Sir John Wyddon who died in 1575. But the church is better known because of the tragic death of one of his descendants here in October 1641. Mary Whiddon was shot at the altar as she was being married, an incident that is said to have inspired R.D. Blackmore's *Lorna Doone.*

To the west of Chagford, an exceptionally pleasant lane leads upstream from **Chagford Bridge** through the wooded valley of the North Teign river. (For 1.5 miles of its length, this lane is joined by the Two Moors Way, the long-distance footpath which runs all the way from Ivybridge on the southern edge of Dartmoor to the Bristol Channel coast.) A rock beside the river known as the **Holed Stone** has a large round cavity. If you climb through this, local people assure you, a host of afflictions from rheumatism to infertility will be cured.

The land to the south of Chagford rises abruptly towards **Kestor Rock** and **Shovel Down**, the sites of impressive Bronze Age settlements and, a little further on, the imposing Long Stone stands at the point where the parishes of Gidleigh and Chagford end and Duchy of Cornwall land begins.

MORETONHAMPSTEAD
16 miles SE of Okehampton on the A382

Moreton, as this little town is known to local people, has long claimed the title of "Gateway to east Dartmoor", a rôle in which it was greatly helped by the branch railway from Newton Abbot which operated between 1866 and 1964. This is the gentler part of Dartmoor, with many woods and plantations, and steep-sided river valleys. Within easy reach are picture-postcard villages such as Widecombe in the Moor, striking natural features like Haytor, and the remarkable Bronze Age stone hut-circle at Grimspound.

The best approach to Moreton is by way of the B3212 from the southwest. From this direction you are greeted with splendid views of the little hilltop town surrounded by fields and with the tower of **St Andrew's Church** piercing the skyline. Built in Dartmoor granite during the early 1400s, the church overlooks the Sentry, or Sanctuary Field, an attractive public park. In the south porch are the tombstones of two French officers who died here as prisoners of war in 1807. At one point during those years of the Napoleonic Wars, no fewer than 379 French officers were living in Moreton, on parole from the military prison at Princetown. One of them, General Rochambeau, must have sorely tested the patience of local people. Whenever news arrived of a French success, he would don his full-dress uniform and parade through the streets.

One of the most interesting buildings in Moreton is the row of **Almshouses** in Cross Street. Built in 1637, it is thatched and has a striking arcade supported by sturdy granite columns. The almshouses are now owned by the National Trust but are not open to the public. Just across the road from the almshouses is **Mearsdon Manor Galleries**, the oldest house in Moreton, dating back to the 14th century. The ground floor of the manor is now a very pleasant traditional English tea room. In total contrast, the remaining rooms contain an astonishing array of colourful, exotic artefacts collected by the owner, Elizabeth Prince, on her trips to the Far East. There are Dartmoor-pony-sized wooden horses, Turkish rugs, Chinese lacquered furniture, finely-carved jade - a veritable treasury of Oriental craftsmanship.

LUSTLEIGH
21 miles SE of Okehampton off the A382

Lustleigh is one of Dartmoor's most popular and most photographed villages. Placed at all

Cottage in Lustleigh

angles on the hillside, it presents a ravishing assortment of 15th and 16th century deeply-thatched, colour-washed cottages, picturesquely grouped around the church. Appropriately for such a genuinely olde-worlde village, Lustleigh keeps alive some of the time-honoured traditions of country life, enthusiastically celebrating May Day each year with a procession through the village, dancing round the maypole, and the coronation of a May Queen. From the village there are some delightful walks, especially one that passes through Lustleigh Cleave, a wooded section of the steep-sided Bovey valley.

BOVEY TRACY

This ancient market town takes its name from the River Bovey and the de Tracy family who received the manor from William the Conqueror. The best-known member of the family is Sir William Tracy, one of the four knights who murdered Thomas à Becket in Canterbury Cathedral. To expiate his crime Sir William endowed a church here, dedicated to St Thomas. That building was destroyed by fire and the present church is

15th century with a 14th century tower. Its most glorious possession is a beautifully carved screen of 1427, a gift to the church from Lady Margaret Beaufort, the new owner of the manor and the mother of King Henry VII.

Bovey Tracy, unlike so many Devon towns and villages, has never suffered a major fire. This is perhaps just as well since its fire-fighting facilities until recent times were decidedly limited. In 1920, for example, the town did have an engine, and five volunteers to man it, but no horses to draw it. The parish council in that year issued a notice advising "all or any persons requiring the Fire Brigade with Engine that they must take the responsibility of sending a Pair of Horses for the purpose of conveying the Engine to and from the Scene of the Fire".

For such a small town, Bovey Tracy is remarkably well-supplied with shops and another interesting place to visit in the town is **Riverside Mill** run by the Devon Guild of Craftsmen. The Guild presents changing craft exhibitions and demonstrations and the mill also contains a Museum of Craftsmanship, a

Willmead Farm, Bovey Tracy

CANONTEIGN FALLS,

nr Chudleigh, Exeter, Devon EX6 7NT
Tel/Fax: 01647 252617

At **Canonteign Falls** the waters from moorland springs and streams on Dartmoor cascade 220 feet down a rocky hillside. It's the highest waterfall in England and a magnificent sight when in full spate. Although the area around the falls was landscaped in the 1700s, it was allowed to become overgrown and astonishingly wasn't restored until 1985. The Falls are located in an area of outstanding natural beauty which offers a breathtaking mix of waterfalls, lakes and cascades, surrounded by spectacular rock formations in a magnificent woodland setting.

There is something here for all the family. On a hot day, visitors can relax in the cool Victorian Fern Garden or take a leisurely stroll around the Wetland Nature Reserve. Youngsters can enjoy the Adventure Area or the indoor play area, as well as the Junior Commando Assault Course, whilst everyone loves the wildfowl and miniature ponies. There's a café serving Devon Cream Teas and appetising home cooked fare, and the Barbecue/Tuck Box serves burgers, snacks, sandwiches and scrumptious Devon Farmhouse Ice Cream. And if you'd like a souvenir of your visit to this splendid natural wonder, you'll almost certainly find something suitable in the Gift Shop here.

THE CARPENTERS ARMS,

Ilsington, Newton Abbot,
Devon TQ13 9RG
Tel: 01364 661215

The picturesque village of Ilsington stands some 500ft up on the edge of Dartmoor, surrounded by woodland. It boasts an impressive medieval church with some fine carvings and a font where the parish's most famous son was baptised in 1586 - John Ford, the celebrated Jacobean dramatist. The village also boasts a lovely old traditional inn, **The Carpenters Arms**, which opened as a simple alehouse in the early 1800s.

The building itself is much older than that, as the ancient dark beams with their display of gleaming horse brasses, bear witness. An open log fire adds to the charm of this welcoming hostelry run by David and Yvonne Mugford. They stock a good range of ales, including Bass, Flowers IPA and Boddington Creamflow. They also offer a wide selection of meals and snacks, amongst which the home made soup of the day is especially popular. Food is available every day between noon and 2pm, and again between 6.30 and 9pm (Sundays, 7-9pm). Customers can enjoy their meal anywhere throughout the inn although there's a special area for children. For parties of 6 or more, bookings are requested. Please note that the Carpenters Arms only accepts cash or a cheque with bank card. A visit to this fine old inn can easily be combined with an excursion to Haytor, perhaps the most famous of the Dartmoor tors, which rises just a couple of miles to the west.

study centre and a shop. Walkers will enjoy the footpath that follows the track bed of the former railway from Moretonhampstead to Newton Abbot, skirting the River Bovey for part of its length

Just to the north of Bovey Tracy is **Parke**, formerly the estate of the Tracy family but now owned by the National Trust and leased to the Dartmoor National Park as its headquarters. There are interpretive displays on all aspects the moor; attractive grounds, in which there is a Rare Breeds Farm; and copious information is available. The Centre can also provide details of the many nature trails, woodland and riverside walks in the area, including one to the famous **Becky Falls** where the Becka Brook makes a sudden 70ft drop.

AROUND BOVEY TRACY

ILSINGTON
3 miles SW of Bovey Tracey off the B3387

Like so many Dartmoor communities, Ilsington was once an important centre of the

wool industry. At the heart of the village is a characteristic trio of late medieval buildings - church, church house and inn. The interior of St Michael's Church is well worth seeing with its impressive array of arched beams and roof timbers which seem to hang in mid-air above the nave. Also of interest are the medieval pew ends, thought to be the only ones in Devon carved with distinctive "poppy head" design; a mid-14th century effigy of a woman; and an elaborately carved 16th century rood screen.

Entry to the churchyard is by way of an unusual lych gate with an upper storey which once served as the village schoolroom. The present structure is actually a replica of the original medieval gate which apparently collapsed when someone slammed the gate too enthusiastically. The nearby church house, dating back to the 1500s, is now sub-divided into residential dwellings known as St Michael's Cottages.

This small village was the birthplace of the Jacobean dramatist John Ford (1586-1639) whose most successful play, *Tis Pity She's A Whore* (1633), is still occasionally revived.

Ilsington is a sizeable parish and includes the three well-known tors of Rippon, Saddle

LOOKWEEP FARM COTTAGES,

Liverton, Newton Abbot, Devon TQ12 6HT
Tel: 01626 833277 Fax: 01626 834412
e-mail: holidays@lookweep.co.uk website: www.lookweep.co.uk

Situated two miles inside the southeastern corner of the Dartmoor National Park, **Lookweep Farm Cottages** provide a delightful setting for a self-catering holiday. The two cottages were sympathetically converted from a traditional stone and cob barn just across the farmyard from the owners' home. The cottages are full of character - timbered with vaulted ceilings, and are exceptionally well equipped with items such as colour TV and video, microwave and washer dryer. Each has a stable door to its own small garden, (garden furniture supplied), and enjoys beautiful views across open fields. Guests have the use of a heated swimming pool, about 12ft by 30ft, which is normally open from May to mid-September, weather permitting. The cottages themselves are available all year round and can each sleep up to 5 persons. Although it's no longer a working farm, Lookweep is surrounded by open farmland and woods. The present owners have horses in the fields and a friendly dog! The farm is just a 4-mile journey from Haytor - the most famous of the Dartmoor tors, located in one of the most spectacular parts of the moor. To the east, the sea is only ten miles away and even closer is the small town of Bovey Tracey, the "Gateway to Dartmoor", which has a wide range of shops, pubs, restaurants, a craft centre, the famous "House of Marbles" and a teapot pottery where children can customise their own mugs.

and **Haytor Rocks**. The latter is perhaps the most dramatic, especially when approached from the west along the B3387, and with a height of almost 1500ft provides a popular challenge for rock climbers.

In the early 1800s, the shallow valley to the north of Haytor Rocks was riddled with quarries which supplied granite for such well-known buildings as London Bridge, the National Gallery and the British Museum.

ASHBURTON
8 miles SW of Bovey Tracey off the A38

This appealing little town lies just inside the boundary of the Dartmoor National Park, surrounded by lovely hills and with the River Ashburn splashing through the town centre. Municipal history goes back a long way here, to 821AD in fact, when the town elected its first Portreeve, the Saxon equivalent of a Mayor. The traditional office continues to the present day, although its functions are now purely ceremonial. But each year, on the fourth Tuesday in November, officials gather to appoint not just their Portreeve but also the Ale Tasters, Bread Weighers, Pig Drovers and even a Viewer of Watercourses.

St Andrews Church, Ashburton

In medieval times, Ashburton's prosperity was based on tin. As one of Devon's four stannary towns, Ashburton benefited from the trade generated by the Dartmoor tinners who were obliged to come here to have their metal weighed and stamped, and to pay the duty. Later, the cloth industry was the town's

THE LAVENDER HOUSE HOTEL & RESTAURANT,
Knowle Hill, Ashburton, Devon TQ13 7QY
Tel: 01364 652697 Fax: 01364 654325

Although only a 3 minute drive from the main Exeter to Plymouth expressway (A38), **The Lavender House Hotel & Restaurant** stands in its own 3-acre landscaped gardens, enjoying glorious views of the Dartmoor National Park. The spacious house dates back to the early 1900s and has been thoroughly modernised and refurbished by the owners, Leon and Karen Roberts.

Guests will find an excellent restaurant serving the finest quality food, based on fresh local produce and prepared to your order by the hotel's Chef de Cuisine. Bar meals are also available in the Lounge Bar, a cosy, comfortable room with leather sofas gathered around the fire. The Lavender House has ten guest bedrooms, all en suite, individually and tastefully decorated, equipped with colour TV and

tea/coffee-making facilities, and most of them with breathtaking views. The hotel's wide range of services includes catering for special dietary requirements, baby sitting facilities, cots and high chairs, packed lunches and much more.

The Lavender House also has a well-equipped Beauty Treatment Room, full conference facilities and, with its beautiful gardens, is a popular venue for wedding receptions. As Leon and Karen say, "We believe in looking after our guests and making them feel totally at home in what is a very special Country House Hotel".

main money-spinner, with several fulling mills along the banks of the Ashburn producing cloth which the East India Company exported to China.

WIDECOMBE IN THE MOOR
8 miles E of Bovey Tracey off the B3212

Just outside Postbridge, a minor road leads to the legendary Widecombe in the Moor. This

Widecombe in the Moor

pleasing village enjoys a lovely setting in the valley of the East Webburn river and the grand old church, with its massive 120ft high granite tower rising against a backdrop of high moorland, has understandably been dubbed the "**Cathedral of the Moors**". Dedicated to St Pancras, the church was built with funds raised by tin miners in the 14th century, and enlarged during the next two centuries. A panel inside the church records the disastrous events of 21st October 1638. A sizeable congregation had gathered for a service when a bolt of lightning struck the tower, dislodging huge blocks of masonry on to the worshippers. Four were killed and a further sixty badly injured. (Local legend maintains that the Devil had been spotted earlier that day spitting fire and riding an ebony stallion across the moor).

In addition to the church, two other buildings are worth mentioning. Glebe House is a handsome 16th century residence which has since been converted to a shop, and Church House is an exceptional colonnaded building which was originally built around 1500

HIGHER VENTON FARM,

Widecombe-in-the-Moor, South Devon TQ13 7TF
Tel: 01364 621235

Only half a mile from the picturesque village of Widecombe-in-the-Moor, **Higher Venton Farm** is a charming 16th century thatched Devon longhouse nestling in the green, unspoilt countryside of the Dartmoor National Park. Once the home of the famous Dartmoor authoress, Beatrice Chase, Higher Venton has been owned by Helen Hicks' family for several generations and their 45-acre farm is still active with sheep, cattle and horses. Helen, assisted by her family 'and Poppy the retriever', offers bed & breakfast guests traditional farmhouse accommodation and good, wholesome cooking using fresh farm produce. Evening meals are also available. There are 2 comfortable double, en suite, bedrooms and one twin room, all of the rooms with washbasins. At Higher Venton your holiday can be as active or relaxed as you wish. For the more energetic, there's a riding stables 5 minutes walk down the lane; a pleasant 15-minute amble brings you to the pretty village of Widecombe-in-the-Moor, renowned for its September Fair and Uncle Tom Cobley and all; and all around lies the rugged beauty of Dartmoor - all 365 square miles of it.

THE ABBEY INN,

30 Buckfast Road, Buckfast, Devon TQ11 0EA
Tel: 01364 642343 Fax: 01364 644067

The Abbey Inn at Buckfast is magnificently positioned on the banks of one of Britain's most beautiful rivers. The River Dart rises on Dartmoor and meanders through Buckfast and Totnes on its way to the ancient port of Dartmouth. The inn was constructed within sight of the ruins of the original Buckfast Abbey in 1750 as a private residence for the owner of the local stone quarry and was named Blackrock House. The new Buckfast Abbey with its magnificent church can be seen from the inn's riverside terrace and prompted the name to be changed to the Abbey Inn some ten years ago.

Opposite the front door of the inn is a footpath that rises steeply to the ruin of Buckfastleigh parish church where the tomb of the squire, Richard Capel, can be seen. It's a fair assumption that Sir Arthur Conan Doyle based his classic tale of The Hound of the Baskervilles on the stories surrounding

this evil man. The Abbey Inn's present proprietors, Liz and Terry Davison, are more renowned for their hospitality and high quality cuisine than for evil goings-on, although their Great Dane dog, Bud, could be mistaken for a relative of the infamous hound and a colony of bats can be seen from the terrace on summer evenings as they leave their cave for a night's hunting!

The inn is situated most conveniently for Dartmoor, lying just inside the National Park, and with the Dart Valley Steam Railway, the Otter Sanctuary and Butterfly Farm all close by.

GLAZEBROOK HOUSE,

South Brent, Devon TQ10 9JE
Tel: 01364 73322 Fax: 01364 72350

Set on the southern slopes of the Dartmoor National Park, within easy reach of the A38, **Glazebrook House** is an elegant mid-Victorian country house surrounded by 4 acres of mature gardens. Privately owned and managed by Fred and Chris Heard, the hotel offers superb en suite rooms, including three 4-poster suites, all beautifully furnished and enjoying lovely countryside and garden views. The stylish restaurant provides first class cuisine - from a

romantic candlelit dinner for two or small dinner parties. The Heards take great pride in the way they present the table d'hôte and à la carte menus with all the dishes prepared with the freshest and finest ingredients under the watchful eye of Chef David Merriman. The hotel's cellar stocks a wide range of fine wines, ensuring there is something to suit every palate. After dinner, guests can relax in the friendly atmosphere of the comfortable lounge bar which boasts a roaring log fire during the winter months. In addition, Glazebrook House has excellent conference facilities and weddings are also a speciality.

During the day, there is plenty to do and see in the neighbourhood. Walking, fishing, golf and horse riding are all available nearby; National Trust properties such as Castle Drogo, Saltram House and Buckland Abbey are on the doorstep and there are many gardens such as Overbecks, The Garden House, Heligan, Trebah and Lukesland to enjoy.

to accommodate those travelling large distances across the moor to attend church services. It was later divided into almshouses then served in succession as a brewery and a school. It is now a National Trust shop and information centre.

The famous fair to which Uncle Tom Cobleigh and his boisterous crew were making their way is still held here on the second Tuesday in September and although it is no longer an agricultural event is still a jolly affair.

From Widecombe, a country lane leads to **Grimspound** which is perhaps the most impressive of all Dartmoor's Bronze Age survivals. This settlement was occupied between 1800BC and 500BC and is remarkably well-preserved. There are 24 hut circles here, some of them reconstructed, and it's still possible to make out the positions of door lintels and stone sleeping shelves. Today, the area around Grimspound is bleak and moody, an atmosphere which recommended itself to Sir Arthur Conan Doyle who had Sherlock Holmes send Dr Watson into hiding here to help solve the case of *The Hound of the Baskervilles*.

Salmon Ladder, Buckfastleigh

NORTH BOVEY
6 miles N of Bovey Tracey off the B3212

In any discussion about which is the "loveliest village in Devon", North Bovey will be one of the leading contenders. Set beside the River Bovey, it is quite unspoiled, with thatched cottages grouped around the green, a 15th century church and a delightful old inn, the Ring of Bells Inn, which like many Devon inns was originally built, back in the 13th century, as a lodging house for the stonemasons building the church. This captivating village seems an appropriate place to end this survey of Dartmoor.

BUCKFASTLEIGH

Buckfastleigh is the western terminus and headquarters of the **South Devon Railway**,

(formerly known as the Primrose Line), whose steam trains ply the 7-mile route along the lovely Dart Valley to and from Totnes. The Dart is a fast flowing salmon river and its banks abound with herons, swans, kingfishers, badgers and foxes. The company also offers a combined River Rail ticket so that visitors can travel in one direction by train and return by boat. The railway runs regular services during the season with the journey taking about 25 minutes each way.

Another popular attraction in Buckfastleigh is the **Buckfast Butterflies & Dartmoor Otter Sanctuary** where a specially designed tropical rain forest habitat has been created for the exotic butterflies. There's an underwater viewing area and both the butterflies and otters can be photographed, with the otters' thrice-daily feeding times providing some excellent photo-opportunities!

A couple of miles south of Buckfastleigh, **Pennywell** is a spacious all-weather family attraction which offers a wide variety of entertainments and activities. Winner of the West Country "England for Excellence" award in 1999, Pennywell also boasts the UK's longest gravity go-kart ride and promises that their Hands-On activities provide something new every half hour.

Another mile or so south, the little church of Dean Prior stands beside the A38. The vicar here at the time of the Restoration was the poet and staunch royalist, Robert Herrick, (1591-1674). Herrick's best known lines are probably the opening of "To the Virgins, to make Much of Time":

Gather ye rosebuds while ye may,
Old Time is still a-flying
And this same flower that smiles today
Tomorrow will be dying.

Herrick apparently found rural Devon rather dull and much preferred London where he had a mistress 27 years his junior. Perhaps to brighten up the monotony of his Devonshire existence, he had a pet pig which he took for walks and trained to drink beer from a tankard. Herrick died in 1674 and was buried in the churchyard where a simple stone marks his "assumed last resting place".

AROUND BUCKFASTLEIGH

BUCKFAST
2 miles N of Buckfastleigh off the A38

Dominating this small market town is **Buckfast Abbey**, a Benedictine monastery

built in the Norman and Gothic styles between 1907 and 1938. If you've ever wondered how many people it takes to construct an abbey, the astonishing answer at Buckfast is just six. Only one of the monks, Brother Peter, had any knowledge of construction so he had to check every stone that went into the fabric. A photographic exhibition at the Abbey records the painstaking process that stretched over thirty years. Another monk, Brother Adam, became celebrated as the beekeeper whose busy charges produced the renowned Buckfast Abbey honey. The Abbey gift shop also offers the famous Buckfast Tonic Wine, recordings of the Abbey choristers and a wide range of religious items, pottery, cards and gifts.

SOUTH BRENT
6 miles S of Buckfastleigh off the A38

Standing on the southern flank of Dartmoor, just within the National Park, South Brent is a sizeable village of some 3000 souls. It can boast a 13th century church with a massive Norman tower, set beside the River Avon, which was once the main church for a large part of the South Hams as well as a

THE PACK HORSE,

1 Plymouth Road, South Brent, Devon TQ10 9BH
Tel: 01364 72283

As its name suggests, **The Pack Horse** inn once served the pack horse traders travelling along what was then the main road between Exeter and Plymouth. Today, the dual carriageway A38 skirts this ancient village on the southern edge of the Dartmoor National Park but it's still a lively little place. The Pack Horse can trace its history back to the early 1600s and, although it has been extended and altered over the years, it still retains much of its old world charm.

Ben Wilkins and his mum Sylvia have owned and run the inn for some 20 years. Both of them cook,

with Ben contributing the spicier dishes and Sylvia offering the traditional favourites. The regular menu is supplemented by daily specials listed on the blackboards and food is served every day from noon until 2pm, and from 7 until 9.30pm. Children are welcome in the back bar; adults can enjoy their meal anywhere in the tavern. The inn's convenient location in the National Park, just a few minutes from the A38, make this an attractive place to stay. The Pack Horse has 3 quality bedrooms available all year round - two doubles and one twin. (Please note that credit cards are not accepted).

considerable area of Dartmoor. Alongside the River Avon are some attractive old textile mills recalling the days when South Brent was an important centre for the production of woollens. In Victorian times, one of the mills was managed by William Crossing whose famous *Crossing's Guide to Dartmoor* provides a fascinating picture of life on the moor in the late 1800s.

In the days of stagecoach travel the town was a lively place with two "posting houses" servicing the competing coaches. It was said that 4 horses could be changed in 45 seconds and a full-course meal served in 20 minutes. The most famous of the coaches, the Quicksilver, left Plymouth at 8.30 in the evening and arrived in London at 4 o'clock the following afternoon - a remarkable average speed of 11 mph, including stops.

IVYBRIDGE
12 miles SW of Buckfastleigh off the A38

The original bridge over the Erme was just wide enough for a single packhorse and the 13th century crossing that replaced it is still very narrow. When the railway arrived here in 1848, Brunel constructed an impressive viaduct over the Erme valley. It was made of wood, however, so that too was replaced in 1895 by an equally imposing stone structure. The town grew rapidly in the 1860s when a quality paper-making mill was established to make good use of the waters of the Erme and has continued to grow as a commuter town for Plymouth.

Serious walkers will know Ivybridge as the southern starting point of the **Two Moors Way**, the spectacular but gruelling 103-mile path across both Dartmoor and Exmoor, finishing at Barnstaple. The trek begins with a stiff 1000ft climb up Butterdon Hill, just outside Ivybridge - and that's the easy bit!

About 5 miles northwest of Ivybridge, the **Dartmoor Wildlife Park** provides an excellent family day out, with more than 150 species of animals and birds to see (see panel on page 108).

CORNWOOD
13 miles SW of Buckfastleigh off the A38

Cornwood is a pleasant village on the River Yealm, a good base from which to seek out the many Bronze Age and industrial remains scattered across the moor. One of the most remarkable sights in Dartmoor is the double line of stones set up on Stall Moor during the Bronze Age. One line is almost 550yds long; the other begins with a stone circle and crosses the River Erme before ending at a burial chamber some two miles distant. There are no roads to these extraordinary constructions, they can only be reached on foot. If you approach Dartmoor from the south, off the A38, Cornwood is the last village you will find before the moors begin in earnest. Strike due north from here and you will have to cross some fifteen miles of spectacular moorland before you see another inhabited place. (Her Majesty's Prison at Princetown, as it happens).

The Duke of Cornwall,

3 Keaton Road, Ivybridge, Devon PL21 9DH
Tel: 01752 892867

Keen followers of football may well recognise the friendly face behind the bar of **The Duke of Cornwall**, just a short walk from the centre of Ivybridge. Dave played for Notts County for seven years and then had a 2-year spell with Torquay United. Photographs, news cuttings and other memorabilia of his career are displayed around the walls of this welcoming hostelry which he runs together with Marie. This attractive stone built pub dates back to the early 1800s when it was built as cottages. Today, the pub offers customers an excellent choice of food every lunchtime and evening (except on Mondays), and it's definitely a good idea to book ahead for weekend dining. Beverages available include 2 real ales as well as a wide range of keg bitters, draught lagers and ciders. Children are welcome to dine, and for fair-weather days there's a pleasant beer garden and patio at the rear of the inn, with the Leat running by. If you are visiting the Duke of Cornwall on a Monday evening, feel free to take part in the regular Quiz Night.

DARTMOOR WILD LIFE PARK,

Sparkwell, nr Plymouth, Devon PL7 5DG
Tel: 01752 837645
website: www.dartmoorwildlife.co.uk

"A wildly different day out" is the promise of the **Dartmoor Wild Life Park** where more than a thousand wild creatures are scattered around 30 acres of beautiful Devon countryside only 3 miles from Plymouth. Many of the animals are close to extinction in their natural environment - their only chance of surviving as a species is through captive breeding in establishments like this.

The Park operates an Adoption Scheme which provides money to help the important breeding programme. Visitors can enjoy a real "Paws-on" experience in the Talk, Touch and Learn all weather facility. There are daily talks with a wide variety of exotic animals and birds, many hand reared, from tarantulas to tiger cubs. Also within the Park is the West Country Falconry Centre which has a large static display and twice-daily flying displays, except Fridays (weather permitting) from Easter to the end of October. Birds on display include the magnificent Bald, Bateleur and Tawny Eagles, Peregrines, Buzzards, Owls, Kestrels and many other falcons.

The Park itself is open every day of the year from 10am until 6pm and other amenities include the Jaguar Restaurant, a 300-seat self-service restaurant which be converted into a dance hall, function room or conference hall. The fully licensed bar is open throughout the day and also within the restaurant block is the gift shop, stocking a full range of souvenirs from T-shirts to the Park's very own Tiger-Poo!

POSTBRIDGE
12 miles NW of Buckfastleigh on the B3212

In prehistoric times, the area around Postbridge was the "metropolis" of Dartmoor as the wealth of Bronze Age remains bears witness. Today, the village is best known for its **Clapper Bridge** which probably dates back to the 13th century and is the best preserved of all the Devon clapper bridges.

Spanning the East Dart River, the bridge is a model of medieval minimalist construction with just three huge slabs of granite laid across solid stone piers. Not wide enough for wheeled traffic, the bridge would originally have been used by pack horses following the post road from Exeter into Cornwall.

Two miles along the road to Moretonhampstead, **Warren House Inn** claims to be the third highest tavern in England. It used to stand on the other side of the road but in 1845 a fire destroyed that building. According to tradition, when the present inn was built its landlord carried some still-smouldering turves across the road to the hearth of his new hostelry and that fire has been burning ever since. It's a pleasant enough sight in summer and must have been even more welcome in the winter of 1963. In that year, the Warren House Inn was cut off by heavy snow drifts some 20ft deep for

Clapper Bridge, Postbridge

Huccaby Bridge, Hexworthy

almost three months and supplies had to be flown in by helicopter. Such a remote inn naturally generates some good tales. Like the one about the traveller who stayed here one winter's night and opening by chance a large chest in his room discovered the body of a dead man. "Why!", said the landlord when confronted with the deceased, "tis only feyther! 'Twas too cold to take 'un to the buryin', so mother salted 'un down!"

DARTMEET
7 miles NW of Buckfastleigh off the B3357

Dartmeet is a picturesque spot where the boulder-strewn East and West Dart rivers join together. At their junction, a single-span

packhorse bridge built in the 1400s crosses the river. Rising in the boggy plateau of north Dartmoor, the Dart and its tributaries drain a huge area of the moor, and run for 46 miles before entering the sea at Dartmouth.

In the days when the tin mines were working, this area was extremely isolated, lacking even a burial ground of its own. Local people had to carry their dead across the moor to Lydford - "Eight miles in fair weather, and fifteen in foul". In good weather, this is grand walking country with a choice of exploring the higher moor, dotted with a wealth of prehistoric remains, or following the lovely riverside and woodland path that leads to the famous Clapper Bridge near Postbridge, about 5 miles upstream.

YELVERTON

This attractive small town stands on the very edge of the moor, enjoying grand views across the Walkham Valley to the north with Brent Tor church, perched on its 1100ft eminence some ten miles away, clearly visible on a good day. The town itself is "flat as a pancake" and with its broad street lined with wide verges, has been described as looking

BADGER'S HOLT,

Dartmeet, Princetown, Devon PL20 6SG
Tel: 01364 631213 Fax: 01364 631475

Dartmeet is a picturesque spot where the boulder-strewn East and West Dart rivers join together. Set beside the river is the well-known and very popular **Badger's Holt**, a fully licensed luncheon and tea room. The speciality of the house is its scrumptious Traditional Devonshire Cream Teas. The menu offers a wide choice of starters, main courses and sweets, as well as sandwiches, snacks and children's meals. The home-made scones can be bought to take away from the gift shop and are highly recommended. The spacious timber building has seating for 150 inside, and room for another 70 outside. Sunday lunch here is good value and very popular. Badger's Holt is open 7 days a week from Mother's Day through to the end of October, from 10am to 6pm; and again during December for Christmas lunch and evening parties. An ideal location for weddings, dinner-dances and other private functions. Exclusive self-catering apartments will be available in a purpose-built complex at the rear of the tea room from January 2001.

"rather like a thriving racecourse"! The town's church looks convincingly medieval, 14th century in style,

According to a local story, Yelverton is one of very few old towns to have been renamed by a railway company. It was originally called "Ella's ford town", or Elfordtown. When the Great Western Railway opened its station here in 1859, the company's officials transcribed the locals' dialect pronunciation of Elfordtown into Yelverton.

In prehistoric times, the area around Yelverton must have been quite heavily populated to judge by the extraordinary concentration here of stone circles and rows, hut and cairn circles, and burial chambers. The B3212 to Princeton passes through this

once-populous stretch of moorland, part of which is now submerged beneath Burrator Reservoir.

AROUND YELVERTON

BERE ALSTON
5 miles SW of Yelverton on the B3257

Set back from the River Tamar, (the boundary here between Devon and Cornwall), Bere Alston was for centuries a thriving little port, transporting the products of Dartmoor's tin mines all around the world. All that commercial activity has long since faded

KNIGHTSTONE TEAROOMS AND RESTAURANT,

Crapstone Road, Yelverton, Devon PL20 6BT
Tel: 01822 853679 Fax: 01822 853649
e-mail: knightstonetea@yahoo.co.uk

Located on the edge of the Dartmoor National Park, **Knightstone** is a quality tea room and also offers bed and breakfast accommodation. The house has an interesting history. It was built in the early 1890s and purchased in the late 1930s by the RAF as a control centre and the surrounding area became RAF Station Harrowbeer. From 1944 to 1946 Harrowbeer was used heavily as a fighter station. Today, Knightstone serves morning teas and coffees, light lunches, cream teas, and traditional Sunday roasts, (booking essential). Everything on the menu is home made, not home cooked, and the kitchen is a chip-free zone! An outside seating area overlooks the moor. Knightstone is licensed and the owners Lucy and Michael Hayes are happy to cater for evening functions. They also welcome bed & breakfast guests for whom 3 rooms are available, 1 double, 1 twin and a single, and the top floor of the former control tower is let as a self contained flat. Please note that the tea room is closed on Mondays and Tuesdays out of season.

THE BURRATOR INN,

Dousland, Yelverton, Devon PL20 6NP
Tel: 01822 853121 Fax: 01822 853281

Located a couple of miles east of Yelverton, within the Dartmoor National Park, **The Burrator Inn** takes its name from the nearby hill and reservoir. It's a spacious and impressive building, more than a hundred years old. Family-run hostelries always seem to be just that little bit more welcoming and The Burrator Inn is

certainly no exception. Your hosts are Mike and June Gale, their sons Jeff and Richard, and daughter Nicola. Together, they have made this stately old inn a popular venue. It's open all day, every day, with food served from 11.00 to 22.00 Monday to Saturday; noon until 22.00 on Sunday. Nicola is the chef and her excellent cuisine is available either à la carte in the separate restaurant or in the bar. Such is the popularity of Nicola's cooking that it's essential to book at weekends for the restaurant. Children are very welcome here - there's a well-equipped play area outside as well as a spacious beer garden. Adults will find pool and darts, and from October through to mid-June there's live music every Saturday night. If you are planning to stay in this lovely part of Devon, The Burrator Inn has 10 attractive guest bedrooms, half of them with en suite facilities.

away but the river here is still busy, although nowadays it is mostly sleek pleasure craft which are seen riding its waters.

A few miles upstream from Bere Alston, **Morwellham Quay** is one of the county's most popular visitor attractions, but just 25 years ago it was a ghost town with the Tamar valley breezes whistling through its abandoned buildings. Then the Morwellham and Tamar Valley Trust was formed, dedicated to restoring this historic site and recreating the busy atmosphere of the 1850s when half the world's copper was passing through the tiny harbour. Morwellham lies 20 miles upstream from Plymouth but the Tamar here was still deep enough for 300-tonne ships to load up with the precious minerals of copper, manganese and arsenic. Known as the Devon Klondyke, Morwellham suffered a catastrophic decline when cheaper sources of copper were discovered in South America.

Nowadays, visitors are greeted by guides in period costume who direct them to the Quay's manifold attractions: a riverside tramway, a tour through the mine, carriage rides, sailing ships, Victorian farmyard and

Shire Horse stables, a museum and slide show, picnic sites and gift shop. The quayside inn has also been restored. Here the labourers on the quay used to meet for ale, food and the latest news of the ships that had set sail from Morwellham. In those days, the news was chalked up on a blackboard: it still is, out of date maybe, but still intriguing.

BUCKLAND MONACHORUM
2 miles W of Yelverton off the A386

A couple of miles west of Yelverton stands **Buckland Abbey** (National Trust), founded in 1278 by Amicia, Countess of Devon, but better known now as the last home of Sir Francis Drake. Drake purchased the former Abbey in 1581 from his fellow-warrior (and pirate), Sir Richard Grenville, whose exploits in his little ship, the *Revenge*, were almost as colourful as those of Drake himself. The two men were not friends, so Drake bought the property anonymously and Sir Richard is said to have been mortified that his arch-rival in public esteem had so deviously acquired the imposing old building. Buckland Abbey remained in the Drake family until 1947

THE EDGCUMBE HOTEL,

2 Fore Street, Bere Alston, Yelverton, Devon PL20 7AD
Tel: 01822 840252

Dating back to the 16th century, the **Edgcumbe Hotel** has had a long and interesting history. In its early days, it was a popular watering-hole for the labourers in the silver mines for which the village was famous. More than 3000 miners were employed and the Bere Alston mines were the main source of supply for a succession of English kings. Later, the village became well known for its flowers and soft fruit - especially black cherries and strawberries. As well as providing the silver miners with their ale, the Edgcumbe has also served as a prison for Spanish sailors in the days of Sir Francis Drake, a hospital and a nunnery.

Fortunately, it has long since reverted to being a hostelry and today this traditional inn with its

low dark beams and small-paned windows is noted for the quality of the ales on offer - Courage Best real ale, John Smith's Smooth and Websters Green Label, along with a good selection of other ciders, lagers and beers. There's an attractive beer garden at the rear where children are welcome. The inn is very much a centre of village life, supporting its own pool, ladies' darts and euchre teams, as well as a football team, and if you are here on a Thursday evening feel free to join in the popular quiz.

when it passed into the stewardship of the National Trust. Since then, the Trust has established a maritime museum at the abbey in which "Drake's Drum" takes pride of place. According to legend, the drum will sound whenever the realm of England is in peril. The drum was brought back to England by Drake's brother, Thomas, who was with the great seafarer when he died on the Spanish Main in 1596. (Rather ignominiously, of dysentery). Buckland Abbey's impressive 14th century tithe barn, 154ft long, houses an interesting collection of vintage carts and carriages.

Buckland Abbey

THE GARDEN HOUSE,

Buckland Monachorum, nr Yelverton, Devon PL20 7LQ
Tel: 01822 854769 Fax: 01822 855358
e-mail: office@thegardenhouse.org.uk
website: www.thegardenhouse.org.uk

Occupying a glorious ten-acre site on the edge of Dartmoor and commanding wonderful views over stunning South Devon landscape, **The Garden House** inspired the Daily Express to ask "Is this the best garden in Britain?" TV star Alan Titchmarsh described it as "A treasure that goes back 400 years". The gardens are home to an astonishing variety of plants which offer a

great wealth and variety of colour and interest throughout the season. One of the most beautiful areas is the terraced walled garden where inspired planting surrounds the ruins of an ancient vicarage.

There's also the opportunity of observing a pioneering, revolutionary approach to gardening. A

visit to the Garden House gives the chance to see how some of the world's great natural sights, from the Mediterranean to South Africa, have inspired the Garden's Manager Keith Wiley in his 'naturalistic' approach to creating sculptures of colour and shape in harmony with nature. Complete your visit by enjoying the delicious home-made light lunches and teas served in the delightful 18th century vicarage. The Garden House is open every day from March 1st to October 31st between 10.30am and 5pm with last admissions at 4.30pm. The owners regret that dogs are not allowed and there is limited access only for disabled visitors.

Drakes Drum

MEAVY
2 miles E of Yelverton off the A386

Once the home of Sir Francis Drake, Meavy is an archetypal Dartmoor village with a part-Norman church, and a delightful white-painted inn, the **Royal Oak** (see panel below). There are some delightful walks all around, especially to the northeast through the woods surrounding Burrator Reservoir.

PRINCETOWN
7 miles NE of Yelverton on the B3212

From Yelverton, the B3212 cuts diagonally across the heart of the moor. Passing through Princeton and on to Moretonhampstead, this is a spectacularly scenic route and should on no account be missed. Princetown, best known for its forbidding **prison**, stands 1400ft above sea level in an area of the moor which is notorious for its atrocious climate. It gets doused with 80 to 100 inches of rain a year, more than three times the average for Exeter which is less than 20 miles away.

That a settlement should be located here at all was the brainchild of one man, Sir Thomas Tyrwhitt, the owner of a local granite quarry. He proposed that a special prison should be built here to house the thousands of troops captured during the Napoleonic wars who were becoming too numerous and unruly for the prison ships moored in Plymouth Sound. The work was completed in 1809 by the prisoners themselves using granite from Sir Thomas' quarry. Paid at the rate of sixpence (2½p) a day, they also built the main east-west road across the moor which is now the B3212, and the famous Devonport leat which supplied water to the dockyard there. Yet another construction was the nearby church of St Mary, a charmless building in whose churchyard stands a tall granite cross in memory of all those prisoners whose bodies lie in unmarked graves. (The mortality rate of the inmates in the early 1800s was 50%). Since around 1900,

THE ROYAL OAK INN,

Meavy, Yelverton, Devon PL20 6PJ
Tel: 01822 852944 e-mail: royaloakinn.meavy@barbox.net

Surrounded by the Dartmoor National Park, the pretty little village of Meavy stands beside the river of the same name. Sir Francis Drake knew Meavy well since he and his family lived locally. He would also have known **The Royal Oak Inn** which dates back to at least 1510 although in his day it was called the Church House Inn because it was owned by the parish church. Today, it's the property of the parish council and run by Zenna and Chris Kingdon, a friendly and welcoming couple who have made this charming traditional hostelry a popular venue. Part of the attraction is the quality of the food on offer - a very varied menu based on local farm produce and daily fish deliveries from the Barbican at Plymouth. The wide choice of beverages includes 4 real ales (one of them named Princetown Jail Ale) and there's always a rotating guest ale. In good weather customers can enjoy their refreshments at the tables outside - where children are welcome - overlooking the village green where the 1000 year old oak from which the inn took its name stands.

THE RAILWAY INN,

Two Bridges Road, Princetown, Yelverton, Devon PL20 6QT
Tel: 01822 890232 e-mail: railwayinnpl20@aol.com

From 1827 onwards a horse-drawn tram connected Crabtree
Wharf in Plymouth to Foggintor Quarries and on to
Princetown. The tramway was converted to a steam railway
in 1883 - hence the name of the **Railway Inn**! This line
closed down eventually in 1956. This splendid old inn is
run by Peter and Julie who arrived here in 1999 after
working for several years on cruise ships. They offer visitors
quality food, ales and accommodation in a traditional, olde-worlde atmosphere. Food is available
throughout the day, from 11am to 9.30pm (10pm at weekends), and the wide choice of beverages
includes real ales, amongst which is a local brew, Dartmoor Pride. Food can be enjoyed in the lounge
or in the attractive beer garden and patio. There are no smoking areas and children are welcome. A
particularly popular feature of The Railway Inn is its full-size skittle alley where visitors can try their
skill at this typical West Country pub sport. And if you are looking for a convenient base for exploring
Dartmoor, the inn has 5 comfortable guest bedrooms, one of which is a double en suite.

prisoners' graves have been marked just with
their initials and date of death. The lines of
small stones are a gloomy sight.

At one time the prison held as many as
9000 French and, later, American inmates but
by 1816, with the cessation of hostilities, the
prison became redundant and was closed.
Princetown virtually collapsed as a result and
it wasn't until 1823 that its granite quarries
were given a new lease of life with the
building of the horse-drawn Dartmoor
Railway, another of Sir Thomas Tyrwhitt's
initiatives. The prison was eventually re-

opened for long-serving convicts in 1850 and
since then it has been considerably enlarged
and upgraded. It is currently in use as a
medium security prison, with around 250
inmates.

Also in the town is the National Park's
Moorland Visitors' Centre which contains
some excellent and informative displays
about the moor, and also stocks a wide range
of books, maps and leaflets. The Centre is
housed in the former Duchy Hotel where Sir
Arthur Conan Doyle stayed while writing
some chapters of *The Hound of the Baskervilles*.

6 Between Dartmoor and Exmoor

Typical Devon Countryside

The area bounded roughly by Tiverton and Crediton in the east, and Okehampton and Great Torrington to the west is one of the quietest and most appealing parts of the county. There are no large towns, no motorways or even dual carriageways. But there are scores of attractive, unspoilt villages with thatched cottages nestling around an ancient church. The winding Devon lanes have discouraged commuters so this is rural Devon at its most "Devonian". The Taw is the largest of its rivers and there are lovely river valleys through which run the Yeo, the Little Dart, the Mole, and the oddly-named Crooked Oak. The landscape throughout is characterised by gently rolling hills which rise to the foothills of Exmoor.

Apart from the period when the wool trade of the Middle Ages was flourishing, the economy of the region has never been buoyant so there are no grand houses or abbeys, and only minimal remains of castles. But the area does contain one of the most interesting churches in the county, at Molland. St Mary's Church had the good fortune to be owned up until the 19th century by the Courtenay family who were ardent Catholics and had no interest in restoring or altering a Protestant house of worship. Consequently, the church still has all its Georgian features intact - most notably the tiers of box pews and an elaborate 3-decker pulpit above which stands a trumpeting angel.

The western part of this region lies in "Tarka Country", so named because of Henry Williamson's story of *Tarka the Otter*, published in 1927. Williamson had rescued an orphan otter cub, named it Tarka and the animal stayed with him until one day it was caught in a rabbit trap. As Williamson was releasing the terrified creature, Tarka slipped from his grasp and disappeared. The author spent months searching up and down the Torridge for Tarka but never saw him again. The Tarka Trail follows the route that Williamson supposed the otter to have followed. Opened by Prince Charles in 1992, the trail includes foot and cycle paths and in all the figure of eight track runs for 175 miles.

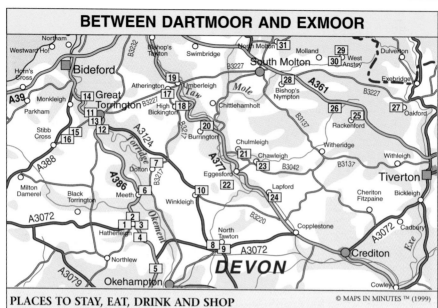

BETWEEN DARTMOOR AND EXMOOR

PLACES TO STAY, EAT, DRINK AND SHOP

© MAPS IN MINUTES ™ (1999)

HATHERLEIGH

Travelling north from Okehampton, (described in the previous chapter), the A386 passes through the village of Follygate. About a mile to the east of the village **Abbeyford Woods** provides some lovely walks, with a particularly lovely stretch running alongside the River Okement. About 6 miles north of Okehampton is the medieval market town of Hatherleigh where the market is still held every Tuesday. The town has been popular for many years as a holiday base for fishermen trying their luck on the nearby River Torridge and its tributary which runs alongside the small town.

A good starting point for an exploration of Hatherleigh is the **Tarka Country Information Point** at Hatherleigh Pottery where there are exhibits detailing the life and countryside in and around this 1000 year old town and you can also pick up leaflets to guide you around Hatherleigh's narrow streets. The leaflets will lead you to the many fascinating small craft and antique shops and to the town's historic buildings of interest.

Hatherleigh was owned by Tavistock Abbey from the late 900s until the Dissolution of the Monasteries in the 1540s and the picturesquely thatched George Hotel is believed to have been built around 1450 as the Abbot's court house. The London Inn also dates from around that time and the Old Church House is thought to be even older.

The town would have possessed an even finer stock of early buildings were it not for a devastating fire in 1840 which destroyed much of the old centre. Fortunately, the 15th century church of St John the Baptist escaped the flames. Set high above the Lew valley, the church's red sandstone walls and sturdy tower still provide a striking focus for this pleasant rural community. Although the church survived the great fire of 1840, a century and a half later hurricane force winds, generated during the storms of January 1990, swashed against its spindly tower and tossed it through the roof of the nave. Thankfully, nobody was in the church at the time.

Until 1966, the Okehampton to Bude railway ran through Hatherleigh. In that year it was closed as part of the notorious "Beeching Cuts". Dr Richard Beeching, a successful businessman until then in the employ of the multi-national company ICI,

SALAR GALLERY,

20 Bridge Street, Hatherleigh, nr Okehampton, Devon EX20 3HY
Tel: 01837 810940 Fax: 01837 810348 website: www.salargallery.co.uk

The small town of Hatherleigh lies at the heart of an agricultural area and is the main shopping centre for this part of North Devon. One of the most interesting of its shops is the **Salar Gallery** which displays a wide selection of arts and crafts by West Country artists. The Gallery is owned and run by Sally Ann Vick and the three separate display areas offer a showcase for all kinds of artefacts. The Exhibition Gallery is devoted to the work of one artist and, between April and December, changes every month - the work of potters and photographers alternating with that of painters etc.

There's a smaller exhibition area for prints of every kind and another front of house area which is a veritable Aladdin's Cave of desirable objects. You'll find silk scarves, 'tattie baskets', wood turnery, exquisite cards and candles, original paintings and sculptures, and much much more. There are pieces to suit every pocket and the range is so wide you will almost certainly find something that appeals to your particular tastes and interests. And what nicer souvenir of a visit to Devon to take home than something created here?

ACORNS,

12 Bridge Street, Hatherleigh, Devon EX20 3HU
Tel: 01837 810479

A life-size pig reclining on a sofa and smoking a cigarette is the centrepiece of the eye-catching display in the front window of **Acorns**, a quintessential English tea room with the extra attraction of pigs! Lots of pigs - pigs sitting on shelves and cabinets; pigs hiding away in nooks and crannies. They are part of Joanne Hobson's collection of more than 300 ornamental pigs of all shapes and sizes, many of them rare. They add a very distinctive touch to this 200-year-old town centre tea room which Joanne owns and runs together with her husband Trevor. As well as serving all the popular teatime treats - Cream Teas, home made cakes, scones, and crumpets, they also offer an extensive menu that ranges from a hearty 'Pig Out Breakfast', through home made pies, main meals, snacks and sandwiches. There's a separate menu for children and Sunday lunch is an Acorns speciality with a choice of roasts at a very reasonable price. Acorns is fully licensed and if the weather permits you can enjoy your food and drink in the tea garden

with its tables and chairs - and more pigs! The Hobsons are happy to cater for functions and parties and if you need help finding the tea room just ask for "That place with the pigs".

THE TALLY-HO COUNTRY INN & BREWERY,

14 Market Street, Hatherleigh, Devon EX20 3JN
Tel: 01837 810306

Lovers of real ales will definitely want to make a bee-line for the **Tally-Ho Country Inn & Brewery** in Market Street. The present brewery began operating in 1990 but its history goes back to a least 1790 when records show that it was then known as The New Inn Brewery. The present brewery is situated at the back of the inn and can be viewed through a large picture window. It can produce 260 gallons of real ales a week and all five ales (4 bitters and 1 mild) are brewed using the traditional full-mash method with English malts and hops. They bear evocative names such as 'Tarka's Tipple', 'Thurgia' (from the Greek word for 'natural magic'), and 'Jollop' - a local name for medicine.

The Tally-Ho is also noted for its quality food which ranges from bar snacks and main meals at lunchtime to a full à la carte menu in the evening. In particular, the desserts, freshly made each day, enjoy an exalted reputation. For those who prefer wine, there's an excellent list of European and New World wines as well as house wines available by the glass or bottle. The Tally-Ho also has a takeaway service of authentic curries. Customers can enjoy their refreshment in the traditional bar with its beamed ceiling or in the secluded beer garden at the rear.

was appointed in 1963 by Prime Minister Harold Macmillan, (and rewarded with the then incredible salary of £40,000 per annum), to sort out what the Conservative government of the day regarded as the mess created by the Labour party's nationalisation of the railways in 1948. Naturally, Dr Beeching's solution was to close every mile of line he could that did not produce a paper profit. The last train on the Hatherleigh to Bude line, a prized local amenity, steamed its way into Cornwall on May 16th 1966, then to a siding, and then to rust. A year earlier, Dr Beeching had been created a Life Baron for his "services to the community".

Long stretches of the old track bed of the railway now provide some attractive walking.

AROUND HATHERLEIGH

MEETH
3 miles N of Hatherleigh on the A386

A mile or so north of Hatherleigh, the A386 crosses the River Torridge and a couple of miles further is the pleasant little village of Meeth whose Old English name means "the meeting of the streams". Indeed, a small brook runs down the hillside into the Torridge. From the early 1700s, Meeth and the surrounding area was noted for its "pipe" and "ball clay" products, generically known as pottery clay. There are still extensive clay works to the northwest of the village.

Meeth's parish church enjoys a picturesque setting and has some Norman features, including an ancient font, and an interesting porch protected by a barrel roof with carved bosses.

But for cyclists and walkers Meeth is much better known as the southern terminus of the **Tarka Trail Cycle/Walkway** which runs northwards through Bideford and Barnstaple, and around the Taw/Torridge estuary to Braunton. The Tarka Country Tourism Association, based in Barnstaple, publishes a comprehensive range of booklets, guides, timetables and videos about the area, as well as stocking Henry Williamson's original novel of 1927, *Tarka the Otter*. For more information from them, telephone 01271 345008.

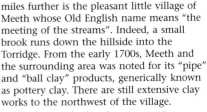

PRESSLAND COUNTRY HOUSE HOTEL,
Hatherleigh, nr Okehampton,
Devon EX20 3LW
Tel: 01837 810871 Fax: 01837 810303
e-mail: accom@presslandhouse.co.uk
website: presslandhouse.co.uk

Located just two miles south of the ancient market town of Hatherleigh, **Pressland Country House Hotel** is a lovely Victorian property set in extensive grounds and enjoying stunning south facing views across to Dartmoor. Pressland House is family run and has a genuinely warm and welcoming atmosphere. The resident owners, Graham and Gill Giles, do all they

can to ensure that guests enjoy their stay. The hotel's public rooms are spacious and guests can relax in either of the two comfortable lounges, one of which has its own bar. The Giles only recently acquired the hotel but the food served here, with its emphasis on freshly prepared local produce, is fast gaining a very good reputation with residents and locals alike. The 3-course dinner menu is changed daily and to compliment your meal the wine list offers an interesting selection of reasonably priced wines from both Europe and the New World.

The 5 spacious and attractive bedrooms all have their own bathroom, (4 are fully en suite), as well as colour TV, clock radio, tea/coffee-making facilities, hair drier - and a view! Please note that Pressland House is a non-smoking establishment and does not take children under 12 or pets. The hotel's location makes it an ideal base for exploring Dartmoor, Exmoor and the North Devon and Cornish coasts. Walking, riding, fishing and golf are all available nearby, as well as many visitor attractions such as Rosemoor Gardens, Dartington Glass and Hatherleigh Farmers Market.

The Crossways Inn,

Folly Gate, nr Okehampton, Devon EX20 3AH
Tel: 01837 52088

The small village of Folly Gate is located on the A386, a couple of miles north of Okehampton. At its heart stands **The Crossways Inn**, a striking black and white building parts of which are believed to date back to the early 1700s. The interior is equally eye-catching with its low beamed ceilings, half-panelled walls, small-paned windows, and a wealth of brasses and ornaments which are polished daily! This traditional hostelry is owned and run by Lynn and Ray Judd who took over here in the summer of 2000 and have quickly established a reputation for good food, good ales and warm hospitality.

All the food served here is cooked and prepared to order, using fresh local produce. There's a wide choice of food on offer, ranging from hearty steaks to vegetarian dishes, from salads to sandwiches, from homemade soup or Garlic Bread to tasty desserts such as home-made Raspberry Pavlova or an orange sorbet. Children under 10 have their own special selection of meals. Adding to the choice, there are daily specials, (amongst which you may well find a tasty Thai dish), and to complement your meal, the inn has a small but interesting selection of wines from around the world. Meals can be taken either in the separate restaurant, in the bar or, weather permitting, in the patio garden at the rear.

Bull & Dragon,

Meeth, Okehampton,
Devon EX20 3EP
Tel: 01837 810325
website: www.bullndragon.co.uk

The village of Meeth was once widely known for its 'pottery clay', an industry which was important here from the early 1700s. The labourers at the extensive Clay Works nearby would certainly have patronised the **Bull & Dragon** which has stood at the centre of the village since the 16th century. It's a picture postcard building with a thatched roof, stone door surrounds and small-paned windows, and the interior is just as inviting - low beams, exposed stone walls, old church settles and lots of nooks and crannies. 'Mine hosts', David and Kim Anderson, are a lively, friendly couple and very good at customer care. Dawn, a highly qualified local chef, manages the kitchen and her menu offers a wide and varied choice of traditional home cooked food. There is also a specials board which regularly changes and where possible makes use of local and seasonal produce.

Meeth makes a good base for exploring Dartmoor and the North Devon and Cornish coasts, so if you are planning to stay in the area, the Bull & Dragon has 3 attractive en suite guest bedrooms available all year round.

DOLTON
6 miles N of Hatherleigh on the B3217

Dolton clusters around its parish church of St Edmund's which boasts a real treasure, a Saxon font more than a thousand years old. Its intricate carvings depict a fantastic menagerie of winged dragons and writhing serpents, with yet more dragons emerging from the upturned face of a man. Their relevance to the Christian message may be a little obscure but there's no denying their powerful impact. This little village, together with its even tinier neighbour, Dowland, seem unlikely candidates to host an international arts festival but each year, during May and June, performers, artists and visitors seek out these two small communities in the heart of Devon.

Just a mile or so to the west of the village flows the River Torridge, immortalised by Henry Williamson in 1927 as the setting for his story of *Tarka the Otter*.

NORTH TAWTON
7 miles E of Hatherleigh off the A3072

Well-known nowadays to travellers along the Tarka Trail, the small market town of North Tawton was once an important borough

RAMS HEAD INN,

South Street, Dolton, North Devon EX19 8QS
Tel: 01805 804255 Fax: 01805 804509
e-mail: ramsheadinn@compuserve.com

Located within easy reach of Dartmoor and the North Devon coast, the Rams Head Inn provides an excellent holday base. The building itself is Grade II listed, dating back to the 1400s and with parts built of cob. There are 5 well-equipped rooms, all en suite with shower or bath, and with TV, direct dial telephone and refreshment tray. The Rams Head is open all day, every day and offers a wide choice of food. Bar snacks and meals are served every lunchtime and evening; the separate restaurant is open from 18.30 to 21.30 every evening.

MURRAY'S,

The Square, North Tawton, Devon EX20 2EW
Tel: 01837 89297

"Where in Devon can you get a 7-course dinner for the set price of £12.50 per person?" (£11 per head if there are 12 or more in your party). The answer is **Murray's** restaurant in North Tawton's market square. You can also get a 3-course lunch for £2.99 and a full carving buffet for weddings and functions for £10 per person.

These remarkable prices are not just a one-off special - Keith Murray, the owner of this very special restaurant, hasn't changed his prices for more than 4 years. And you won't find starvation-size servings either. An accomplished chef with wide experience in catering all around the UK, Keith offers wholesome and appetising food in hearty portions and expects to maintain these prices throughout

the currency of this book. In Keith's view, his restaurant not only has the cheapest but also the best food in Devon, a claim which his many customers undoubtedly agree with. Murray's isn't licensed but you are welcome to bring along their own tipple - and there's no corkage charge.

Keith also offers another money-saving attraction in an adjacent annex where you'll find a range of refurbished leather, suede and sheepskin jackets and coats. There are around 200 to choose from and all are less than the price of a shirt!

governed by a portreeve, an official who was elected each year until the end of the 19th century. This scattered rural community prospered in medieval times but the decline of the local textile industry in the late 1700s dealt a blow from which it never really recovered - the population today is still less than it was in 1750. The little town also suffered badly from the ravages of a series of fires which destroyed most of the older and more interesting buildings. However, a few survivors can still be found, most notably **Broad Hall** (private) which dates back to the 15th century.

KAYDEN HOUSE HOTEL,

High Street, North Tawton,
Devon EX20 2HF
Tel: 01837 82242

Located just a few miles from the Dartmoor National Park, North Tawton provides a convenient base for exploring the Park's spectacular scenery. And a good place to stay in North Tawton is the **Kayden House Hotel**, a charming old hostelry which dates back to the 18th century. In summer, the front of the hotel is ablaze with multi-coloured hanging baskets and window boxes of flowers. The Kayden is owned and run by Nicholas and Amanda Waldron, both of whom have been trained in hotel management and worked with major hotel groups before settling in North Tawton.

Nicholas is the chef and his regularly-changing menus offer a good choice of meat, fish and vegetarian dishes with both table d'hôte and à la carte menus available. Everything is prepared and cooked to order, using fresh local produce wherever possible. Main meals are served in the separate restaurant, immaculate with its crisp linen tablecloths and glittering crystal glass; light meals, snacks and sandwiches are available in the bar. Nicholas' favourite subject is wine, which explains the quality and variety of the wines on offer and also the wine-related items displayed around the walls. If you are planning to stay in this scenic area, the hotel has 7 guest rooms, all of them en suite and with a 3-diamonds rating from the English Tourist Board.

NEWLANDS FARM,

Dowland, Winkleigh, Devon EX19 8PQ
Tel: 01805 804442 Fax: 01805 804618

If you are looking for a relaxed holiday 'far from the madding crowd', you'll find just the thing at Newlands Farm, located deep in the heart of mid-Devon. This is Tarka the Otter country where it is still a pleasure to walk the flower-bedecked lanes or wander around the fields of Newlands Farm. The farm is pesticide-free, so wild life and flowers thrive. The Tarka footpath is just 200 yards from the farm and only a couple of miles away is Halsdon Nature Reserve which borders the beautiful River Torridge. Stafford Moor, also only 2 miles distant, is the largest trout fishery in the West Country and expert tuition is available. Newlands Farm offers self-catering accommodation in a well-equipped mobile home, situated in half an acre of mature gardens and enjoying lovely view of open countryside with Dartmoor on the horizon. There's a private garden with picnic table and, inside, 3 bedrooms (1 double, 2 twins), shower and washroom, separate WC, and a kitchen with gas cooker and fridge. The lounge/dining area has a gas fire, colour TV and radio. The owners of Newlands Farm are Ralph and Mary Gent.

WINKLEIGH
6 miles NE of Hatherleigh on the B3220

This attractive village with its open views across to Dartmoor is believed to have been a beacon station in prehistoric times. When the Normans arrived they built two small castles, one at each end of the village. They were probably intended as bases for hunting in the nearby park - the only Devon park to be mentioned in the Domesday book. For centuries Winkleigh was an important local trading centre with its own market, fair and borough court. Today, it's a peaceful little place with thatched cottages nestling up to the mainly 15th century church which has a richly carved and painted wagon roof where 70 golden-winged angels stand guard over the nave.

GREAT TORRINGTON

A good place to start exploring Great Torrington is at **Castle Hill** which commands grand views along the valley of the River

Torridge. (There's no view of the castle: that was demolished as long ago as 1228: its site is now a bowling green). On the opposite bank of the river is the hamlet of Taddiport where the tiny 14th century church by the bridge was originally the chapel of a leper hospital: its inmates were not permitted to cross over into Torrington itself.

Not many churches in England have been blown up by gunpowder. That was the fate however of the original **Church of St Michael and All Angels**. It happened during the Civil War when General Fairfax captured the town on February 16th, 1645. His Royalist prisoners were bundled into the church which they had been using as an arsenal. In the darkness, the eighty barrels of gunpowder stored there were somehow set alight and in the huge explosion that followed the church was demolished, 200 men lost their lives, and Fairfax himself narrowly escaped death. The present spacious church was built five years later, one of very few in the country erected during the Commonwealth years.

Torrington's **May Fair** is still an important event in the local calendar, and has been

THE ROYAL EXCHANGE,

86 New Street, Great Torrington,
Devon EX38 8BH
Tel/Fax: 01805 623395

The Royal Exchange has won awards for its floral displays and the colourful array of tubs, window boxes and hanging baskets prove they were well-earned. This attractive old pub, parts of which date back some 400 years, is just what you would hope to find in a traditional English inn - lots of old beams, a friendly relaxed atmosphere and good, wholesome food. The sandwiches, savouries, pies and pastries are all home made from fresh produce and the Sunday roast provides especially good value for money. The Royal Exchange is a free house so there's an excellent selection of drinks. Darts and pool are available and to the rear of the inn a spacious and pleasant garden.

Your hosts, Paul Skitral and Jane Hampton, came to the hospitality business after careers in the banking world. A lively and enthusiastic couple in their thirties, they have made a great success of this charming old inn. It's located in the town centre with the famous Dartington Crystal showroom only a quarter of a mile away and, for walkers and cyclists, the Tarka Trail is also nearby. And if you arrive on the first Thursday in May, you'll find Torrington's May Fair in full swing, complete with maypole dancing.

ORFORD MILL,

nr Torrington, Tel: 01271 850611
Bookings through Best Leisure, North Hill, Shirwell,
Barnstaple, Devon EX31 4LG

Set within its own 3 acres of grounds, **Orford Mill** with its Manor House and former corn and timber Mill has been lovingly and sympathetically converted into an outstanding range of self-catering apartments and cottages. The choice "Owlery Oak" which sleeps 7 plus a cot, to "Mill Pool" which sleeps 3, or 2 plus cot. All the accommodation has quality furnishings and decoration, comprehensively equipped kitchens, a telephone for outgoing calls and duvets, linen and

bath towels are all provided.

"Tarka", a single-storey cottage which sleeps 4, reminds visitors that this is the heart of Tarka the Otter country. Indeed, Tarka is reputed to have hidden from the hounds Deadlock within the mill pool here. The old mill and its waterwheel (still operational) stand alongside the River Torridge, noted for its good fishing. In addition to its lovely riverside setting and spacious grounds with streams and waterfalls, the Orford Mill complex also offers visitors an indoor heated swimming pool, fitness room, games room and a secure children's play area. The Mill's grounds adjoin those of the famous RHS gardens at Rosemoor, "the Wisley of the West", Torrington and the famous Dartington Crystal showrooms are less than a mile away, and the scenic attractions of Exmoor and Dartmoor, the North Devon and Cornwall coasts, are all within easy reach.

FURZE FARM,

nr Great Torrington,
North Devon EX38 7HA
Tel: 01805 623360

Furze Farm was first recorded in 1332 when Robert atte Forse (Robert of Forse) was assessed in the sum of 3 shillings (15p) as his contribution to the subsidy roll, or poor tax.

Over the years the house has been modified and extended but a significant survival of the past is the linenfold panelling in the hall which is of a type used in the 1500s. The farmhouse is currently a Grade II listed building and the home of Beryl Heard and her husband who has farmed here for many years. They welcome bed & breakfast guests to this peaceful and relaxing spot.

There are 3 guest bedrooms, all with private facilities, a guests' TV lounge, and a full English breakfast is included in the tariff. Furze Farm, which is non-smoking throughout, is open all year except for Christmas and the New Year. The house is conveniently situated for the Tarka Trail with its picturesque walks and cycle track and Great Torrington, renowned for Dartington Glass and Rosemoor Gardens, is little more than a mile away. A short drive will bring you to Westward Ho! and other splendid beaches, to Clovelly and its steep cobbled street, and to the market towns of Bideford and Barnstaple.

since 1554. On the first Thursday in May, a Queen is crowned, there is maypole dancing in the High Street, and a banner proclaims the greeting *"Us be plazed to zee 'ee"*.

The town can also boast one of the West Country's leading tourist attractions, **Dartington Crystal**, where visitors can see skilled craftsmen blowing and shaping the crystal, follow the history of glass-making from the Egyptians to the present day, watch a video presentation, and browse amongst some 10,000 square feet of displays. The enterprise was set up in the 1960s by the Dartington Hall Trust to provide employment in an area of rural depopulation: today, the beautifully designed handmade crystal is exported to more than 50 countries around the world. Tel: 01805 623797.

About a mile south of Great Torrington, the Royal Horticultural Society's **Rosemoor Garden** occupies a breathtaking setting in the Torridge Valley. The 40-acre site includes mature planting in Lady Anne's magnificent garden and arboretum; a winding rocky gorge with bamboos and ferns beside the stream, and a more formal area which contains one of the longest herbaceous borders in the country. There are trails for children, a picnic area and an award-winning Visitor Centre with a licensed restaurant, plant centre and shop. The garden is open all year round except on Christmas Day.

AROUND GREAT TORRINGTON

WEARE GIFFORD

3 miles NE of Great Torrington off the A386

This appealing village claims to be the longest riverside village in England, straggling for almost two miles along the banks of the Torridge. Weare Gifford (pronounced *Jifford*) has a charm all its own, suspended in time it seems to belong to the more peaceful days of half a century ago. The villagers even refused to have full street lighting installed, so avoiding the "street furniture" that blemishes so many attractive places.

Another attraction in the village is a fine old 15th century manor house, **Weare Gifford**

SEA LOCK COTTAGE (ETC***), SEA LOCK CAMPING BARN,

7 Annery Kiln, Weare Giffard, Bideford,Devon EX39 5JE
Tel: 01237 477705 Mobile: 0786 602 6194 e-mail: ahwills@annerykiln.freeserve.co.uk

For anyone exploring the delightful "Tarka Country" especially on foot, by bike or even canoe, **Sea Lock Cottage** or **Sea Lock Camping Barn** provide perfect bases. Overlooking Halfpenny Bridge on the River Torridge, they stand in a peaceful and unspoilt valley with backdrops of oak woodlands. The area is rich in wildlife. You are more than likely to see herons, buzzards, kingfishers and maybe even an otter. The property has direct access to the Tarka Trail and boasts its own private nature reserve, ponds with ducks and geese, and a newly-created saltmarsh habitat. Lord Rolle's Canal (1825-70s) once ran through it and there are substantial remains where it enters the river at the sea lock. The award-winning Devon Bike-Bus which operates along the Coast to Coast Cycle Route(NCN 27) stops close by.

Sea Lock Cottage offers well-appointed, self-catering accommodation sleeping up to 5 people. For those seeking more basic facilities Sea Lock Camping Barn sleeps up to 16, in 3 rooms, with shared common room and kitchen area which may be booked by bed, room or sole use. There is also a small campsite beside the Barn. Pets by arrangement.

The owners, Adrian and Hilary Wills, have been involved in conservation and enhancement of their property for 25 years and with their local knowledge can help you enjoy your holiday fully. Having travelled extensively in Australia, Canada and Europe they welcome all holiday-makers especially international visitors.

THE OLD RECTORY,

Langtree, nr Torrington, North Devon EX38 8NF
Tel/Fax: 01805 601602
e-mail: Theoldrectorydevon@hotmail.com

Langtree village sits on a hilltop deep in the North Devon countryside and from **The Old Rectory** there are grand views across to Dartmoor. Built around 1840, the house stands in an acre of mature gardens and there's a pleasant covered terrace where you can sit and admire the view. Another attractive feature of the garden is the ornamental pool with golden orfe. The Old Rectory is the home of Susan and Terry Lee, a lively and humorous couple both of whom work in the teaching profession.

They have 3 guest bedrooms (1 double, 1 twin, 1 single), all of them extremely spacious and attractively furnished in period style with colour co-ordinated soft furnishings. Each room has its

own private bathroom and is equipped with television and hospitality tray. Guests have the use of the residents' lounge which is also very spacious and has some striking friezes on the high walls. Here you can relax in front of the open fire and there's also a television set provided. At breakfast time there's a choice of a traditional full English breakfast or a lighter Continental option. During the day, there's plenty to keep you busy with Dartmoor, Exmoor and the spectacular North Devon and Cornwall coast all within easy driving distance.

BARNS FARM CARAVAN & CAMPING,

Langtree, Great Torrington, Devon EX38 8NF
Tel: 01805 601409 Fax: 01805 601551/0870 2849518 Mobile: 07890 211 960
e-mail: Barnsfarm@tarka-country.co.uk   website: www.tarka-country.co.uk/barnsfarm

Caravan and camping sites that offer real peace and privacy are the exception rather than the rule but Barns Farm Caravan & Camping is one such exception. Banked mounds planted with shrubs and trees separate the individual sites and the whole park is lavishly supplied with lawned areas and masses of foliage. The site is open from April to October, children are welcome as are dogs under control. Amenities include water supply, toilet and waste disposal. The site is level and takes full advantage of the far-reaching views of Exmoor, Dartmoor and Bodmin Moor - an ideal location for those wishing to explore the area's natural beauty.

Langtree, a typically inviting small Devon village of about 500 people, is just a few minutes walk

away. Here you'll find a traditional inn serving a good selection of meals and snacks, a shop-cum-Post Office, church, chapel and a small playing field. The Tarka Trail is only a mile and a half distant and other nearby attractions include Dartington Crystal at Great Torrington (3.5 miles) and the RHS Rosemoor Gardens (1 mile) whose 32 acres of themed gardens are worth a visit at any time of the year. A little further afield are the splendid beaches at Instow and Westward Ho! and for a truly memorable experience take the boat trip to Lundy Island with its thousands of multi-coloured puffins.

THE VILLAGE SHOPPE & TEA ROOM B&B,

Atherington, Umberleigh, North Devon EX37 9HY
Tel: 01769 560248

The people of Atherington used to claim that you could see the whole of Devon from their hilltop village. Not strictly true, but the views certainly are spectacular and if you stay for bed and breakfast at The Village Shoppe and Tea Room you can gaze at them to your heart's content. Chris and Jo Hart run this versatile establishment which stands in the picturesque village square. On the other side of the square rises the tower of Atherington's ancient church, famous for its unique rood loft dating back to the 1530s.

The Shoppe isn't quite as old. It was built in the 17th century and was originally a coaching inn.

Today, the Harts offer their guests 2 very comfortable bedrooms, (1 double, 1 twin), hearty English breakfasts and, within easy reach, all the scenic splendours of Exmoor and the Devon coast. Before setting off to explore the countryside, you can stock up in the shop which carries a wide range of general provisions and gifts and also serves as the village off licence. Later in the day you can return for a Devon Cream Tea and other teatime treats in the appealing tea room which is housed in a restored oak-beamed room with a splendid inglenook fireplace.

COUNTRY WAYS,

Little Knowle Farm, High Bickington,
Umberleigh, Devon EX37 9BJ
Tel: 01769 560503
e-mail: kate.price@virgin.net
website: www.devon-holiday.co.uk

For a self-catering holiday in an incredibly peaceful corner of North Devon, **Country Ways** would be hard to beat. The name actually covers 3 beautifully converted barns hidden away on a small farm with lovely gardens and magnificent views. Children love it here since there are lots of friendly animals, many of them rare breeds. There's also a games area and barbecues and the splendid beaches at Croyde and Westward Ho! are an easy drive away. The three cottages are individually named. The Cuckoo's Nest, which sleeps six, has 3 bedrooms and a luxury bathroom downstairs, and a large open plan living room/kitchen upstairs.

The Stables is a single storey cottage designed with the wheelchair user in mind and sleeps 4; while The Den is a lovely couples cottage sleeping two. The Cuckoo's Nest and The Den both have a

Highly Commended 4-key rating; The Stables has a Highly Commended 3-key rating and is Category 2 in the National Accessible Scheme. All the accommodation is centrally heated and visitors can adjust the thermostats to suit themselves. The kitchens are modern and well-equipped, and both heating and electricity are included in the price as are bed linen, towels and tea towels. You only need to bring your own beach towels and cot bedding if required. There is also a laundry room on site and at the time of writing a Fitness Suite is being constructed for the more energetic!

THE GABLES ON THE BRIDGE,

Umberleigh, North Devon,
EX37 9AB
Tel: 01769 560461

Umberleigh village sits beside the River Taw, famous for its salmon and trout and the inspiration for Henry Williamson's stories of *Tarka the Otter* and *Salar the Salmon*. The village still boasts its own railway station on the Barnstaple to Exeter line, better known nowadays as the "Tarka Line" since it closely follows the River Taw on its way to Barnstaple Bay. Only a 100 yards or so from Umberleigh Station, The Gables on the Bridge offers a wide range of refreshments during the day as well as overnight accommodation. Breakfasts, morning coffee, lunches and Devon Cream Teas are served in the attractive Conservatory at the rear of the house. Look out for the grape vine which is now more than 100 years old.

The area around Umberleigh is grand walking country and Myra and Tony Pring, who own The Gables, have prepared a useful sketch map with detailed directions to guide visitors to the major places of interest. Distances vary from 3 miles to 8 miles and if you'd like to spend a couple of days following all three of the walks, The Gables has 3 attractive guest rooms where you can stay overnight, all of them en suite and all with tea/coffee making facilities. Downstairs, guests have the choice of a TV lounge or a cosy, quiet lounge in which to relax, and breakfasts are served in the separate dining room. Salmon and sea trout fishing can be arranged for guests if required.

PORTSMOUTH ARMS,

Burrington, Umberleigh, North Devon EX37 9ND
Tel: 01769 560397

Only two hostelries in Britain have a railway station named after them, rather than the other way around. The Portsmouth Arms, near the village of Burrington, is one of those two. The inn was well-established here at least 100 years before the railway arrived in 1873 and named its station after the pub. The inn had adopted its own name from the Lord Portsmouth on whose estate it stood. Today, the Portsmouth Arms Station is a popular stopping-off point for travellers on the "Tarka Line", as the Barnstaple to Exeter route is now known. The Portsmouth Arms inn is a spacious building with a Lounge Bar, Saloon Bar and separate restaurant and the interior decoration is quite fascinating. Many brass and copper items adorn the walls and there's also an intriguing range of suits of armour, coats of arms and heraldic shields, many of them with connections to Lord Portsmouth.

Maureen Casey is the landlady here. She comes from Liverpool and has that wicked sense of humour only Merseysiders seem to possess. A lively place, the Portsmouth Arms also offers an excellent choice of home cooked traditional English Pub Food - anything from a freshly-prepared sandwich to chicken or beef dishes, curries, pies and pasties. And if you plan to be anywhere near the Portsmouth Arms on a Sunday lunchtime, make a booking well ahead for the legendary Sunday roast.

Hall. Although its outer walls were partially demolished during the Civil War, the splendid gatehouse with its mighty doors and guardian lions has survived. Inside, the main hall has a magnificent hammer-beam roof, and several of the other rooms are lined with Tudor and Jacobean oak panelling. For centuries, the house was the home of the Fortescue family and in the nearby church there is an interesting "family tree" with portraits of past Fortescues carved in stone.

ATHERINGTON
7 miles NE of Great Torrington on the B3217

A landmark for miles around, **St Mary's Church** stands in the picturesque square of this hilltop village and is notable for a feature which is unique in Devon - a lavishly carved and alarmingly top-heavy rood loft. Created by two carvers from Chittlehampton in the 1530s, it is an exceptionally fine example of their craft. The church also contains striking effigies of Sir John Wilmington, who died in 1349, and his wife; a window of medieval glass; and well-preserved brasses of Sir John Basset, (died 1529), his two wives and twelve children.

HIGH BICKINGTON
6 miles E of Great Torrington on the B3217

Two miles south of Atherington is another hilltop village. Standing at almost 600ft above sea level, the village commands excellent views in all directions. It boasts a fine 16th century inn, The George, which is set amongst a delightful group of thatched cottages, and a parish church dating back to the 1100s which is renowned for its exceptional collection of carved bench and pew ends. There are around 70 of them in all: some are Gothic (characterised by fine tracery); others are Renaissance (characterised by rounded figures). More recent carving on the choir stalls depicts an appealing collection of animals and birds.

Exmoor River

BURRINGTON
8 miles NE of Great Torrington off the A377

This picture postcard village of thatched and whitewashed cottages is also perched on top of a hill, offering yet more glorious views. Equally unspoilt is the early-16th century church with its unusual granite arcade and an impressive wagon roof decorated with carvings of angels.

SOUTH MOLTON

This pleasant small market town, thankfully now bypassed by the A361 North Devon link road, has been a focus of the local agriculture-based economy since Saxon times, and in common with many such towns throughout Devon was a centre of the wool trade in the late Middle Ages.

In the heart of the old town lies Broad Street, so broad as to be almost a square, and distinguished by some handsome Georgian and Victorian civic architecture. Among the noteworthy buildings to be found here are the **Market Hall and Assembly Rooms**, the eccentric **Medical Hall** with its iron balcony and four Ionic columns, and the **Guildhall** of 1743 which overhangs the pavement in a series of arches.

RED LION HOTEL

East Street, Chulmleigh, Devon EX18 7DD
Tel: 01769 580384 Fax: 01769 580217

Chulmleigh lies in the heart of 'Tarka the Otter' country and when the Red Lion Hotel was built in the 1700s it was a busy place on the old High Road between Crediton and Barnstaple. Then a new road was constructed through the Taw valley and Chulmleigh became a peaceful backwater. The Red Lion stands in the centre of the town and is very much a 'local community pub'. Every Sunday morning, a group of regulars gather here to plan fund-raising activities for charities. They've dubbed themselves the 'Sunday Morning Club' and in one corner of the tavern there's a collection of their photographs.

Dennis Govier is the landlord of this lively pub which is very traditional in its atmosphere - low-beamed ceilings and old prints and photographs around the walls. Darts and other pub games are available. The Red Lion offers a wide variety of bar meals, many of which are available to take away. There is also a separate dining room where the menu includes steaks and fish dishes together with a selection of Chinese meals.

For special occasions, The Red Lion has a function room which can cater for up to 60 guests.

THE LYMINGTON ARMS

Lama Cross, Wembworthy,
Devon EX18 7SA
Tel/Fax: 01387 83572

Located on the edge of the village and within easy reach of The Tarka Trail and Eggsford Forest, The Lymington Arms is a charming old inn which was built around 1820 by Lord Chichester for his son. (The Chichester family owned an extensive estate here). It became a coaching inn and still retains something of that atmosphere. Hunting scenes hang on the walls of the restaurant where customers are assured of an 'Eating Experience' - excellent food,

freshly prepared and based mainly on local produce. There's a Carvery on Thursdays and Sundays and for the less hungry a good choice of bar meals and snacks. Devotees of real ales will find a choice of 3 and wine lovers are pampered with an extensive list of wines from all around the world.

Outside, there's a courtyard garden in Mediterranean style, with stone tables shaded by parasols, and a children's play area. Patrons can also enjoy a game of skittles or pool, or try their hand at the shove ha'penny board. There's a function room for special occasion and a large private car park. A good time to visit The Lymington Arms is in July when it hosts a lively Beer Festival but the outstanding cuisine is available all year round.

AROUND SOUTH MOLTON

CHULMLEIGH
9 miles SW of South Molton off the A377

With its narrow cobbled lanes, courtyards and quiet squares, Chulmleigh is a delight to explore. Sprawled across the hills above the leafy valley of the Little Dart river, it is one of several attractive small towns in mid-Devon which prospered from the wool trade in the Middle Ages and then declined into sleepy, unspoilt communities. Chulmleigh's prosperity lasted longer than most since it was on the old wagon route to Barnstaple but in 1830 one of the newfangled turnpike roads was constructed along the Taw valley, siphoning off most of its trade. A quarter of a century later the Exeter to Barnstaple railway was built along the same route, the final straw for Chulmleigh as a trade centre. But this charming small town has been left with many original thatched cob cottages which cluster around a fine 15th century church noted for its lofty pinnacled tower and, inside, a wondrously carved rood screen that extends 50ft across the nave and aisles.

LAPFORD
11 miles S of South Molton on the A377

Remarkably, this small community still has its own railway station. Passenger numbers have been much augmented since British Rail's rather prosaic "Exeter to Barnstaple route" was re-christened as the "Tarka Line". The original name may have been lacklustre but the 39-mile journey itself has always been delightful as it winds slowly along the gentle river valleys of the Yeo and the Taw.

Lapford stands high above the River Yeo, its hilltop church a famous local landmark for generations: *"when yew sees Lapford church yew knaws where yew'm be"*. It's well worth a visit since the 15th century rood screen inside is regarded as one of the most exquisitely fashioned in the country. There are 5 bands of the most delicate carving at the top and above them rise modern figures of the Holy Family, (Jesus, Mary and John), surmounted by the original ornamental ceiling with its carved angels gazing down from the nave roof.

RACKENFORD
9 miles SE of South Molton off the A361

Set on the hillside above the Little Dart River, Rackenford has posed something of a problem for historians who can't work out the origins of its name. What is certain though is that there was a settlement here at the time of the Domesday Book and that in the 1400s it was prosperous enough to build an impressive church. Like many others in this area, it has a striking black and white wagon roof, embossed with leaves and flowers, and with 13 angels of carved oak perched on the corbels.

GREAT BURRIDGE FARM,

Cheldon, Chawleigh, Chulmleigh, Devon EX18 7HY Tel: 01363 83818
e-mail: shelleyweeks@smartone.co.uk website: www.tuckedup.com/greatburridge.html

Great Burridge Farm looks as pretty as a picture with its whitewashed walls and neat, thatched roof. This inviting B&B is hidden away deep in the heart of mid-Devon - but don't worry, Shelley will send you detailed, easy-to-follow directions. When you do arrive at Burridge, you'll find a picturesque family farmhouse set in the stunning wooded valley of the Little Dart River. There's just one guest bedroom: a pretty, centrally-heated en suite double, furnished with a comfy antique brass bed, stripped pine and Laura Ashley linens. Television and tea/coffee making facilities are also provided. The atmosphere is relaxed and informal and guests can come and go at any time. Guests can relax in the cosy sitting room or in the secluded garden. Dinner is optional - although not licensed guests are welcome to bring their own wine - and is sometimes taken en famille around the refectory table in the farmhouse kitchen. Delicious packed lunches can also be provided. Located almost exactly halfway between the Dartmoor and Exmoor National Parks, Great Burridge Farm provides an ideal base for exploring this lovely part of the country.

RUDGE FARM,

Lapford, Crediton, Devon
EX17 6NG
Tel: 01363 83268

Only windows and doors peek out from the rampant foliage smothering the front wall of this lovely old farmhouse. Very old farmhouse, in fact - some of its timbers have been precisely dated to the spring of 1315! Rudge Farm enjoys an idyllic setting, surrounded by lawns, trees, a pond and a stream. Peacocks strut freely around the grounds of this 200-acre family farm, turning up each morning outside the front door for their breakfast. David and Marion Mills are the owners of the farm and they welcome self-catering guests to a completely self-contained wing of the house. There's a large sunny drawing room with a granite fireplace and woodburning stove and furnished with plenty of comfortable chairs, colour TV and a comfortable large settee. Together with the 3 upstairs bedrooms (1 double en suite, 1 family and 1 twin), the wing can accommodate up to 8 people. There a well-equipped beamed kitchen with an adjacent utility room which contains a deep freeze and automatic washing machine. Children are especially welcome at Rudge Farm. In addition to the barbecue, there's a swing, climbing frame and other outdoor games, including a boat for the pond. Marion also keeps a good supply of indoor games, books and puzzles for both adults and children. Located in almost the exact centre of Devon, Rudge Farm is ideal as a base for exploring the whole county.

WORTHY FOLLY

Rackenford, Tiverton, Devon EX16 8EF
Tel/Fax: 01884 881308

Set in seventy glorious acres of Devon parkland, woodland and open meadows, Worthy Folly provides a wonderfully tranquil setting for a perfect country holiday. Built in 1980, Worthy Folly possesses all the characteristics of an old country house but is also equipped with all modern amenities. Lovers of country pursuits staying here are spoiled for choice: fishing, riding, driven and rough shooting, clay pigeon shooting, bird watching and guided walks are just some of the options available. Anglers can fish for salmon and sea trout on the River Mole (which can be rented during the season), with evening sea trout fishing also available. Or you might just want to explore Worthy Folly's twenty acres of

meadows which include a small lake which holds carp, a duck pond and numerous Deer Wallows where you can watch red deer taking their daily dip. For the more adventurous, the owners of Worthy Folly, Dick and Simone Williams, can arrange an Exmoor Safari with a local driver and guide. Located just 20 minutes from the M5, Worthy Folly is the perfect base from which to explore Exmoor, Dartmoor and the lovely Devon coastline. Guests can stay on either a B&B, or B&B and dinner basis, or on special all-inclusive holidays with all meals provided.

Exmoor

BISHOP'S NYMPTON
4 miles SE of South Molton off the A361

Bishop's Nympton, King's Nympton, George Nympton, as well as several Nymets, all take the Nympton or Nymet element of their names from the River Yeo which in Saxon and earlier times was known as the Nymet, meaning "river at a holy place". Bishop's Nympton has a long sloping main street, lined with thatched cottages, and a 15th century church whose lofty, well-proportioned tower is considered one of the most beautiful in Devon. For many years the church had a stained glass window erected in Tudor times at the expense of Lady Pollard, wife of Sir Lewis, an eminent judge and leading resident of the village. Sir Lewis told the author of *The Worthies of Devon*, John Prince, that he was away on business in London at the time and the details of the design were entrusted to his wife. At the time Sir Lewis left for town, he and his wife already had 21 children, 11 sons and 10 daughters. "But his lady caused one more child than she then had to be set there: presuming that, usually conceiving at her

CREACOMBE PARSONAGE FARM,

Parsonage Cross, Creacombe, Rackenford, Tiverton, Devon EX16 8EL
Tel: 01884 881441 Fax: 01884 881551
e-mail: creaky.parson@dial.pipex.com

Situated in open countryside with views over mid-Devon to Dartmoor in the distance, **Creacombe Parsonage Farm** offers a wide choice of accommodation styles. This small working farm has been absorbing the tranquillity of rural Devon since the 17th century. It's an ideal spot to rest for a few days, lazing in the fields, wandering along the leafy lanes, riding horseback or, if you feel more active, exploring the scenic splendours of North Devon and Exmoor.

In the main house there are three bedrooms (1 family, and 2 twins which are also available as singles) for bed & breakfast guests. All the rooms are equipped with wash hand basins, colour TV and tea/coffee making facilities. One room also has an en suite toilet. The nearby Camping Barn is suitable for small groups who require a dry base for their activities. Cooking facilities and a small fridge are available if required. Another option is a luxury 3-bedroom caravan which is fully equipped and sleeps up to 6 people. The caravan is situated in its own area of the campsite, a short distance from the farmhouse where all meals, including packed lunches, are available if required. Whichever form of accommodation you choose, you will be welcome in the spacious guests' lounge, in the garden, and indeed anywhere around the farm.

There's more. Christine Poole an accomplished needlecraft enthusiast, together with her partner John Harris, (who runs this versatile complex) hosts weekend retreats during which help will be given to hone your skills in embroidery, patchwork and 3-dimensional needlework.

THE RED LION,

Rookery Hill, Oakford, Devon EX16 9ES
Tel/Fax: 01398 351219

Located in the beautiful and unspoilt Exe valley, an area of outstanding natural beauty, Oakford is an attractive village clustered around the beautiful church of St Peter with its lofty 15th century tower. **The Red Lion** stands at the heart of the village with its beer garden, patio and car park actually on the other side of the road. It's believed to have been a 17th century coaching inn and the interior with its inglenook fireplace, brasses and copper items evokes that period. A collection of porcelain plates along with vintage irons and bottles of all ages, shapes and sizes adds to the charm.

Steve and Sheila Elliott, the owners of the Red Lion, extend a warm welcome to their patrons, offering real ales, an extensive wine list, an excellent pub menu using fresh local produce wherever possible, and a non-smoking restaurant. At weekends the Elliotts always offer something special in addition to the normal menu and they also hold popular theme evenings. The inn is an ideal base for exploring glorious Devon and Somerset and has very comfortable and clean en suite twin and double bedrooms including a four poster for that special occasion, all provided with tea and coffee-making facilities. Breakfast at the Red Lion is rather special, with croissants and freshly-squeezed oranges part of the wholesome fare.

CROSSE FARM,

Bishops Nympton, South Molton,
North Devon EX36 4PB
Tel: 01796 550288

Crosse Farm looks absolutely delightful with its neatly thatched roof and ancient stone walls. It's a traditional Devon Longhouse, dating back to the 12th century and standing in lovely open countryside close to the Exmoor National Park. This working farm is the home of Dawn and David Verney and their three children, who have 400 ewes and 70 beef cattle and grow 120 acres of corn and maize. There are also around 120 cows which children love to watch as they are being milked. Visitors will find some beautiful walks all around and the Verneys can offer you some fun fishing on the River Yeo. Land Rover rides around the farm are also very popular. A little further afield are the glorious beaches of the North Devon coast and the spectacular scenery of Exmoor.

Self-catering accommodation is in one wing of the farmhouse. Downstairs, there's a shower room and a fully equipped kitchen with dishwasher, washing machine, 4-ring electric cooker, fridge/freezer, microwave and use of tumble drier. The kitchen has plenty of units and worktop space. The cosy lounge/dining area has comfortable sofas and chairs to seat 6 people, a colour television and log effect fire. Upstairs, there are 3 attractively furnished bedrooms. Two of them are twins one of which has a vanity unit, the third is the spacious en suite master bedroom - 18ft by 18ft and enjoying magnificent views of the valley. Linen and towels are included and there is a safe enclosed garden.

husband's coming home, she should have another. Which, inserted in expectation, came to pass in reality". The oddest thing about the story is that Lady Pollard not only correctly predicted the forthcoming child, but also its sex.

WEST ANSTEY
7 miles E of South Molton off the B3227

The tiny hamlet of West Anstey lies just a mile or so from the Somerset border. **The Two Moors Way** passes by just a little to the east and the slopes on which the hamlet stands continue to rise up to the wilds of Exmoor. Despite being so small, West Anstey nevertheless has its own church, which boasts a fine Norman font and an arcade from the 1200s but is mostly 14th century. The area around West Anstey is one of the emptiest corners of Devon - grand open country dotted with just the occasional farm or a tiny cluster of cottages dotting the landscape.

MOLLAND
5 miles E of South Molton off the A361

Hidden away in a maze of lanes skittering across the foothills of Exmoor, Molland is one of Devon's "must-visit" villages for anyone interested in wonderfully unspoilt churches. Following the sale of the village in the early 1600s, **St Mary's Church** stood within the estates of the Courtenay family. During and following the Commonwealth years, the Courtenays remained staunch Catholics and showed no interest in restoring or modernising the Protestant parish church. So today you will still find a Georgian screen and tiers of box-pews, whitewashed walls, an elaborate 3-decker pulpit crowned by a trumpeting angel and a colourful Royal Arms blazoned with the name of its painter, Rowlands.

Despite their Catholic principles, three late-17th and early-18th century members of the Courtenay family are commemorated by some typically flamboyant monuments of the time.

DUNSLEY FARM,

West Anstey, nr South Molton, Devon EX36 3PF
Tel/Fax: 01398 341246

For a self-catering holiday in wonderfully peaceful surroundings it would be hard to beat Dunsley Farm, hidden away on the edge of the Exmoor National Park. A Grade II listed building, the 16th century farmhouse is situated overlooking a lovely valley of meadows and woodland. There are two ponds, well-stocked with tench, rudd, roach and carp, and a nesting kingfisher is usually to be seen nearby. Dunsley is a working farm with beef, sheep and lambs, and visitors are welcome to walk around but dogs must be kept on a lead and children supervised.

The cottage consists of two bedrooms: a large room with one double and one single bed, and a smaller room with twin beds. The bathroom has bath and shower, sink and immersion heater - electricity is provided by a £1 coin slot meter. There's a large lounge with colour TV, electric heaters throughout, plus a high chair and cot for smaller guests. The kitchen is well equipped with cooker, fridge, washing machine, microwave and tumble drier. All linen is provided, pets are welcome and the cottage is available all year round.

The farm is well placed to see the sights of Exmoor - Tarr Steps, Dunster and Dulverton are all within easy reach. Riding stables can be found nearby or you can just relax in the farm's garden (easy chairs provided) and just let the world go by.

JUBILEE HOUSE,

Highaton Farm, West Anstey, South Molton,
North Devon EX36 3PJ
Tel: 01398 341312 Fax: 01398 341323
e-mail: denton@exmoorholiday.co.uk
website: www.exmoorholiday.co.uk

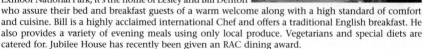

"Come as a guest, leave as a friend" is the motto at **Jubilee House**, an elegant modern house surrounded by its own 35-acre farm and mature gardens. Located on the edge of the Exmoor National Park, it's the home of Lesley and Bill Denton who assure their bed and breakfast guests of a warm welcome along with a high standard of comfort and cuisine. Bill is a highly acclaimed international Chef and offers a traditional English breakfast. He also provides a variety of evening meals using only local produce. Vegetarians and special diets are catered for. Jubilee House has recently been given an RAC dining award.

There's a choice of 2 double rooms and 3 single rooms serviced by two bathrooms, with gas central heating throughout. All the rooms are comfortable with matching pine furniture and unusual tapestry wall-hangings. A spacious lounge is available for guests, generously furnished with a TV and music system and a log burner stove to make you feel at home. A recent addition to Jubilee House's amenities which has proved very popular is the therapeutic hot tub spa on the spacious patio. Facilities are also

available for anyone wishing to bring their own horse, with ample stabling and grazing. Jubilee House stands on the Two Moor Walk and the Dentons are happy to transport any baggage on to your next stop. There are many other walks and attractions within easy reach that would interest the whole family.

ETB/RAC 4 diamonds and RAC Sparkling Diamond and Warm Welcome award. Please note that Jubilee House is non-smoking throughout.

ZEALES,

East Street, North Molton,
North Devon EX36 3JQ
Tel: 01598 740356 Fax: 01598 740157
e-mail: zeales@libertysurf.co.uk

Located on the edge of the Exmoor National Park, North Molton was in medieval times a royal manor. It became an important iron ore mining centre during the reign of Elizabeth I but by the early 1800s that industry had fizzled out. Today North Molton is a peaceful agricultural village set around a small square dominated by the mighty tower of All Saints Church. It's worth stepping inside the church to see the 'wineglass' pulpit with its 18th century sounding board and the fine tomb of Richard Bampfylde who lies surrounded by figures of his 12 sons and five daughters.

Richard's tomb was erected around the time that **Zeales** was being built. This attractive old house with its whitewashed walls has a Grade II listed building status and the building is full of charm and character. Surrounded by mature gardens, it's the home of Martin and Stella Hickman, both of whom used to work in education. They offer a warm welcome to bed & breakfast guests who will find this delightful house provides a friendly and relaxing base from which to explore Exmoor and North Devon. Zeales has 3 guest bedrooms, all en suite, very spacious and beautifully furnished with everything colour co-ordinated and with every conceivable extra provided. Guests also have the use of the residents' lounge with its log fire and colour television. A traditional full English breakfast is included in the tariff and evening meals of home cooked English dishes are available by arrangement. A one-bedroom self-contained holiday flat furnished to a high standard is also available.

River Barle and Cow Castle, Exmoor

Also within Molland parish lies Great Champson, the farm where in the 18th century the Quartly family introduced and developed their celebrated breed of red North Devon cattle.

NORTH MOLTON
3 miles N of South Molton off the A399 or A361

Tucked away in the foothills of Exmoor, North Molton was once a busy wool and mining town. At intervals from Elizabethan times until the late 1800s, copper and iron were extracted from the hills above the town and transported down the valley of the River Mole and on to the sea at Barnstaple. Evidence of abandoned mine workings are still visible around the town as well as remains of the old Mole Valley tramway.

North Molton's 15th century parish Church of All Saints reflects the small town's former industrial importance. It's a striking building with a high clerestory and a 100ft pinnacled tower which seems rather grand for this rather remote community. Several notable features have survived. There's a part-medieval "wine-glass" pulpit complete with sounding board and trumpeting angel, a rood screen, some fine Jacobean panelling, and an extraordinary 17th century alabaster monument to Sir Amyas Bampfylde depicting the reclining knight with his wife Elizabeth reading a book and their 12 sons and 5 daughters kneeling nearby. The figures are delightfully executed, especially the small girl with plump cheeks holding an apple and gazing wide-eyed at her eldest sister.

Also interesting is the church clock which was purchased in 1564 for the then exorbitant price of £16.14s 4d. However, it proved to be a sound investment since it remained in working order for 370 years before its bells chimed for the last time in 1934.

Just to the west of the church is a fine 16th century house, Court Barton (private). The iconoclastic biographer and critic Lytton Strachey (1880-1932) stayed here with a reading party in 1908. It seems that the eminent writer greatly enjoyed his stay, reporting enthusiastically on the area's "mild tranquillities", and a way of life which encompassed "a surplusage of beef and Devonshire cream,.....a village shop with bulls'-eyes,.....more cream and then more beef and then somnolence".

7 Bideford and the West Coast

The delightful riverside town of Bideford and the world-famous village of Clovelly cascading down the cliffside are just two of the prime attractions of this scenic corner of the county.

An outstanding stretch of the South West Coast Path follows the broad curve of Bideford Bay to the great headland of Hartland Point - such a conspicuous feature that almost 1900 years ago it was shown on Ptolemy's famous map of the known world. A few miles north of the point lies Lundy Island, a huge granite breakwater famous for its puffins and its stamps. The island also offers some exhilarating walks, with grand views, some 400 different birds, the unique breed of Lundy ponies, a tavern, lighthouse - and the chance to see the last indigenous black rats to have survived in Britain.

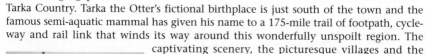
Lighthouse, Lundy Island

Bideford is one of the main "staging posts" in Tarka Country. Tarka the Otter's fictional birthplace is just south of the town and the famous semi-aquatic mammal has given his name to a 175-mile trail of footpath, cycleway and rail link that winds its way around this wonderfully unspoilt region. The captivating scenery, the picturesque villages and the relaxed lifestyle help to explain why so many visitors fall under its spell. To prepare yourself for exploring Tarka Country, a visit to the interpretation centre housed in a 1950s railway carriage at the restored Bideford Station is strongly recommended.

Stoke Church

As well as the natural beauties of the area, one of Devon's most impressive churches is to be found at Hartland where the Church of St Nectan contains what many regard as the finest carved rood screen in the county. Tapeley Park Gardens and Northam Burrows Country Park both provide satisfying outings while family parties have the choice of two popular venues, the Big Sheep and the Milky Way, both of which provide a wide range of activities for both adults and children.

Apart from Bideford itself, there are no towns of any size in this region - but hundreds of delightful villages and hamlets awaiting the traveller through what, for many, is the country's best-kept secret.

BIDEFORD AND THE WEST COAST

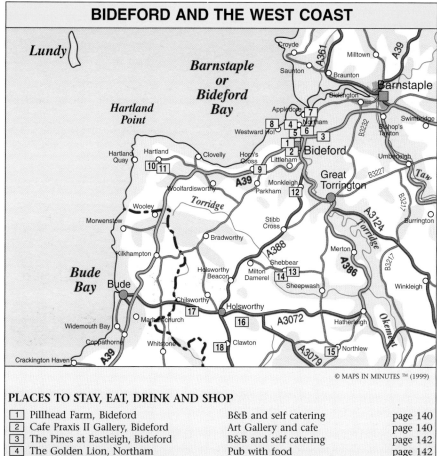

Lundy

Barnstaple or Bideford Bay

Hartland Point

Croyde
Milltown
A361
Saunton
Braunton
A39
Barnstaple
Bickington
Swimbridge
Appledore [7]
Bishop's Tawton
B3232
Westward Ho! [8] [4] Northam
[5] [6]
[3]
[1]
Horn's Cross [2] Bideford
Littleham
Umberleigh
Taw
Hartland Quay [10][11]
Hartland
Clovelly
[9]
Great Torrington
B3227
A39
Monkleigh
Parkham [12]
Woolfardisworthy
Torridge
Wooley
Morwenstow
Stibb Cross
Burrington
A312A
B3217
Bradworthy
A388
Merton
B3217
Kilkhampton
Holsworthy Beacon
Milton Damerel [14] [13]
Shebbear
A386
Bude Bay
Bude
Sheepwash
Winkleigh
Chilsworthy
Holsworthy
Widemouth Bay
Marhamchurch [17]
[16]
A3072
Hatherleigh
Okement
Coppathorne
Whitstone [18]
Clawton
A3079
[15] Northlew
Crackington Haven
A39

© MAPS IN MINUTES ™ (1999)

PLACES TO STAY, EAT, DRINK AND SHOP

[1]	Pillhead Farm, Bideford	B&B and self catering	page 140
[2]	Cafe Praxis II Gallery, Bideford	Art Gallery and cafe	page 140
[3]	The Pines at Eastleigh, Bideford	B&B and self catering	page 142
[4]	The Golden Lion, Northam	Pub with food	page 142
[5]	Yeoldon House Hotel, Northam	Hotel and restaurant	page 144
[6]	Cross House and Cottages, Northam	Self catering	page 144
[7]	Coach and Horses, Appledore	Pub with food	page 145
[8]	The Village Inn, Westward Ho!	Pub, food and accommodation	page 146
[9]	Sea Breeze, Horns Cross	Bed and breakfast	page 146
[10]	Mettaford Farm Cottages, Hartland	Self catering	page 148
[11]	Hart Inn, Hartland	Pub with food	page 148
[12]	The Bell Inn, Monkleigh	Pub with food	page 150
[13]	Backway Farm, Shebbear	B&B on working farm	page 151
[14]	Wootton Farm, Shebbear	B&B on working farm	page 152
[15]	East Worth Farmhouse, Northlew	B&B with evening meal	page 152
[16]	Claw Cottage, Hollacombe	B&B with evening meal	page 154
[17]	The Barton, Pancrasweek	B&B with evening meal	page 154
[18]	The Hollies, Clawton	B&B on working farm	page 155

PILLHEAD FARM,

Bideford, North Devon EX39 4NF
Tel: 01237 479337 Fax: 01237 479337

Only 1.5 miles from Bideford *Pillhead Farm* offers 3 self-catering cottages as well as traditional farmhouse bed and breakfast in a choice of delightful rooms. The 130 acre sheep and cereal farm has been owned by the Hill family for almost one hundred years, with Diana and Richard Hill representing the fourth generation. Their bed and breakfast guests stay in the (non-smoking) main house where there's a choice of rooms with private facilities, TVs, refreshment facilities. Included in the tariff is a really good farmhouse breakfast which will set you up for the day and evening meals are available by arrangement.

The self-catering cottages are all set around a central courtyard with a swimming pool, paddling pool, patio, barbecue and picnic area. (Bed & breakfast guests also have the use of these amenities). Two of the cottages have private gardens and one, The Cider House, has been especially designed for a couple. About 300 years old, The Cider House was formerly the location of the farm cider press and stable - parts of the press together with many traditional features have been incorporated into the conversion. Outside the main season, the Hills offer short self-catering breaks of three nights or more at any of the cottages. Whichever form of accommodation you prefer, there's plenty to keep you occupied. Coarse fishing, golf, horse riding, walking and cycling are all available locally; the coastal footpath and the Tarka Trail are only a short distance away, and the farm is well located for all the many beaches and visitor attractions of glorious North Devon.

CAFÉ PRAXIS II GALLERY,

1 & 2 Market Place, Bideford, North Devon EX39 2DR
Tel: 01237 423353

For the best coffee in Bideford along with an interesting display of paintings, the place to make for is the **Café Praxis II Gallery** in the old Market Place. The 'II' is there because the Director of the gallery, Robin Hall, established a similar café-cum-gallery in Bristol before moving to North Devon in 1997. The ground floor is divided, with the café on one side, the gallery on the other, while the first floor is devoted entirely to works of art. There's always a wide range of subjects on display and there are exhibitions by local artists which change every four weeks or so. Whatever your artistic tastes, you'll almost certainly find something here that pleases you and at prices to suit every pocket.

The aroma of freshly ground coffee drifts through the gallery and the Italian style beverage really is superb. To accompany it, there's an excellent choice of salads (with garlic bread), snacks, savouries and sandwiches. Home made soups, filled French sticks and vegetarian dishes all add to the choice. And if you are not a coffee drinker, choose from the range of herbal teas, soft drinks and organic fruit juices.

BIDEFORD

Named the "Little White Town" by Charles Kingsley, this attractive town set beside the River Torridge was once the third busiest port in Britain. The first bridge across the shallow neck of the Torridge estuary was built around 1300 to link Bideford with its aptly-named satellite village, East-the-Water. That bridge must have been very impressive for its time. It was 670ft long, and built of massive oak lintels of varying length which created a series of irregular arches between 12 and 25ft apart. These erratic dimensions were preserved when the bridge was rebuilt in stone around 1460, (the old bridge was used as scaffolding), and despite widening during the 1920s they persist to this day. Unusually, Bideford Bridge is managed by an ancient corporation of trustees, known as *feoffees*, whose income, derived from property in the town, not only pays for the upkeep of the bridge but also supports local charities and good causes. A new high-level bridge a mile or so downstream, opened in 1987, has relieved some of the traffic congestion and also provides panoramic views of the town and the Torridge estuary.

Bideford received its Market Charter from Henry III in 1272, (on May 25th to be precise) and markets still take place every Tuesday

Town Shops, Bideford

and Saturday. Since 1883 they have been held in the splendid **Pannier Market** building, reckoned to be one of the best surviving examples of a Victorian covered market. Along with local produce, there's a huge selection of gifts, crafts, and handmade goods on offer: "Everything from Antiques to Aromatherapy!"

As we've noticed at Dartmouth and Salcombe, Devon ports seemed to specialise in particular commodities. At Bideford it was tobacco from the North American colonies which brought almost two centuries of prosperity until the American War of Independence shut off supplies. Evidence of this golden age can still be seen in the opulent merchants' residences in Bridgeland Street, and most strikingly in the **Royal Hotel** in East-the-Water, a former merchant's house of 1688 with a pair of little-seen plasterwork ceilings which are perhaps the finest and most extravagant examples of their kind in Devon.

It was while he was staying at the Royal Hotel that Charles Kingsley penned most of *Westward Ho!* A quarter of a million words long, the novel was completed in just seven months. There's a statue of

Bridge over the River Torridge, Bideford

THE PINES AT EASTLEIGH,

nr Bideford, North Devon EX39 4PA
Tel: 01271 860561 Fax: 01271 861248
e-mail: barry@thepinesateastleigh.co.uk
website: www.thepinesateastleigh.co.uk

Set in 7 acres of beautiful North Devon countryside, **The Pines at Eastleigh** is a Grade II listed building dating back to Georgian times. It's the home of Barry and Jenny Jones who offer their guests comfortable accommodation on either a bed and breakfast or self-catering basis. The house stands on a quiet lane, once the main road to Barnstaple and only a couple of miles from the ancient port of Bideford. Bed & breakfast guests stay in the attractively converted stables block where most of the rooms are at ground floor level overlooking the courtyard. All rooms have en suite facilities, central heating, Teletext TV, light refreshments and direct dial telephones. Guests have the use of a lounge whose picture windows frame views across the garden to the fields. Here, visitors can help themselves to a drink from the bar, listen to music or browse the books, magazines and maps.

Evening meals are available by arrangement and you can complement your meal with wine from the personally selected list.

Self-catering guests are accommodated in two nearby cottages. Everything is included in the price - linen, towels, heating, even telephone calls, grocery pack and cancellation insurance.

Cots and high chairs are available, there's secure storage for cycles, canoes etc, and pets are welcome. Non-smoking establishment - credit cards accepted.

THE GOLDEN LION,

36 Cross Street, Northam,
North Devon EX39 1BS
Tel: 01237 474594

On October 31st, 1865, the *Bideford Gazette* reported a serious incident at **The Golden Lion**. The landlord, Mr William Rooke, was demonstrating the firing mechanism of a gun to a customer when it went off, wounding a servant girl "named Littlejohns in the neck and bosom". Fortunately, the wound was not fatal and "on consciousness returning, the girl said she did not think her master tried to do it". Such incidents

happily are not regular occurrences at The Golden Lion, lively place though it is. The inn has darts, skittles and pool teams in local leagues and its own pool room and skittle alley where they can hone their skills. Your hosts here are Derek and Cynthia Askie, a friendly and welcoming couple who have made the inn a popular venue. Derek is ex-RAF and the couple are the proud owners of a Norton motorcycle. The Golden Lion's bar has a very traditional atmosphere, with lots of old prints and photographs of local scenes, and outside there's an attractive beer garden. If you're feeling peckish, the inn offers a simple but wholesome choice of sandwiches and rolls, with an occasional roast at Sunday lunchtime. (Incidentally, the pub's name comes from a ship crewed by Northam men which sailed to meet the Spanish Armada).

Kingsley, looking suitably literary, on Bideford Quay. Broad and tree-lined, the Quay stands at the foot of the narrow maze of lanes which formed the old seaport, a pleasant reminder of the town's maritime past.

Just round the corner from the Quay, on the edge of Victoria Park, is the **Burton Museum & Art Gallery**, opened in 1994. The Museum includes some interesting

St Helens Church, Lundy Island

curios such as Bideford harvest jugs of the late 1700s, and model ships in carved bone made by French prisoners during the Napoleonic wars. The Gallery has frequently changing exhibitions with subjects ranging from automata to kites, quilts to dinosaurs, as well as paintings by well-known North Devon artists.

One excursion from Bideford that should not be missed is the day trip to **Lundy Island** on the supply boat, the *MS Oldenburg*. Lundy is a huge lump of granite rock, 3 miles long and half a mile wide, with sheer cliffs rising 500ft above the shore. Its name derives from the Norse *lunde ey*, meaning puffin island, and these attractive birds with their multi-coloured beaks are still in residence, along with many other species. More than 400 different birds have been spotted on Lundy, and you might also spot one of the indigenous black rats for whom the island is their last refuge. The island has a ruined castle, a church, a pub, a shop selling souvenirs and the famous stamps. There's even a hotel, but if you hope to stay overnight you must book well ahead.

About 3 miles north of Bideford, on the east bank of the Torridge, are the lovely grounds of **Tapeley Park Gardens**. Within its 20-acre site are four distinctly different themed areas, each one home to a rich and fascinating variety of flowers, trees, shrubs

and vegetables. The well-known Italian terrace borders, created in the late 19th century, have been renovated in recent years, and other attractions include a walled Kitchen Garden, an Organic Permaculture garden (which incidentally finds a good use for old carpets), woodland and lakeside walks, a plant shop and a tea room. The gardens are open 10am - 5pm from Easter to October, but closed on Saturdays. Tel: 01271 342371.

AROUND BIDEFORD

NORTHAM
2 miles N of Bideford on the A386

It was at Northam, three years after William the Conqueror's triumph at Hastings, that the slain King Harold's three illegitimate sons landed here from Ireland with a force of more than 60 ships. Their attempt to regain the throne from William was mercilessly put down at a site to the south of the town which is still known as Bloody Corner. Today, Northam is a busy little place with some elegant Georgian houses on Orchard Hill and a fine church tower which has been a landmark for mariners across many generations.

YEOLDON HOUSE HOTEL,
Durrant Lane, Northam, Bideford,
Devon EX39 2RL
Tel: 01237 474400 Fax: 01237 476618
e-mail: yeoldonhouse@aol.com
website: www.yeoldonhousehotel.co.uk

Set beside the River Torridge, with lawns sloping down towards the river, **Yeoldon House Hotel** combines yesterday's charms perfectly with today's comforts. Real hospitality and a refreshingly casual atmosphere awaits the visitor to this striking mid-Victorian building originally built for the owner of Appledore shipyard.

The elegant "Soyer's" restaurant, named after the famous Victorian chef Alexis Soyer, looks out over the lawns to the river and has an air of casual elegance where visitors feel comfortable in any attire. The daily changing menu offers an imaginative cuisine based on fresh fish, meat and vegetables from the area. Home-made desserts provide a perfect conclusion to a delicious meal which you can complement with a selection of international wines. In the morning, ease into your day with a Traditional English or Continental breakfast whilst watching the sun rise over the River Torridge. Each of the bedrooms at Yeoldon House holds its own charm - the cosy country style rooms, the grand four poster room, or the split level room with its own balcony and lounge area. All rooms are en suite with colour TV, tea/coffee-making facilities and direct dial telephone. The hotel is owned and run by the Steele family, Brian and Jennifer and their sons Colin and Christopher, who assure their guests of personal attention to ensure an enjoyable and memorable stay.

CROSS HOUSE & COTTAGES,
Fore Street, Northam, Bideford,
North Devon EX39 1AN
Tel: 01237 472042

Located above the village of Northam, an ancient village mentioned in the Domesday Book, **Cross House & Cottages** offer "home-from-home" self-catering accommodation. Cross House itself is a charming historic Grade II listed house dating back to the 18th century. A very spacious self-contained wing of the house, which sleeps up to 7 plus a cot, is available for guests. The rooms are full of character, with exposed beams, original slate floor and an inglenook fireplace.

Nearby, Cross Cottage is a one-bedroomed cottage, ideal for couples. Guests staying at Cross House Wing and Cross Cottage have full use of the lovely walled garden of the main house. A third property, Florence Cottage, is a Grade II listed fisherman's cottage located in the heart of Appledore, a unique Georgian fishing village with narrow lanes all leading down to the quay. The cottage combines olde worlde charm with modern amenities. There's a quaint open plan lounge/kitchen with character beams and exposed stone walls, and two country print co-ordinated bedrooms, one double and one twin.

All the Cross House properties have fully equipped kitchens with electric cooker, washing machine, fridge freezer, microwave, toaster and slow cooker. The owners, Cyma and Charlie Cassar, make every effort to ensure that "like many before you, you come as a guest and leave as a friend". Close to beaches and moors it is an excellent base for touring or simply relaxing. Pets welcome with well-behaved owners.

APPLEDORE
3 miles N of Bideford on the A386

Overlooking the Taw-Torridge estuary, Appledore is a delightful old-world fishing village of narrow winding lanes and sturdy fishermen's cottages from the 18th and 19th centuries. The streets of the old quarter are too narrow for cars although not, it seems, for the occasional small fishing boat which is pulled up from the harbour and parked between the buildings, where all types of fishing can be arranged and you can even go crabbing from the quayside. It seems appropriate that the **North Devon Maritime Museum** should be located in this truly nautical setting. Housed in a former shipowner's residence, the museum contains a wealth of seafaring memorabilia, a photographic exhibit detailing the military exercises around the estuary in preparation for the D-Day landings during World War II, a reconstructed Victorian kitchen, and much more.

Also well worth a visit is the Appledore Crafts Company in Bude Street. This co-operative of 14 leading local craftspeople offers visitors a wide range of craft items ranging from furniture and paintings, ceramics, glass and textiles, metalwork and knitwear.

A pleasant little excursion from Appledore is the short ferry ride across the Torridge estuary to Instow, home of the North Devon Yacht Club, where there is another excellent beach.

WESTWARD HO!
2 miles N of Bideford on the B3236

Is there any other place in the world that has been named after a popular novel? Following the huge success in 1855 of Charles Kingsley's tale of Elizabethan derring-do, a company was formed to develop this spectacular site with its rocky cliffs and two miles of sandy beach. The early years were troubled. A powerful storm washed away the newly-built pier and most of the houses. When Rudyard Kipling came here in 1874 as a pupil at the United Services College he described *Twelve bleak houses by the shore*. Today Westward Ho! is a busy holiday resort well worth visiting for its 3 miles of golden sands and the nearby

COACH & HORSES,

5 Market Street, Appledore, Devon EX39 1PW
Tel: 01257 474470

Just 50 yards from the water's edge, the **Coach and Horses** is the place to go for good food and drink - and to catch up on all the local news! This is very much a community pub and when a new owner bought it, 300 of the regulars organised a petition for the popular landlords, Kevin and Janet Vincent, to be kept on as managers. And so they were. They were farmers for many years before deciding on a change of direction. Janet's cooking is undoubtedly one reason for their popularity. She prepares everything on the extensive menu herself - anything from steaks to sandwiches, soups to lasagne, curries and much more.

In good weather, enjoy your meal in the pleasant beer garden at the rear. Darts are popular at the Coach and Horses and so too is euchre - the pub sustains two very accomplished teams. Additional entertainment is provided by Morris Dancers who regularly visit the inn. Appledore itself is a delightful place to explore with its narrow streets and views over the Taw-Torridge estuary. In the days of sail this was a busy shipbuilding centre and its history is told in the town's North Devon Maritime Museum.

THE VILLAGE INN,

Youngaton Road, Westward Ho! Devon EX39 1HU
Tel: 01237 477331 Fax: 01237 425183

Close to the sea front and all the village shops and amenities, **The Village Inn** is a striking building with primrose walls and imposing double-fronted bay windows. Originally a farmhouse, and one of the first buildings in Westward Ho!, it has been extended over the years. Your hosts are the Hudson family, Julie and Stuart, and their daughter Clare who looks after the kitchen. They describe the inn as "Everything that a Village Inn should be" and indeed it is. There's a wonderfully traditional ambience in the spacious, high ceilinged rooms, and an open fire adds to the welcoming atmosphere.

Naturally, the inn offers traditional Sunday lunches and at other times a choice of delicious home cooking. Choose from the extensive bar menu or from the ever-changing daily specials board. There are vegetarian choices and special diets can be catered for given advance notice. A Free House, the inn also offers a good range of well pulled pints. If the weather is favourable, there's a pleasant beer garden at the rear where you can enjoy your refreshments. Recently, the Hudsons completely refurbished 4 upstairs rooms and these are now available for guests. The rooms are all en suite, light and airy with colour TV, generous courtesy trays - and sea views.

SEA BREEZE,

West Goldworthy Farm, Horns Cross, nr Bideford, Devon EX39 5DQ
Tel: 01237 451650

Enjoying panoramic views of the enchanting Devon countryside, **Sea Breeze** provides wonderful peace and tranquillity while at the same time being within easy reach of North Devon's many attractions. It's the home of John and Jo Slee who welcome bed and breakfast guests to their attractive modern house. There are two guest bedrooms, one on the ground floor, the other on the first floor with a large balcony from which to admire those superb views. One is a family room, the other a double. Both are en suite and equipped with TV and tea/coffee making facilities. A "ruinous" traditional English breakfast with all the options is included in the tariff and guests have the use of a comfortable lounge. The house is within easy walking distance of the glorious North Devon coast, fishing and golf are available nearby, and the picture postcard village of Clovelly is a mere 5 miles away. Keen walkers will surely want to explore a stretch of the North Devon Coast Path which passes nearby - Hartland Point lies about 12 miles to the west, the splendid beach at Westward Ho! about 6 miles to the north.

Northam Burrows Country Park, 670 acres of grazed burrows rich in flora, fauna and migratory birds, and offering tremendous views across Bideford Bay. There's also the Royal North Devon Golf Club, the country's oldest golf links, which is open to holiday members.

An unusual event at Westward Ho! is the **Pot Walloping Festival** which takes place in late spring. Local people and visitors join together to throw pebbles which have been dislodged by winter storms back onto the famous ridge, after which exercise pots of a different kind also get a walloping.

A couple of miles south of Westward Ho!, on the A39 road to Bude, is **The Big Sheep** which The Good Guide to Britain 1997 voted the "Devon Family Attraction of the Year". Its owners promote The Big Sheep as "a working farm turned wacky tourist attraction". Amongst the wide variety of entertainment offered, the rather bizarre sheep racing and duck trialing events are apparently amongst the most popular. More conventional attractions include regular demonstrations of cheese making, sheep-shearing, sheepdog trialing and adventure playgrounds. Open daily all year, 10am-6pm. Tel: 01237 477916.

WOOLFARDISWORTHY
11 miles SW of Bideford off the A39

Naturally, you don't pronounce Woolfardisworthy the way it looks. The correct pronunciation is *Woolsery*. The extraordinary name goes back to Saxon times when the land was owned by Wulfheard who established a *worthig*, or homestead, here.

A mile or so north of the village, alongside the A39, is another family entertainment complex, the **Milky Way Adventure Park**. The Park includes a huge indoor play area (for both children and adults) where you can test your archery and laser target shooting skills, a Pets Corner where children are encouraged to cuddle the animals, a Bird of Prey Centre, a Sheep Dog Training and Breeding Centre, "Toddler Town" - a safe play area for very young children, a Sports Hall, a

miniature railway, and a "Time Warp Adventure Zone". The complex is open daily during the season, and weekends at other times. Tel: 01237 431255

CLOVELLY
12 miles SW of Bideford off the A39

Even if you've never been to Devon, you must have heard of this unbelievably quaint and picturesque village that tumbles down a steep hillside in terraced levels. Almost every whitewashed and flower-strewn cottage is worthy of its own picture postcard and from

Steep Cobbled Road, Clovelly

the sheltered little harbour there is an enchanting view of this unique place. One reason Clovelly is so unspoilt is that the village has belonged to the Rous family since 1738 and they have ensured that it has been spared such modern defacements as telegraph poles and "street furniture".

Clovelly Harbour

METTAFORD FARM HOLIDAY COTTAGES,

Mettaford Farm, Hartland, Devon EX39 6AL
Tel: 01237 441249 website: mettafordfarm.co.uk

Enjoying a peaceful and exceptionally attractive location in an Area of Outstanding Natural Beauty, **Mettaford Farm Holiday Cottages** were converted from original stone barns around 14 years ago. They have been totally refurbished, recently redecorated and equipped to very high standards whilst retaining many original features such as beamed ceilings and cottage style latched doors. Each of the 8 cottages has its own garden area with benches, table and barbecue, and three of them have ground floor bedrooms, toilet and bathing facilities. The cottages are set in 13 acres of well-tended grounds with a wooded streamside nature trail linking the coarse fishing and ornamental ponds. The site

offers an outstanding range of leisure amenities - a 6-hole golf course, a first class 30ft by 15ft heated indoor pool, a very spacious, well-equipped games room with table tennis, pool table and darts with croquet, short tennis and badminton lawns nearby. There's also a small children's play area, a laundry room, pay phone and a small licensed shop for basic provisions. The farm is only 2 miles from the lovely National Trust coast path and just over a mile from the centre of Hartland with its shops and pubs. The picture postcard village of Clovelly is a few minutes drive away and the superb beaches at Westward Ho! and Bude are also within easy reach.

HART INN,

The Square, Hartland,
North Devon EX39 6BL
Tel: 01237 441474

Located right in the centre of this long, straggling village, the **Hart Inn** looks absolutely delightful with its cream walls and many-coloured hanging baskets. The interior is just as pleasing to the eye - low, beamed ceilings, glinting brass and copper items, jugs, porcelain and other knick-knacks dispersed around the walls all add to the charm. Step into one of the family/dining rooms and you'll instantly realise why it's called the Cobbler's Room. Ranged around the walls is a display of vintage boots, shoes and cobblers tools, many donated by local people. They depict Hartlands last cobbler and the 'circle of life' i.e. varieties of footwear worn by the very young through to the elderly. The other main room Frank & Spencer's Shoppe (non-smoking) is equally interesting. Its walls are adorned with household bric-a-brac from yesteryear and murals of old family favourite brand labels which complement the theme as does the artists view of a bygone time through the trompe l'oeil windows. Very eye-catching.

In addition to these unusual features, the inn is also well-known locally for the quality and scope of the food on offer. The extensive choice ranges from hearty main courses to jacket potatoes, and from vegetarian options to children's choices, as well as daily specials. In good weather, enjoy your food and drink in the secluded beer garden at the rear. This lively inn is very much at the heart of village life, sustaining not just ladies and men's darts and skittles teams but also teams for pool, euchre and even football.

The only access to the beach and the beautifully restored 14th century quay is on foot or by donkey, although there is a Land Rover service from the Red Lion Hotel for those who can't face the climb back up the hill. The only other forms of transport are the sledges which are used to deliver weekly supplies. During the summer months there are regular boat trips around the bay, and the *Jessica Hettie* travels daily to Lundy Island with timings that allow passengers to spend some six hours there, watching the seals and abundant wildlife.

The Clovelly Pottery, opened in 1992, displays an extensive range of items made by Cornish and Devon potters. In the nearby workshop, for a small fee, you can try your own hand at throwing a pot.

This captivating village has some strong literary connections. It features as "Steepway" in the story *A Message from the Sea* by Dickens and Wilkie Collins. Charles Kingsley (*The Water Babies; Westward Ho!*) was at school here in the 1820s and the Kingsley Exhibition

Rocky Coastline, Clovelly

explores his links with the village. Next door, the Fisherman's Cottage provides an insight into what life was like here about 80 years ago. And the award-winning Visitor Centre has an audio-visual show narrating the development of Clovelly from around 2000BC to the present day.

HARTLAND
15 miles SW of Bideford on the B3248

This pleasant village with its narrow streets and small square was once larger and more important than Bideford. Hartland was a royal possession from the time of King Alfred until William the Conqueror and continued to be a busy centre right up to the 19th century. It was at its most prosperous in the 1700s and some fine Georgian buildings survive from that period. But the most striking building is the parish **Church of St Nectan** which stands about 1.5 miles west of the village. This is another of Devon's "must-see" churches. The exterior is impressive enough with its tower, 128ft high, but it is the glorious 15th century screen inside which makes this church one of the most visited in the county. A masterpiece of the medieval woodcarvers' art, its elegant arches are topped by four exquisitely fretted bands of intricate designs. The arches are delicately painted, reminding one yet again how colourful English churches used to be before the vandalism of the Puritan years. As well as the screen, the church's other treasures include a highly decorated Norman font, a magnificent Gothic tomb chest of gleaming black stone and some ancient Tudor benches.

In the churchyard is the grave of Allen Lane who, in 1935, revolutionised publishing by his introduction of Penguin Books, paperback books which were sold at sixpence (2.5p) each.

Back in Hartland village, anyone interested in attractive stoneware will want to visit the **Hartland Pottery** in North Street. Here you can watch Clive C. Pearson and his team involved in the various processes of making their oven to table ware. Functional oil lamps are a popular item, and Clive's own favourite pieces are Chun-glazed, a particularly lovely deep blue glaze that originated during the Sung Dynasty, 960-1279 AD.

From the village, follow the signs to **Hartland Abbey**. Founded in 1157, the

Abbey was closed down in 1539 by Henry VIII who gave the building and its wide estates to William Abbott, Sergeant of the Royal wine cellars. His descendants still live here. The house was partly rebuilt in the mid-18ᵗʰ century in the style knows as Strawberry Hill Gothic, and in the 1850s the architect George Gilbert Scott added a front hall and entrance. The Abbey's owner, Sir George Stucley, had recently visited the Alhambra Palace in Spain which he much admired. He asked Scott to design something in that style and the result is the elegant Alhambra Corridor with a blue vaulted ceiling with white stencilled patterns. The Abbey has a choice collection of pictures, porcelain and furniture acquired over many generations and, in the former Servants' Hall, a unique exhibition of documents dating from 1160. There's also a fascinating Victorian and Edwardian photographic exhibition which includes many early

Coastline, Hartland Quay

photographs. The Abbey is open May-September on Wednesdays, Bank Holiday Sundays and Mondays, from 2pm-5.30pm.

A mile further west is **Hartland Quay**. Exposed to all the wrath of Atlantic storms, it seems an inhospitable place for ships, but it was a busy landing-place from its building in 1566 until the sea finally overwhelmed it in 1893. Several of the old buildings have been

THE BELL INN,

Monkleigh, Bideford, North Devon, EX39 5JS
Tel: 01805 622338

Located in the heart of this picturesque village, **The Bell Inn** looks the very picture of a traditional Devon hostelry with its thatched roof and whitewashed upper storey. The interior is just as inviting - low-beamed ceilings, small-paned windows and lots of gleaming brass and copper all add to the welcoming atmosphere. The Bell is a lively place. In addition to all the popular pub games - darts, pool, dominoes and cards, there's a piano in the bar and the inn hosts regular folk music and jazz evenings.

The pub is also a showcase for the work of local artist Chris Collingwood whose oil paintings are displayed around the walls, along with those of April Doubleday whose works also adorn the ladies' lavatory! A major attraction here is the quality of the food. Mine hosts Jock and Sue insist that The Bell is "a pub serving good food - not a restaurant with a bar". Their menu offers an excellent choice of "Hot & Spicy" curries, a selection of "Not Hot or Spicy" dishes and a good range of vegetarian options. The Bell also serves cream teas which, if you're lucky with the weather, can be enjoyed in the beer and tea garden at the rear.

Monkleigh is the kind of place where you'll probably want to linger - if so, why not take advantage of Maggie's Cottage next door which has 3 guest bedrooms, (two doubles and a single).

Lighthouse, Hartland Point

converted into a comfortable hotel; another is now a museum recording the many wrecks that have littered this jagged coastline.

About three miles to the north of the Quay, reached by winding country lanes, is **Hartland Point**. On Ptolemy's map of Britain in Roman times, he names it the "Promontory of Hercules", a fitting name for

this fearsome stretch of upended rocks rising at right angles to the sea. There are breathtaking sea and coast views and a lighthouse built in 1874.

LITTLEHAM
3 miles S of Bideford off the A386

A tiny village set on hills above the River Yeo, Littleham comprises just a few houses, an ancient church, and an excellent pub, the Crealock Arms. Unusually for Devon, church and pub stand at opposite ends of the village: St Swithin's on a winding byway to the north-east; the Crealock Arms at the end of a lane to the south-west. They are linked, though, by the inn's name, for the grandest thing in the church is the impressive memorial to General Crealock, a distinguished Victorian soldier and local landowner, whose tomb stands nearly six feet high.

MONKLEIGH
5 miles S of Bideford on the A388

Monkleigh parish church also contains a striking monument, an ornate canopied tomb

BACKWAY FARM,
Shebbear, Beaworthy, Devon EX21 5HN
Tel/Fax: 01409 231259

If you are looking for a quiet and peaceful holiday, it would be hard to find a better location than **Backway Farm**, tucked away in the countryside between Holsworthy and Hatherleigh. The stone and tile farmhouse dates back some 150 years and stands in 170 acres of a working dairy farm. The owner, Margaret Johns, is Devon born and bred, and she has been welcoming bed and breakfast guests to her charming home for some years now. There are 4 guest bedrooms, 1 of them en suite and all of them attractively furnished and decorated. The spacious rooms are well-equipped with television and

hospitality trays and they all enjoy wonderful views across open countryside to Dartmoor. A traditional English breakfast 'with all the options' is included in the tariff.

Backway Farm is conveniently located for exploring the north Cornwall and Devon coasts, and for visiting famously picturesque villages such as Clovelly. A short drive southwards will bring you to the celebrated beauty spot of Lydford Gorge which stands on the edge of the Dartmoor National Park - 365 square miles of mostly wild and rugged terrain which has been designated as an area of outstanding natural beauty.

WOOTTON FARM,

Shebbear, Beaworthy,
Devon EX21 5QW
Tel: 01409 281248

Farmhouse holidays continue to grow in popularity and at **Wootton Farm**, deep in the west Devon countryside, it's easy to understand why. The house is a traditional Devon longhouse and stands in 230 acres of a working dairy and mixed farm. It's the home of Mr and Mrs Quance, both of them locally born and bred. They have two guest bedrooms, comfortably furnished to the highest standards and equipped with tea and coffee-making facilities. Both rooms enjoy stunning views across open countryside to Dartmoor. There are some lovely walks in the neighbourhood and the Cornish and North Devon coasts are both within easy reach.

Shebbear itself is a pleasant little village, its houses grouped around a large square. The church boasts a Norman doorway and a 14th century effigy of a lady but the village is perhaps best known for its 'Devil's Stone'. This is a large boulder at the foot of an oak tree on the green. Every Guy Fawkes' Day, men from the village ring the church bells then turn the boulder over with sticks and levers. The bells are then rung again. Whatever was the original significance of this curious ceremony, it has long since been forgotten.

EAST WORTH FARMHOUSE,

Northlew, Okehampton,
Devon EX20 3PN
Tel: 01409 221757

Nestling in unspoilt countryside a mile from the village of Northlew, **East Worth Farmhouse** is a delightful 17th century Devon longhouse which has been lovingly refurbished to modern standards while retaining the atmosphere and charm of a bygone era. It's the home of Rosalind Haddon, a welcoming hostess who greets arriving bed & breakfast visitors with

afternoon tea and cakes. She is also a superb cook and you are strongly recommended to take advantage of the optional evening meal. Rosalind will happily cater for vegetarian and other dietary requirements if she is notified in advance.

The premises are not licensed but guests are welcome to bring their own wine or other tipple. Guests have the use of their own sitting/dining room which is well-provided with books and games as well as TV and radio, and are welcome to stroll or sit in the relaxing atmosphere of the tranquil garden with its wonderful views. The farmhouse has 2 guest bedrooms, both en suite and both, like the rest of the house, non-smoking. This peaceful retreat provides an excellent base for exploring Dartmoor, Exmoor and the coasts of North Devon and Cornwall, with visitor attractions such as Rosemoor Gardens, the Tarka Trail and Tintagel village all within easy reach.

containing the remains of Sir William Hankford who was Lord Chief Justice of England in the early 1400s. He lived at nearby Annery Park and the story goes that having been troubled by poachers Sir William instructed his gamekeeper to shoot anyone he found in the park at night. The gamekeeper did indeed see a figure passing through the park, fired and discovered to his horror that he had killed his master.

SHEBBEAR
13 miles S of Bideford off the A388

This attractive village is set around a spacious square laid out in the Saxon manner with a church at one end and a hostelry at the other. Lying in a hollow just outside St Michael's churchyard is a huge lump of rock, weighing about a ton, which is known as the **Devil's Stone**. According to local legend, the boulder was placed here by Old Nick who challenged the villagers to move it, threatening that disaster would strike if they could not. Every year since then, on November 5th (a date established long before the Gunpowder Plot of 1605), a curious ceremony has taken place. After sounding a peal of bells, the bell ringers come out of the church and set about the stone with sticks and crowbars. Once they have successfully turned the stone over, they return in triumph to the bell tower to sound a second peal.

SHEEPWASH
22 miles S of Bideford off the A3072 or A386

Sheepwash is yet another Devon community to have been devastated by fire. The conflagration here occurred in 1742 and the destruction was so great that for more than ten years the village was completely deserted. Slowly, the villagers returned, built new houses in stone, and today if you want the essence of Devon distilled into one location, then the village square at Sheepwash is just about perfect. Along one side stands the famous Half Moon Inn, renowned amongst fishermen; on another, the old church tower rises above pink-washed thatched cottages, while in the centre, cherry trees shelter the ancient village pump.

Just south of the village, the minor road crosses the River Torridge and there's a rather heartening story about the bridge here. Until

well into the 1600s, the only way of crossing the river was by means of stepping stones. One day, when the river was in full spate, a young man attempting to return to the village was swept away and drowned. His father, John Tusbury, was grief-stricken but responded to the tragedy by providing money to build a bridge. He also donated sufficient funds for it to be maintained by establishing the Bridgeland Trust and stipulating that any surplus income should be used to help in the upkeep of the church and chapel. The Trust is still in operation and nowadays also funds outings for village children and pensioners.

NORTHLEW
26 miles S of Bideford off the A3072

As at Sheepwash, the thatched cottages and houses stand around a large central square which is dominated by a charming 15th century church standing on the hilltop above the River Lew. The church is noted for its Norman remains and the exceptional (mainly Tudor) woodwork in the roof, bench ends and screen. Also of interest is one of the stained glass windows which features four saints. St Thomas, to whom the church is dedicated, is shown holding a model of the church; St Augustine, the first Archbishop of Canterbury, holds the priory gateway, while St Joseph carries the Holy Grail and the staff which grew into the famous Glastonbury thorn tree. The fourth figure is simply clad in a brown habit and carries a bishop's crozier and a spade. This is St Brannock who is credited with being the first man to cultivate the wild lands of this area by clearing woodland and ploughing and could therefore be regarded as the patron saint of farmers.

HOLSWORTHY
18 miles SW of Bideford on the A388/A3072

Wednesday is a good day to visit Holsworthy. That's when this little town, just four miles from the Cornish border, holds its weekly market. This is very much the traditional kind of street market, serving a large area of the surrounding countryside and with locally-produced fresh cream, butter, cheese, and vegetables all on sale. The town gets even livelier in early July when it gives itself over to the amusements of the three-day-long **St Peter's Fair**. The Fair opens with the curious

CLAW COTTAGE,

Hollacombe, Holsworthy,
Devon EX22 6NP
Tel: 01409 253638
e-mail: kathymeyer1@compuserve.com

Set within one and a quarter acres of mature gardens, **Claw Cottage** is nominally the property of Kathy and Derek Meyer but, as they admit, is actually owned by their three cats, Rufus, Orlando and Pyewacket. (Which means that only cat-loving dogs can be accommodated). The cottage offers a good standard of accommodation and privacy as the Meyers only take up to 6 guests in their non-smoking home. There are 3 guest bedrooms, an en suite double with 4-poster bed, an en suite twin room and a double room with private loo and shower. All rooms have tea/coffee-making facilities and colour television. Visitors are welcome to make use of the delightful stream-bordered garden for bird-watching or just to relax in. A traditional English breakfast is included in the tariff and evening meals are available by arrangement. Where possible, these are based on locally reared or grown meat, poultry, fish and vegetables.

The cottage is situated on a cycle route and two mountain bikes are available for the use of visitors. The small market town of Holsworthy is less than three miles away. In addition to the weekly cattle and pannier markets and a monthly furniture auction, the town has several major fairs throughout the year. The Cornish resort of Bude, well known for its annual Jazz Festival, is a 20-minute drive away and there are numerous other local attractions, including Adventure Parks, an Otter Sanctuary, potteries, fishing and Nature Trails.

THE BARTON,

Pancrasweek, Holsworthy, Devon EX22 7JT
Tel: 01288 381315

Occupying a lovely position amongst the rolling hills of west Devon, **The Barton** offers comfortable bed and breakfast accommodation in a friendly and relaxing atmosphere. A traditional Devon longhouse of stone and tile, The Barton stands in an acre of garden surrounded by open farmland. This is great walking country and your hosts, Christine and Richard Chant, can guide you to some of the best areas. (The Tarka Trail, for example, is just a short distance away). The Barton has 3 guest rooms, all en suite and individually styled. The spacious rooms are fully equipped, with a hospitality tray in each. A traditional English breakfast is included in the tariff and evening meals, based on fresh local produce, are available on request.

Pancrasweek's unusual name comes from its Church of St Pancras and the old English word wic, meaning a hamlet or farmstead. The village lies close to the Cornish border and the North Devon coast with its picture postcard villages such as Clovelly is also within easy reach. A few miles to the east stretch the wild wastes of Dartmoor and another half hour's drive will bring to the historic cathedral city of Exeter.

old custom of the **Pretty Maid Ceremony.**
Back in 1841, a Holsworthy merchant
bequeathed a legacy to provide a small
payment each year to a local spinster, under
the age of 30 and noted for her good looks,
demure manner and regular attendance at
church. Rather surprisingly, in view of the
last two requirements, the bequest still finds a
suitable recipient each year.

Holsworthy's most striking architectural
features are the two Victorian viaducts that
once carried the railway line to Bude. The
viaducts stride high above the southern edge
of the town and, since they now form part of
a footpath along the old track, it's possible to
walk across them for some stunning views of
the area.

An interesting feature in the parish church
is an organ built in 1668 by Renatus Hunt for
All Saints Church, Chelsea. In 1723, it was
declared worn out but was nevertheless
purchased by a Bideford church. There it gave
good service for some 140 years before it was
written off once again. Removed to
Holsworthy, it has been here ever since.

The area around Holsworthy is particularly
popular with cyclists. There are three clearly-
designated routes starting and finishing in
the town, and it also lies on the "West
Country Way", a 250-mile cycle route from
Padstow to Bristol and Bath which opened in
the spring of 1997.

CLAWTON
21 miles S of Bideford on the A388

A good indication of the mildness of the
Devon climate is the number of vineyards
which have been established over the last
thirty years or so. Clawford Vineyard in the
valley of the River Claw is a good example.
Set in more than 78 acres of vines and
orchards, the vineyard's owners welcome
visitors to sample their home-grown wines
and ciders, and in the autumn to watch that
year's vintage being produced.

THE HOLLIES,

Clawton, Holsworthy,
Devon EX22 6PN
Tel: 01409 253770

Set in the attractive countryside of
North Devon, near the Cornish
border, **The Hollies** provides an ideal
base for touring Devon and
Cornwall. This spacious modern
house is the home of Graham and
Rosemary Colwill who feel sure that
anyone who stays for a week or more,
leaves looking ten years younger! The
Hollies stands on a working farm
with pleasant views of the
neighbouring lake and vineyard, and
with many animals to see including

sheep, lambs and calves. There's an extensive lawn area for playing games and a sunny patio for
relaxing. Accommodation consists of 3 en suite bedrooms - two double rooms and one family or twin
bedroom. All are very well-appointed and equipped with every conceivable extra including television
and tea/coffee-making facilities. A traditional English breakfast is served and evening meals are available
by arrangement. Children are welcome.

This area of Devon is a bird-watcher's paradise, due to the many different habitats of open moorland,
secluded valleys, rolling hills, ancient woodland and, of course, the coastline. Riding, pony trekking
and lake fishing are available nearby and there are golf courses at Holsworthy and Bude. Bude also has
a lovely beach. To the east, the Dartmoor National Park is within easy reach; to the west, a short drive
brings you to the dramatic Cornish coast.

8 The North Devon Coast

The glorious stretch of coastline that runs from Barnstaple Bay to the Somerset border offers some of the grandest coastal scenery in the country, and a beach, Woolacombe, which has been named as one of the Top Ten Beaches in the world. This 3-mile expanse of golden sands has also gained both the Blue Flag accolade for safety and cleanliness, and a Premier Resort Award for the quality of its amenities. There are other fine beaches at Instow and at Croyde which is popular with wind-surfers riding the mighty Atlantic breakers.

The three major settlements in this area are Barnstaple, Ilfracombe and Braunton. The latter two are pretty much the same size, but Ilfracombe is a fully-fledged town, Braunton still officially a village. As if to compensate for hurt pride, Braunton now claims the distinction of being the "largest village in the country".

Most of the other settlements are genuinely villages, or hamlets, linked by a network of country lanes meandering around rolling hills, while the twin villages of Lynton and Lynmouth, linked by a unique water-powered cliff railway, exert an irresistible allure with their romantic setting and almost Mediterranean charm. The area

St Peters Church, Barnstaple

has been popular with holiday-makers for almost 200 years so there's a huge variety of traditional visitor attractions as well as more recent allurements such as go-karting.

Valley of the Rocks, Lynton

Amongst the older buildings, Arlington Court is notable for the eclectic collections amassed by its last owner, Rosalie Chichester, during the course of a long life, and the now redundant church at Parracombe, a "time warp" building still just as it was in the 18th century.

To the west is the Exmoor National Park, only one third of which lies in Devon. The moor rises sharply with the highest point (1600ft) near Kinsford Gate which is easily reached by a minor road and provides a spectacular viewpoint. The surrounding uplands are scattered with numerous prehistoric barrows and standing stones. Much less bleak than Dartmoor, this is hill farming country with sheep, cattle and ponies, although in the higher areas red deer still roam freely.

THE NORTH DEVON COAST

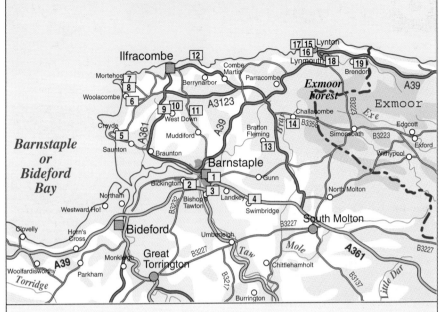

© MAPS IN MINUTES ™ (1999)

PLACES TO STAY, EAT, DRINK AND SHOP

NORTH HILL,

nr Barnstaple Tel: 01271 850611
Bookings through Best Leisure, North Hill, Shirwell,
Barnstaple, Devon EX31 4LG

A mile long drive meanders its way upwards through a beautiful wooded valley teeming with wildlife - deer, foxes, badgers, buzzards, herons and woodpeckers. At the end of the drive is the group of cottages known as **North Hill**, a perfect hideaway deep in the rolling hills of North Devon. All of these self-catering cottages have exposed beams full of characteristic charm and individuality, some retaining many original features. There are 8 of them, offering accommodation ranging from 2 people plus a cot, up to 6 plus cot. All are furnished to a very high standard with fitted carpets, pine furniture, matching linen and curtains, full size cooker, fridge freezer, microwave, colour television and video recorder.

Every cottage has its own woodburner as well as central heating. Guests have the use of a 33ft indoor heated swimming pool which is open all year, a large kiddies paddling pool and whirlpool spa

all of which are heated to a comfortable 88°F whatever the weather outside. Other facilities include an all weather tennis court, games room with pool table and table tennis, fitness room, sauna room with sunbed and shower, while outside there's large safe and well-equipped playground for children. You might well find enough here to occupy you throughout your stay, but then you'd be missing the scenic splendours of the North Devon coastline with its superb beaches, resort towns such as Ilfracombe, or the rugged beauty of Exmoor and "Lorna Doone Country".

THE OLD BARN,

Tews Lane, Bickington, Barnstaple, Devon EX31 2JU
Tel: 01271 372195 Fax: 01271 375133

The old road from Barnstaple to Bideford, the B3233, passes through the village of Bickington which lies alongside the little River Lemon just before it flows into the River Taw. Cottages cluster around the ancient church and for walkers along the South West Coast Path which runs nearby, Bickington provides a convenient refreshment stop in the form of The Old Barn Inn. It's a family run business with Andrea and Mike Drinkwater, aided by their daughter Amanda, offering customers good food and real ales. The pool table, dart board and large screen TV are always available.

Dating back some 150 years, the inn is full of character with lots of beams and decorated with old farm implements. There are large seating areas throughout. One wall is devoted to a "Rogues' Gallery" - a photographic montage of all the regulars, mounted and framed!

At lunchtimes there's a good choice of traditional oven baked jacket potatoes, ploughman's, baguettes and hot bar meals with additional choices for children and vegetarians. The evening menu, served between 19.00 and 21.30, presents some appetising choices such as Salmon steak with lime and fennel sauce, and chicken breast in white wine and mushroom cream, with a range of vegetarian meals, all complimented by a comprehensive wine list. To finish the meal, a superb range of desserts. Ample car parking space is available.

BARNSTAPLE

Barnstaple enjoys a superb location at the head of the Taw estuary, at the furthest point downstream where it was possible to ford the river. The first bridge across the Taw was built in the late 1200s, but the present impressive structure, 700ft long with 16 arches, dates from about 1450 although it has been altered and widened many times.

Visitors will immediately realise that Barnstaple takes its floral decorations very seriously. The town began its association with the Britain in Bloom movement in 1991 and just five years later crowned its efforts by winning the Gold award for the "Prettiest Floral Town in Europe" in the Entente Florale Competition. Wherever you turn you may well find a magnificent display - a haycart full of flowers outside the police station and civic centre, for example, a giant postage stamp modelled in blossoming plants outside the Post Office, or a stunning model of a train (again, all created in flowers) at the entrance to the railway station.

The town's love of floral exuberance may be one of its most endearing features but Barnstaple is also the administrative and commercial capital of the region, a pre-eminence it already enjoyed when the Domesday Book recorded the town as one of only four boroughs in the county. Back then, in 1086, Barnstaple had its own Mint and, already, a regular market. More than nine centuries later, the town still hosts produce markets every Tuesday and Friday, but the **Pannier Market** is open every weekday. This huge, glass-roofed building covering some 45,000 square feet was built in 1855 and its grandiose architecture resembles that of a major Victorian railway station, (London's St Pancras springs to mind). Each day of the week at the market has a different emphasis: crafts on Monday and Thursday, for example, antiques on Wednesday. The Market takes it name from the pannier baskets, (two wicker baskets connected by a leather strap draped across the back of a donkey, pony or horse), in which country people in those days would carry their fruit and vegetables to town.

Butchers Row, Barnstaple

Just across the road from the Pannier Market is **Butchers Row**, a quaint line of booth-like Victorian shops built mostly of wood and with brightly painted wooden canopies. When they were built, back in 1855, they were occupied exclusively by butchers, but now you'll find a much wider variety of goods on sale - seaweed amongst them. Every week during the summer season at least 300lbs of this succulent algae are sold, most of it ending up as a breakfast dish, served with bacon and an egg on top.

Pannier Market, Barnstaple

In Barnstaple's High Street stands the rather austere **Guildhall**, built in the Grecian style in 1826 and now housing some interesting civic memorabilia: - portraits, municipal regalia and silverware. Nearby, the Church of St Peter and St Paul dates back to the early 1300s. After having its spire twisted by a lightning strike in 1810, it suffered even more badly later that century under the heavy hand of the Victorian restorer, Sir Gilbert Scott. Much more appealing are the charming 17th century Horwood's Almshouses nearby, and the 15th century St Anne's Chapel which served for many years as the town's Grammar School. During the late 17th century John Gay, author of *The Beggar's Opera*, was numbered amongst its pupils.

Another interesting museum has the unusual distinction of being housed in a former signal box. The **Lynton and Barnstaple Railway Museum** (free) records the history of the narrow-gauge railway that ran between Barnstaple to Lynton from 1898 to 1935. Barnstaple is also the northern terminus of the **Tarka Line**, a lovely 39-mile route that follows the gentle river valleys of

the Yeo and the Taw where Tarka the Otter had his home. The railway is actually the main line route to Exeter but has been renamed in honour of one of the area's major visitor attractions.

As at Tiverton, the 17th century well-to-do residents of Barnstaple were given to charitable endowments. As well as Thomas Horwood's almshouses, Messrs. Paige and Penrose both bequeathed substantial funds for almshouses, and in 1659 Thomas' wife, Alice, paid for the building in Church Lane of a school for "20 poor maids". It is now a coffee house.

A slightly later building of distinction is **Queen Anne's Walk**, a colonnaded arcade with some lavish ornamentation and surmounted by a large statue of the Queen herself. Opened in 1708, it was used by the Barnstaple wool merchants who accepted that any verbal bargain they agreed over the Tome Stone was legally binding. The building stands on the old town quay from which, in 1588, five ships set sail to join Drake's fleet against the Armada.

One of Barnstaple's most enduring industries has been pottery, made here

THE THREE PIGEONS,

Village Street, Bishops Tawton, Devon EX32 0DG
Tel: 01271 372269

Formerly a coaching inn, **The Three Pigeons** still has the low beamed ceilings of that era and the traditional atmosphere is enhanced by the dark wood furnishings and a wealth of old prints and photographs of the village. Today this welcoming tavern is very much at the heart of the community, maintaining its own football team and offering customers a choice of skittles, darts, euchre and pool. Mine hosts at this lively pub are Bryan and Carol Godwin, both of whom had many years experience in the licensed trade in the Midlands before moving to this attractive corner of Devon. The Three Pigeons is open all day, every day, with a good choice of wholesome home made food available from noon until 21.00. The regular menu offers a good selection of main dishes, jacket potatoes, burgers, sandwiches, baguettes, an all day breakfast and vegetarian options, along with

Barnstaple in Spring

daily specials. The home made soup, pies and pasties are especially recommended. Devotees of real ales will find themselves well provided for and there's also an extensive choice of other brews, spirits and wines.

Bishops Tawton village, just a mile or so out of Barnstaple, is not over-supplied with listed buildings but it can boast a very unusual one. - a sociable 3-seater outside lavatory. This amenity has not been used for forty years or more but it still looks perfectly serviceable.

Queen Anne's Walk, Barnstaple

continuously since the 13th century. In Litchdon Street, the **Royal Barum Pottery** welcomes visitors to its workshop, museum, and well-stocked shop.

Walkers along the Tarka Trail will know Barnstaple well as the crossover point in this figure-of-eight long-distance footpath. Inspired by Henry Williamson's celebrated story of *Tarka the Otter*, the 180-mile trail wanders through a delightful variety of Devon scenery - tranquil countryside, wooded river valleys, rugged moor line, and a stretch of the North Devon coast, with part of the route taking in the **Tarka Line** railway in order to get the best views of the locations described in the novel. A guide book is available covering the whole trail and there are pamphlets detailing individual sections.

AROUND BARNSTAPLE

LANDKEY
2 miles SE of Barnstaple off the A361

Landkey boasts a fine church with some impressive memorials (well worth visiting) and also the distinction of being the only village bearing this name in Britain.

Historians believe that it is derived from *Lan*, the Celtic word for a church, and the saint to which it was dedicated, Kea. An enduring legend claims that St Kea rowed over from Wales with his personal cow on board determined to convert the pagans of north Devon to Christianity. Sadly, these benighted people were not persuaded by his eloquence, so they chopped off his head. Not many public speakers could cope with that kind of negative response, but St Kea calmly retrieved his severed head and continued, head in hand, to preach the Gospel for many years.

BISHOPS TAWTON
3 miles S of Barnstaple on the A377

Bishop's Tawton takes its name from the River Taw and the medieval Bishop's Palace that stood here until the reign of Henry VIII and of which a few fragments still stand. The village today is not over-endowed with listed buildings but it can boast a very unusual one, a sociable three-seater outside lavatory which has been accorded Grade II Listed status. This amenity has not been used for forty years or more (and the brambles which have invaded it would make it rather uncomfortable to do so) but it still looks perfectly serviceable.

SWIMBRIDGE
5 miles E of Barnstaple on the A361

For almost half a century from 1833 this attractive village was the home of the Rev. John "Jack" Russell, the celebrated hunting parson and breeder of the first Jack Russell terriers. A larger than life character, he was an enthusiastic master of foxhounds and when his Bishop censured him for pursuing such an unseemly sport for a man of the cloth, he transferred the pack into his wife's name and continued his frequent sorties. He was still riding to hounds in his late 70s and when he died in 1880 at the age of 87 hundreds of people attended his funeral. Russell was buried in the churchyard of St James', the church where he had been a diligent pastor. He was gratefully remembered for his brief sermons, delivered as his groom waited by the porch with his horse saddled and ready.

Mostly 15th century, the **Church of St James** is one of Devon's outstanding churches, distinctive from outside because of its unusual lead-covered spire. Inside, there is

ANIMAL FARM COTTAGES,

East Kerscott, Swimbridge, Barnstaple,
North Devon EX32 0QA
Tel/Fax: 01271 831138
e-mail: animalfarmcottages@lineone.net
website: www.animal-farm-cottages.com

Animal lovers will feel very much at home at **Animal Farm Cottages**, two charming self-catering cottages located in the heart of North Devon. The 4-acre property is also a refuge for a varied group of abandoned animals which Lynn and Steve Marshall have taken to their hearts. The animals have been featured on Channel 4's popular Pet Rescuers programme and currently there are swans, geese, ducks, chickens, goats, a cow, a pig and a donkey all being looked after here.

There are two cottages to rent. Cider Press Cottage is a 17th century cider house which has been converted to a fully equipped 3-bedroomed cottage yet retains the original cider press and many exposed beams. Overlooking the duck pond (fenced in) is Orchard Cottage, formerly a stables and also dating back to the 17th century. Orchard Cottage can accommodate up to 6/7 and Cider Press up to 6 visitors. There is ample off road parking and a large communal garden with BBQ, garden furniture and climbing frame/swings. Please note that, because of the farm animals, dogs are not allowed.

The cottages make an ideal base for exploring the scenic beauty of North Devon which is one of only three areas in the UK still classed as tranquil! It's only a mile to the nearest village, Swimbridge, which has a public house, small shop, post office and a church whose pastor was once the Rev John (Jack) Russell who introduced the famous Jack Russell terrier. The nearest beach is approximately 10 miles away and Exmoor National Park is easily accessible.

ST HELEN'S PRIORY,

Hobbs Hill, Croyde, North Devon EX33 1NE
Tel: 01271 890757 www.sthelenspriory.co.uk

Just a short walk from Croyde's famous beach, **St Helen's Priory** is a beautiful thatched building which was previously part of a 17th century priory and is now run as a small hotel and restaurant. It is one of the oldest properties in the village and although secluded in its own grounds of over an acre lies right in the heart of this picturesque village. Inside, the Priory retains much of its original charm and character with winding corridors, oak floors, beams to walls and ceilings, but also offers comfortable and roomy accommodation with all modern amenities. Guests have the use of an attractive lounge with oak floors and two inglenook fireplaces and also a small conservatory/reading room which leads to a residents' private gardens with an old water well and fish ponds. There's also a lush tea garden - open to all - where you can enjoy home made cakes, lunches or the speciality of the house, Devon Cream Teas. St Helen's has its own licensed restaurant and bar which offers an extensive menu and a full wine list. Croyde village itself is well-known for its Gem, Rock & Shell Museum and in addition to Croyde's own superb beach there are miles of golden sands at Saunton, Putsborough and Woolacombe, all just minutes away.

a wealth of ecclesiastical treasures: a richly carved rood screen spanning both the nave and the aisles, an extraordinary 18th century font cover in the shape of an elongated octagonal "cupboard", a fine 15th century stone pulpit supported by a tall pedestal and carved with the figures of saints and angels, and a wonderful nave roof with protective angels gazing down. Collectors of unusual epitaphs will savour the punning lines inscribed on a monument here to John Rosier, a lawyer who died in 1658:

> Lo, with a Warrant
> sealed by God's decree
> Death his grim Seargant
> hath arrested me
> No bayle was to be given,
> no law could save
> My body from the prison
> of the grave.

The village itself has some elegant Georgian houses and a pub which in 1962 was renamed after Swimbridge's most famous resident. Jack Russell societies from around the world frequently hold their meetings here.

MUDDIFORD
4 miles N of Barnstaple on the B3230

From Barnstaple to Ilfracombe, the B3230 winds through a pretty valley, passing along the way through attractive little villages. Despite the rather unappealing name, Muddiford is one of them. The village really did get its name from the "muddy ford" by which medieval travellers used to cross the river here.

Less than two miles to the east of Muddiford, **Marwood Hill Gardens** offers visitors some 18 acres of trees and shrubs, many of them rare and unusual. The collection was started more than half a century ago and now includes an enormous number and variety of plants. The three lakes, linked by the largest Bog Garden in the West Country, are busy with ducks and multi-coloured carp. From spring, when camellias and magnolias are in bloom, through to the brilliant hues of Autumn, the gardens provide a continuous spectacle of colour.

BRAUNTON
6 miles NW of Barnstaple on the A361

Braunton claims the rather odd distinction of being the largest village in Devon. It is certainly a sizeable community, spreading along both sides of the River Caen, with some handsome Georgian houses and a substantial church reflecting Braunton's relative importance in medieval times. The church is dedicated to St Brannoc, a Celtic saint who arrived here from Wales in the 6th century. It's said that his bones lie beneath the altar of the present 13th century church, a story which may well be true since the building stands on the site of a Saxon predecessor. What is certainly true is that the church contains some of the finest 16th century carved pews to be found anywhere in England. Many of the carvings depict pigs, a clear allusion to the ancient tradition that St Brannoc was instructed in a dream to build a church where he came across a sow and her litter of seven pigs. Arriving in North Devon some time during the 7th century, the saint happily discovered this very scene at the spot where Braunton's church now stands.

There is further evidence of Saxon occupation of this area to be found in **Braunton Great Field**, just to the southwest of the village. This is one of very few remaining examples of the Saxon open-field strip system still being actively farmed in Britain. Around 350 acres in total, the field was originally divided into around 700 half-acre strips, each of them a furlong (220yds) long, and 11yds wide. Each strip was separated by an unploughed "landshare" about one foot wide. Throughout the centuries, many of the strips have changed hands and been combined, so that now only about 200 individual ones remain.

CROYDE
10 miles NW of Barnstaple on the B3231

Croyde is renowned for its excellent beach with, just around the headland, another 3-mile stretch of sands at Saunton Sands, one of the most glorious, family-friendly sandy beaches in the West Country. The sands are backed by 1,000 acres of dunes known as **Braunton Burrows**. The southern part of this wide expanse is a designated nature reserve

THE RED BARN,

Woolacombe, North Devon EX34 7DF
Tel: 01271 870264

Just a hundred metres from Woolacombe's famous beach stands The Red Barn which has been owned by the Ashford family since the 1960s. Angus Ashford is the third generation of his family to run this lively restaurant and bar. Given its sea front location and panoramic views out to sea, it's not surprising to find that Angus is a keen surfer, as are many of the staff here. Several are active members of the Surf Life Saving Champions Club and their passion for this exhilarating sport is evident in the Red Barn's unusual décor. The theme of course is surfing, and along with various trophies there's a wealth of surfing memorabilia - prints, paintings and a fascinating collection of vintage, locally-made surf boards.

Surfers tend to work up healthy appetites and the Restaurant/Bar menu here seems designed to satisfy them, and indeed anyone who really enjoys their food. Along with traditional hot meals like country Ham & Eggs, or cod fried in home made batter, there are steaks and grills, curries and chillis, grilled beef or vegetarian burgers, speciality omelettes and an All Day Breakfast. In addition, you'll find ploughmans, jacket potatoes, freshly-cut, amply-filled sandwiches, and even more choices in the blackboard list of the chef's daily specials. Food is served all day, every day of the year and if you are a devotee of real ales, there's a choice of 5 different brews, along with traditional West Country ciders. Children are welcome at this family-oriented hostelry and will surely enjoy the large patio overlooking the beach.

NORTH MORTE FARM CARAVAN & CAMPING PARK,

Mortehoe, Woolacombe, North Devon EX34 7EG
Tel: 01271 870381 Fax: 01271 870115
e-mail: enquiries@northmortefarm.co.uk
website: www.northmortefarm.co.uk

Adjoining National Trust land and only 500 yards from Rockham Beach, North Morte Farm Caravan & Camping Park is set in some of the most spectacular countryside in the south-west. Set high up on the cliff top, the Park enjoys some stunning views and if you follow the coastal path breathtaking vistas open up at every turn. Woolacombe with its two miles of golden sands is close by and another short walk will bring you to the ancient village of Mortehoe.

The Park offers a wide choice of 4, 6 and 8-berth holiday homes to rent. Each is fully equipped, except for linen, and has parking for 2 cars alongside. (Please note, dogs are not permitted). A separate area

provides pitches for tents, dormobiles and touring caravans, with electric hook-ups available. The park has a very well-equipped children's play area and other amenities include a shop and off-licence, hot showers and flush toilets, and a laundry room with washing machines, spin drier and tumble dryers, plus hair drying and ironing facilities. This popular holiday area offers a wide variety of activities - fishing, golf, horse riding, sailing and boating, tennis and squash, and even hang-gliding are all available locally. Also within easy reach are visitor attractions such Arlington Court, Dartington Glass Factory, a wildlife park, gardens, museums, potteries and much, much more.

Croyde Bay

noted for its fluctuating population of migrant birds as well as rare flowers and insects.

WOOLACOMBE
13 miles NW of Barnstaple on the B3343

The wonderful stretch of golden sands at Woolacombe is justifiably regarded as the finest beach in North Devon. This favoured resort lies between two dramatic headlands, both of which are now in the care of the National Trust. The sands and rock pools lying between these two outcrops are a delight for children, (along with the swing boats and donkey rides), and surfers revel in the monster waves rolling in from the Atlantic.

Back in the early 1800s, Woolacombe was little more than a hamlet whose few residents sustained a precarious livelihood by fishing. Then, suddenly, the leisured classes were seized by the craze for sea bathing initiated by George III at Weymouth and enthusiastically endorsed by his successor George IV at Brighton. Inspired by the economic success of those south coast towns, the two families who owned most of the land around Woolacombe, the Fortescues and the Chichesters, began constructing villas and

hotels in the Regency style, elegant buildings which still endow the town with a very special charm and character. Many friends of the Fortescue and Chichester families regarded their initiative as a suicidally rash enterprise. Woolacombe was so remote and the roads of North Devon at that time still so primitive, little more than cart tracks - who, they asked, would undertake such an arduous journey? During the first few years only a trickle of well-to-do visitors in search of a novel (and comparatively inexpensive resort) found their way to Woolacombe. But their word of mouth recommendations soon ensured a steady flow of tourists, a flow which has swelled to a flood over subsequent years. Today, Woolacombe beach is still as beautiful as it was then and it also now basks in the bureaucratic glow of a European Commission "Seaside Award". To qualify for the EC's "coveted yellow and blue flag" that comes with the award, no fewer than 28 "exacting criteria" have to be fulfilled. These range from clearly sensible requirements - the sea water should be unpolluted; lifeguards, first aid and disabled facilities should all be provided and easily available - to the stern

Putsborough Sand, Woolacombe

EASEWELL FARM,

Mortehoe, Woolacombe, North Devon EX34 7EH
Tel/Fax: 01271 870225

Well off the beaten track, Easewell Farm Holiday Park and Golf Club offers an outstanding range of amenities, so much so that it has been awarded the prestigious 5 ticks rating by the West Country Tourist Board. Set amidst glorious rolling hills, this family site offers touring pitches, camping, a rented cottage, a static caravan and an abundance of on site activities. There's an indoor heated pool, games

room, indoor bowls, skittles, table tennis, and adventure playground. You can relax in the spacious bar, enjoy a meal in the restaurant or buy one from the takeaway. On a practical level, there's a well-stocked shop, modern toilet blocks with free hot showers, a fully equipped launderette, a dishwashing area, electric hook-ups and 'Super Sites' which provide paved hard standing, TV aerial, water, drainage, electricity and night light. The Park's popular purpose-built 9-hole golf course has a par of 33 and provides a stern test for both experienced golfers and beginners: clubs, balls and trolleys are available for hire from the Golf Shop.

The site is just a few miles from Ilfracombe with its shops, restaurants and entertainment, while Woolacombe's magnificent Bay with its miles of award winning golden sands is just 5 minutes by car. For horse lovers, riding is available at the nearby Stables; boat trips can be taken from Ilfracombe for either fishing or a pleasure cruise; and the Tarka Trail provides miles of track for a breathtaking walk or bike ride through some of the county's most stunning scenery.

FAIRVIEW FARM COTTAGES,

West Down, nr Woolacombe, North Devon EX34 8NE
Tel: 01271 862249 www.fairviewfarm.co.uk

The small self-catering complex of cottages at Fairview Farm consists of picturesque converted stone and cob farm buildings situated around a lawned courtyard, all set in 13 acres and surrounded by rolling Devon countryside with fine rural views, and yet within a few minutes drive of the finest beaches the south west has to offer.

There is a choice of 1,2 and 3 bedroom cottages, all being bright and airy with modern fitted kitchens, including microwaves, and with full gas central heating for those out-of-season breaks.

Within the grounds there exists an extensive array of facilities including a championship all-weather tennis court, a 5 acre 9-hole pitch and putt course, croquet lawn, a vast safe indoor play barn for young children with ride-on toys, ball pond and giant wendy-house, an outside play area with swings, climbing frame and trampoline, plus a well-equipped games room with table-tennis, pool table and amusements. Extensive parking and storage facilities are available and, with so much land, well-behaved dogs are welcome and easily exercised away from other guests.

Ideally situated for easy access to the west-facing surfing beaches, or the rocky bays to the north, and yet equally suited as a base for walking the dramatic South West Coast Path or the moors and valleys of Exmoor itself, Fairview Farm offers a holiday, and a welcome, second to none.

stipulation that "Dog control and poop scoop by-laws should be displayed on the promenade".

Just outside the town, **Once Upon a Time** provides a huge variety of entertainment for younger children - indoor and outdoor play area, crazy golf, a young scientist's room, children's driving school, train rides, animated fairy tales, an "ocean of plastic balls to play through in the Wild Boar Adventure Trail, and much more.

MORTEHOE
14 miles NW of Barnstaple off the B3343

Mortehoe is the most north-westerly village in Devon and its name, meaning "raggy stump", reflects the rugged character of the Morte peninsula. In this pretty stone-built village.

Mortehoe's part-Norman church is certainly worth a visit. It's a small cruciform building with a 15th-century open-timbered wagon roof, an interesting early 14th century table tomb, a bell in the tower which may be the oldest in Devon, and a wonderful series of grotesquely carved Tudor bench ends. The church is also notable for the large mosaic of 1905 which fills the chancel arch. Designed by Selwyn Image, the Slade Professor of Art at Oxford, the mosaic was created by the same craftsmen who did the mosaics in St Paul's Cathedral.

A short walk from Mortehoe village leads you to the dramatic coastline, mortally dangerous to ships, but with exhilarating views across to Lundy Island. Much of this clifftop area is in the guardianship of the National Trust which also protects nearby Barricane Beach (notable for being formed almost entirely of sea shells washed here from the Caribbean), and the three-mile stretch of Woolacombe Sands.

WEST DOWN
9 miles NW of Barnstaple off the A361

This village of whitewashed houses beside the River Caen is mostly notable for its tiny church with a nave barely 15ft wide. Mostly rebuilt in the 17th and 18th centuries, the church has nevertheless retained a fine oak roof from the 1300s, a Norman font which was discovered buried beneath the floor, and

HIDDEN VALLEY CARAVAN PARK AND RESTAURANT,

West Down, nr Ilfracombe, Devon EX34 8NU
Tel: 01271 813837 Fax: 01271 814041
e-mail: hvpdevon@aol.com
website: www.hiddenvalleypark.com

Nestling in a beautiful wooded valley, Hidden Valley Caravan Park has been showered with awards, most notably the AA's accolade of 'Best Park in the South West, 1997-98'. The Park's secluded location attracts a wealth of wild life. Wild ducks often join the tame ones on the lake, herons seem to appear from nowhere, fishing for their breakfast, buzzards glide gracefully overhead; kingfishers, squirrels and red deer have all been spotted here. The Park is ideal for children. The adventure playgrounds with their aerial glides, climbing nets, sand pits and swings will keep them happy for hours. There's also a game room where they can play pool while Mum and Dad have a quiet drink. Adults will appreciate the Lounge Bar/Restaurant overlooking the lake where they can choose from a very extensive menu,

enjoy a Devon Cream Tea in the afternoons or select a takeaway meal. Other amenities include a well-stocked shop and off licence, modern toilet blocks equipped to the highest standards, laundry room and ironing facilities, TV hook-ups to all pitches and facilities for freezing ice packs. There are some lovely woodland walks in and around the valley and North Devon's glorious Golden Coast with its miles of golden sands is just a short drive away.

a rare wooden figure of Sir John Stowforth, Justice of the Common Pleas in the 1300s. He is shown wearing the robes of a Serjeant-at-Law and much of the original colouring has survived.

ILFRACOMBE

Like Barnstaple, Ilfracombe takes its floral decorations very seriously - during the 1990s the town was a consistent winner of the Britain in Bloom Competition. Between June and October the town goes "blooming mad" with streets, parks and hotels awash with flowers. Ilfracombe also promotes itself as a "Festival Town" offering a wide variety of events. They include a Victorian Celebration in mid-June when local people don period costumes, and a grand costume ball and a fireworks display all add to the fun, to the National Youth Arts Festival in July, a Fishing Festival in early August, a Carnival Procession later that month, and many more.

A recent addition to the town's amenities is **The Landmark**, a striking building with

Harbour Entrance, Ilfracombe

what look like two gleaming white truncated cooling towers as its main feature. This multi-purpose arts centre has a 480-seat theatre, cinema screening facilities, a spacious display area and a café-bar with a sunny, sea facing terrace.

With a population of around 11,000, Ilfracombe is the largest seaside resort on the North Devon coast. Up until 1800, however, it was just a small fishing and market town

CENTERY FARM,

Bittadon, North Devon EX31 4HN Tel: 01271 866676
e-mail: all@centery-farm.freeserve.co.uk www.centery-farm.freeserve.co.uk

Nestling in a valley just north of the parish of Bittadon, Centery Farm offers visitors friendly, informal hospitality on either a self-catering or bed & breakfast basis. The present farmhouse is believed to have occupied this site for many hundreds of years and has been modernised to a high standard whilst retaining its sense of history. The wealth of oak beams and open log fires give the house great charm and character. Bed & breakfast guests are accommodated in the main house where the well-appointed bedrooms have large en suite facilities (with bath and shower), there are comfortable dining and sitting rooms, and guests are free to come and go at will. For those who prefer self-catering, Honeysuckle Cottage, adjacent to the farmhouse, sleeps 6 in comfort.

Pets are welcome at Centery Farm, (there are even 'bring-your-own-horse' facilities), and the farmhouse overlooks a large duck pond abounding with wildlife. Your hosts, David and Annie Rickard, are keen conservationists and can arrange guided wildlife outings, including one to the famous Red Deer. Horse riding and carriage driving are also available locally, as are fishing, golf, and surfing. For garden lovers, Marwood Gardens, Tapley Park and the Royal Horticultural Society's Rosemoor Garden are easily accessible as are various other attractions for young and old alike.

Ilfracombe Harbour

and sea water therapies. The **Tunnel Baths**, with their extravagant Doric façade, were opened in Bath Place in 1836, by which time a number of elegant residential terraces had been built on the hillside to the south of the old town.

The arrival of the railway in 1874 brought an even larger influx of visitors to Ilfracombe. Much of the town's architecture, which could best be described as "decorated Victorian vernacular", dates from this period, the new streets spreading inland in steeply undulating rows. Around the same time the harbour was enlarged to cope with the paddle steamers bringing in tourists from Bristol and South Wales. Today, visitors can take advantage of regular sailings from that harbour to Lundy Island, as well as cruises along the spectacular Exmoor coast.

For walkers, the coastal path here provides some spectacular scenery, whether going west to Capstone Point, or east to Hillsborough Hill.

Just to the east of Ilfracombe, at Hele Bay, **The Old Corn Mill & Pottery** is unique in North Devon. Dating back to the 16th century, the mill has been lovingly restored from near dereliction and is now producing

relying entirely on the sea both for its living and as its principal means of communication.

The boundaries of the old town are marked by a sheltered natural harbour to the north, and a part-Norman parish church boasting one of the finest medieval waggon roofs in the West Country half-a-mile away to the south.

The entrance to Ilfracombe harbour is guarded by Lantern Hill, a steep-sided conical rock which is crowned by the restored medieval chapel of **St Nicholas.** For centuries, this highly conspicuous former fishermen's chapel has doubled as a lighthouse, the light being placed in a lantern at the western end of the building. St Nicholas must surely be the only ecclesiastical building in the country to be managed by the local Rotary Club - it was they who raised the funds for its restoration. From the chapel's hilltop setting there are superb views of Ilfracombe, its busy harbour and the craggy North Devon coastline.

Like so many west country resorts, Ilfracombe developed in response to the early-19th century craze for sea bathing

Ilfracombe Coastline

100% wholemeal stone-ground flour for sale. In Robin Gray's pottery, you can watch him in action at the potter's wheel and try your own skill in fashioning slippery clay into a more-or-less recognisable object. If you really want to keep the result, the pottery will fire and glaze it, and post it on to you.

Half a mile or so south of the mill, set in a secluded valley, **Chambercombe Manor** is an 11th century mansion which was first recorded in the Domesday Book. Visitors have access to eight rooms displaying period furniture from Elizabethan to Victorian times, can peek into the claustrophobic Priest Hole, and test their sensitivity to the spectral presences reputed to inhabit the Haunted Room. Outside, the 4 acres of beautiful grounds contain wildfowl ponds, a bird sanctuary and an arboretum.

AROUND ILFRACOMBE

BERRYNARBOR
4 miles E of Ilfracombe off the A399

Nestling in a steep-sided combe, Berrynarbor is a wonderfully unspoilt village set around St

Peter's which, with its 96ft high tower, is one of the grandest churches in North Devon. Inside, there is an interesting collection of monuments, many of them memorials of the Berry family, once the owners of the nearby 15th century manor house which later became the village school.

COMBE MARTIN
5 miles E of Ilfracombe on the A399

Just a short distance from Berrynarbor, on the other side of the River Umber, is another popular resort, Combe Martin. There's a good sandy beach here and a short walk will take you to one of the secluded bays. An added attraction, especially for children, is the large number of rock pools amongst the bays. In the village itself, the main street is more than two miles long, reputed to be the longest in the country and features a wide selection of inns, cafés and shops. As well as the **Combe Martin Museum**, there is also the **Combe Martin Motorcycle Museum**, and on the outskirts of the village, a **Wildlife and Dinosaur Park** where life-sized animated dinosaurs lurk in the woods! The 25-acre site also shelters 250 species of real animals, including a large and lively collection of apes

WATERMOUTH COVE HOLIDAY PARK,

Watermouth Cove, Berrynarbor,
nr Ilfracombe, North Devon EX34 9SJ
Tel: 01271 862504

Set amidst 27 acres of spectacularly beautiful coastline, **Watermouth Cove Holiday Park** offers holidaymakers a well laid out caravan site with comprehensive amenities and a whole host of activities both in the park itself and nearby. The private beach is a wonderland for children, magical caves and marvellous rocks keeping them spellbound for hours. The calm, shallow waters of the bay are perfectly safe for

youngsters and for adults the rocks around the beach and headland provide some of the best coastal fishing to be found - from mackerel to the really big fish. There are two freshwater swimming pools set in a lovely walled garden, a children's playground and indoor playroom, another recreation room with TV, pool table and darts, and a small amusement arcade.

The Park is owned and run by the Parr family, Alan and Christine, their two daughters and son. They have equipped the site with every conceivable amenity - a shop catering for everything you're likely to need, attractive toilet facilities kept in tip-top condition, constant hot water for showers and washing facilities, electric hook ups, a launderette and a licensed Clubroom where live entertainment is provided most nights during the season. This outstanding site also has limited hard-standing facilities available for motor homes and caravans and a small number of luxurious chalets to rent.

Adjacent to the Park is the delightful Watermouth Harbour overlooked by Watermouth Castle, a grand mansion completed in 1823 which has some fascinating displays which even include a collection of early vacuum cleaners!

Combe Martin Coastline

A remarkable architectural curiosity in the village itself is **The Pack o' Cards Inn**, built by Squire George Ley in the early 18th century with the proceeds of a highly successful evening at the card table. This Grade II listed building represents a pack of cards with four decks, or floors, thirteen rooms, and a total of 52 windows. Inside there are many features representing the cards in each suit.

and monkeys. Within the park are animal handling areas, an "Earthquake Ride", a dinosaur museum and oriental gardens. There's an otter pool and daily sea lion shows and falconry displays, and if you book ahead you can experience the unique thrill of swimming with the sea lions.

BRATTON FLEMING
15 miles SE of Ilfracombe off the A399

Although the official boundary of the Exmoor National Park lies 3 miles to the east, Bratton Fleming definitely has a moorland feel to it. If you can get access to the church tower, there are glorious views across field and valleys to the sea, some 12 miles distant.

No one seems to have a kind word for its much restored 15th century church but about three miles northwest of the village is a building which should certainly be visited.

Arlington Court is an imposing National Trust property which was home to the Chichester family from 1534 until the last owner, Rosalie Chichester, died childless in 1949. (Sir Francis Chichester, famous as an aviation pioneer and as the first solo round-the-world sailor, was born two miles away at Shirwell). The present house was built in 1822 to an unambitious design by the Barnstaple architect, Thomas Lee, and extended some forty years later by Sir Bruce Chichester who also added the handsome stable block. When he died in 1881, he left the house and its 2775-acre park to

Combe Martin Bay

WHITE HART INN,

Bratton Fleming,
North Devon EX31 4TA
Tel/Fax: 01598 710344

Bratton Fleming stands on a hillside some 700ft above sea level, close to the Somerset border and the wild acres of the Exmoor National Park. Located in the heart of the village, The White Hart has a history that stretches back some 300 years and is reflected in the stone slab floors, low beamed ceilings and many nooks and crannies. Settles and old church pews add more character to the traditional atmosphere. The local village team has made the White Hart their headquarters which explains the photographs and caricatures of cricketing heroes displayed around the walls. This charming old tavern is run by Helen McLeod and Juliette Reilly, two enthusiastic young ladies whose friendly and welcoming manner contribute greatly to the popularity of the White Hart. It's a lively hostelry with pool and darts (in a separate area), regular quiz nights and live music at the weekends. During the summer, weather permitting, barbecues are held in the attractive garden at the rear.

Another major attraction here is the food. Helen and Juliette offer a comprehensive menu with something for every palate and size of appetite. Fresh fish, including local trout, is a speciality, but there's also a wide choice of steaks and other meat, poultry, pasta and vegetarian dishes. For lighter appetites, the choice ranges from home made soup or pâté, 'loaded' jacket potatoes, freshly cut 'doorstep sandwiches', hot crusty baguettes, beef burgers, pizzas, an all day breakfast or home cooked ham and egg. Children's portions are available and to complement your meal, there's an extensive selection of real ales, lagers, ciders, spirits and wines.

If you are planning to stay in this scenic corner of the county, the White Hart has recently opened a brand new guest bedroom. It's a double room, fully furnished to the highest standard and equipped with television and hospitality tray. From this comfortable base, Exmoor and the manifold attractions of North Devon are all within easy reach. Only a mile or so from the village is the unique narrow gauge Exmoor Steam Railway; another couple of miles will bring you to the Exmoor Zoological Park or Arlington Court (National Trust), a lovely early 19th century building housing collections of every kind - model ships, costume, pewter, shells and even horse drawn carriages.

A little further afield are the picturesque coastal villages of Lynton and Lynmouth; Ilfracombe with its wealth of seaside resort attractions; the glorious beaches at Woolacombe, Croyde and Staunton; and, if you are a keen walker, you could follow part of the spectacular South West Coast Path which runs for 518 miles from Minehead in Somerset to Bournemouth.

his daughter Rosalie, along with a staggering mountain of debts. Only 15 years old when she inherited the estate, Rosalie managed to keep it intact and stayed on at Arlington Court until her death at the age of eighty-three.

The interior today is really a museum reflecting Rosalie's varied interests. There are displays of her collections of porcelain, pewter, shells, snuff boxes, and more than a hundred model ships, some made by French soldiers captured during the Napoleonic wars.

Intriguingly, Rosalie never saw the most valuable work of art amongst her possessions. After her death, a water-colour by William Blake was discovered on top of a wardrobe where it had lain forgotten for over 100 years. It is now on display in the white drawing room.

During her lifetime, Rosalie Chichester transformed the grounds of Arlington Court into something of a nature reserve. She ordered the building of an 8-mile long perimeter fence to protect the native wildfowl and heron populations. The Shetland ponies and Jacob sheep grazing the fields today are descendants of those introduced by Rosalie. Another of her eclectic interests is evident in the 18th century stable block which houses a unique collection of horse-drawn carriages she saved from destruction, in which rides are available at most times.

About 5 miles to the east of Arlington Court, **Exmoor Zoological Park** is home to more than 170 species of unusual and exotic animals and birds. The residents of the 12 acres of gardens here range from pygmy marmosets to tarantulas, from penguins to catybara. Children can enjoy close encounters with many of the more cuddly animals, there are informative talks by the keepers but, as in any zoo, the most magnetic visitor attraction is the feeding time for the various animals.

CHALLACOMBE
15 miles SE of Ilfracombe on the B3358

Famous for its ancient inn, the Black Venus (see panel below), Challacombe stands just inside the Exmoor National Park with the Edgerley Stone which marks the border with Somerset only a mile and a half away. There

THE BLACK VENUS INN,

Challacombe, nr Barnstaple, Devon
Tel: 01595 763251

Believed to be the only hostelry in England bearing this name, The Black Venus Inn is a splendid old stone-built inn enjoying a wonderful situation in the Exmoor National Park. Japonica clings to its walls and there's a well-maintained beer garden to the side, a lovely setting in which to enjoy the fare on offer. Inside, this historic 16th century building is full of Devon character and charm: the low ceilings still have the original beams intact, the stone fireplace in the restaurant has a hand carved wooden surround and on the walls are vintage agricultural implements.

For landlords Jennie and Adrian Lidbury, the Black Venus is their first pub and they have taken to it extremely well. Jennie is skilled in alternative medicine and also has the gift of being a medium; Adrian is a former engineer. Their open and friendly personalities have made the inn a popular place with both visitors and locals. Concentrating on local ales and cider, the bar is a cosy place to enjoy a drink or a snack and there is also a comprehensive menu available in the restaurant, offering a wide choice supplemented by daily specials. Jennie's butcher and greengrocer guarantee fresh, local produce. Located in the heart of walking and riding countryside, this is a charming inn that is well worth seeking out.

THE DENES,

15 Longmead, Lynton, Devon EX35 6DQ
Tel/Fax: 01598 753573
Website: www.thedenes.com e-mail: j.e.mcgowan@btinternet.com

An excellent base for exploring the glorious coastline and countryside around Lynton is **The Denes**, an imposing 3-storey house parts of which date back to Georgian times. It's the home of John and Sally McGowan, a friendly and welcoming couple with a commitment to making sure their guests have a comfortable and relaxing stay. They offer a choice of en suite double or family room, family room with shared bathroom, or double room with private bathroom. All the rooms are beautifully furnished and equipped with hospitality trays; some have their own television. Alternatively, guests are welcome to relax in the lounge with other residents for their evening's entertainment. Evening meals are provided with a choice from the 3-course menu which can be geared to suit your requirements. Following the meal, coffee and mints are served in the lounge. If you are travelling with a young child, baby sitting can be arranged.

Around the house are displayed paintings by Sally's father, an accomplished artist whose works can be purchased - an ideal souvenir of your visit. Sally is also an artist and, like her husband, committed to personal fitness. John regularly takes on the challenge of marathon runs. You may not feel quite so

energetic but there's plenty to keep you occupied in this lovely part of Devon. The Denes is situated at the entrance to the Valley of Rocks, a well-known local beauty spot strewn with extraordinary rock formations. The twin towns of Lynton and Lynmouth offer many sporting activities: sea and river boat trips as well as a range of shops and the famous Cliff Railway that links them. Nearby are the popular resorts of Combe Martin, Ilfracombe and Woolacombe to the west; Porlock and Minehead to the east.

Whatever your particular interest, you will almost certainly find a location nearby where you can indulge it. In Lynmouth itself, there's Exmoor's Brass Rubbing Centre; a little further afield are Dunster Castle and Cleeve Abbey; while the unspoilt acres of the Exmoor National Park stretch for miles to the south and east. The Garden Gnome Reserve might be rather a specialised interest but Tropiquaria near Watchet will almost certainly appeal to all the family. Walkers and cyclists will surely enjoy following the Tarka Trail and walkers have the spectacularly scenic South West Coast Path to explore. It's the longest of Britain's long-distance paths and extends for 613 miles from Minehead in Somerset to Bournemouth, passing through Lynton en route.

was a settlement here in the days of the ancient Britons and it was they who gave the village its name. Experts cannot agree whether the name means "cold valley" or "calves' valley" but as one of them points out, either interpretation would be valid, "for the wind is never still here, and the moorland raises good beef cattle".

PARRACOMBE
13 miles E of Ilfracombe off the A39

The redundant **Church of St Petrock** is notable for its marvellously unspoilt interior, complete with 15th century benches, 17th century box pews, a Georgian pulpit and a perfectly preserved musician's gallery. Perhaps most striking of all is the unique gated screen between the chancel and the nave which bears a huge tympanum painted with the royal arms, the Lord's Prayer, the Creed and the Ten Commandments. We owe the church's survival to John Ruskin who led the protests against its intended demolition in 1879 after another church was built lower down the hill.

We are now in the Exmoor National Park,

crossing hog-backed hills where rivers fall 1500ft in less than four miles. The views are entrancing, preparing the traveller for the quite astonishing loveliness of those inseparable twins, Lynton and Lynmouth, just a few miles further on.

LYNTON
17 miles E of Ilfracombe, off the A39

Lynton and Lynmouth, though often mentioned in the same breath, are very different in character. Lynton is the younger of the two settlements and sits atop a great cliff 600ft high; Lynmouth, far below, clusters around the junction of the East and West Lyn rivers just before they reach the sea.

Lynton is a bright and breezy village, its houses and terraces mostly Victorian. The **Exmoor Museum**, housed in a restored 16th century house, has an interesting collection of the tools and products of bygone local craftsmen and other exhibits recounting local history.

To the west of Lynton, about a mile or so along a minor road, is one of the most remarkable natural features in Devon, the

CROFT HOUSE HOTEL,

Lydiate Lane, Lynton, North Devon EX35 6HE
Tel/Fax: 01598 752391
e-mail: jane.woolnough@lineone.net
website: www.smoothhound.co.uk/hotels/crofthou.html

Just five minutes walk from the town centre, **Croft House Hotel** is a delightful Grade II listed building dating back to 1828. It's situated in a quiet lane in the old town, within easy walking distance of the Valley of Rocks and the famous Cliff Railway which connects the town to Lynmouth with its picturesque harbour. Croft House is the home of Jane and Terry Woolnough who offer visitors a choice of bed & breakfast or bed, breakfast and evening meal, as well as special winter breaks when your third night's accommodation is free. Evening meals are served by candlelight in the pleasant dining room where Jane provides an appetising 3-course meal with plenty of choice, including vegetarian options. Guests can take advantage of the fully licensed bar for a drink before or with dinner, and after dinner settle down in the lovely walled patio garden with another perhaps! You can also enjoy afternoon tea in the garden.

Croft House has 7 guest bedrooms, six of which are en suite and the seventh has its own private facilities. Three of the rooms have 4-poster beds to add that extra touch of romance to your stay and if you really want to impress you can arrange with the Woolnoughs to have flowers and wine waiting in your room.

Valley of the Rocks. When the poet Robert Southey visited the area in 1800, he was most impressed by this natural gorge *"covered with huge stones...the very bones and skeletons of the earth; rock reeling upon rock, stone piled upon stone, a huge terrific mass'"* In *Lorna Doone*, the author R.D. Blackmore transforms the site into the "Devil's Cheesering" where Jan Ridd visits Mother Meldrun who is sheltering under "eaves of lichened rock". And it was after walking along the clifftop path, more than 1300ft above the sea, in company with William Wordsworth and his sister Dorothy that S. T. Coleridge was inspired to write his immortal *Rime of the Ancient Mariner.*

LYNMOUTH

18 miles E of Ilfracombe on the A39

Lynton is connected to its sister-village Lynmouth by an ingenious cliff railway which, when it opened on Easter Monday, 1890, was the first of its kind in Britain. A gift from Sir George Newnes, the publisher and newspaper tycoon, the railway is powered by water, or rather by two 700-gallon water tanks, one at each end of the 450ft track.

Alford House Hotel,

3 Alford Terrace, Lynton, Devon EX35 6AT
Tel/Fax: 01598 752359
e-mail: bookings@alfordhouse.freeserve.co.uk

Nestling on the slopes of the most beautiful coastline in Devon, **Alford House Hotel** is a charming Georgian-style, 8-bedroom hotel which enjoys a panoramic vista to be envied! It's privately owned and run by Roy, Amanda and Martyn Ayers who pride themselves on the excellence of the food served here, with a menu that offers a wide choice to meet everyone's taste. A stunning location, personal, friendly service, and the comfortable en suite bedrooms (most with sea views and some with 4-poster beds) make Alford House ideal for a relaxing holiday.

Millslade Country House Hotel & Restaurant,

Brendon, Lynton, North Devon EX35 6PS
Tel: 01598 741322 Fax: 01598 741355
e-mail: bobcramp@millslade.freeserve.co.uk

A perfect base for exploring Exmoor in general and Lorna Doone country in particular, the **Millslade Country House Hotel & Restaurant** is set in beautiful grounds with the River East Lyn running alongside. The owners, Bob and Gillie Cramp, recently abandoned the glamorous world of film production, (Bob was a director/cameraman, and is still a keen photographer; Gillie was a set dresser), to run this small country house hotel. Originally an early-18th century coaching inn, it has a spacious residents' lounge with a log fire, an interestingly stocked bar and an elegant dining room. Bob is an accomplished cook who bases his cuisine on the best of seasonal and locally-sourced specialities. A typical dinner menu might offer Grilled Goat's Cheese on Ciabatta with a mixed salad as a starter, Roasted Cod in a Sauce

Verte amongst the main courses, and a delectable Strawberry Romanoff in a Brandy Basket on a Strawberry Coulis as a dessert choice.

The hotel has 6 guest rooms, all doubles and all en suite, and each is generously equipped to make your stay as enjoyable as possible. If you are looking for an active holiday, you'll find plenty to keep you busy - riding, shooting, or fishing for salmon or trout on the hotel's stretch of river, or exploring on foot the beauty and wildlife of Exmoor and Lorna Doone Country. You are welcome to bring your dog with you - even your horse since local stabling is available by arrangement.

Valley of the Rocks, Lynton

When the tank at the top is filled, and the one at the bottom emptied, the brakes are released and the two passenger carriages change place.

For centuries, the people of Lynmouth subsisted on agriculture and fishing, especially herring fishing and curing. By good fortune, just as the herring shoals were moving away to new waters, the North Devon coast benefited from the two new enthusiasms for "Romantic" scenery and sea bathing. Coleridge and Wordsworth arrived here on a walking tour in the 1790s, Shelley wrote fondly of his visit in 1812, and it was Robert Southey, later Poet Laureate, who first used the designation "the English Switzerland" to describe the dramatic scenery of the area. The painter Gainsborough had already described it as "the most delightful place for a landscape painter this country can boast". One of the most picturesque villages in Devon, Lynmouth also has a tiny harbour surrounded by lofty wooded hills, a curious Rhenish Tower on the pier, and do seek out Mars Hill, an eye-ravishing row of thatched cottages.

Understandably, this lovely setting acts as a magnet for artists and craftspeople. People

EXMOOR'S BRASS RUBBING & HOBBYCRAFT CENTRE,

Woodside Craft Centre, Watersmeet Road, Lynmouth,
North Devon EX35 6EP
Tel/Fax: 01598 752529

Exmoor's Brass Rubbing & Hobbycraft Centre provides an ideal outing for all the family - admission is free, you only pay for any materials you use. Visitors can discover the simple craft of Brass Rubbing in a relaxed and friendly atmosphere with instruction, supervision and materials provided. The Centre contains more than 150 exact facsimiles of brasses dating from 1277. The huge variety of subjects includes knights, ladies, clergy, animal footrests, even a skeleton.

The centre also sells ready made brass rubbings in various sizes and colours which make unique presents. They are also available in stylish green

cylinders for sending by mail. Also much in demand are the specially designed plates depicting such subjects as an Exmoor stag or pony, eagle and Celtic brasses, views of Lynmouth Harbour and the famous Cliff Railway, children's stories and the ever popular 'No Smoking' skeleton. The spacious premises also house an extensive selection of crafts, gifts and cards. The Centre has excellent facilities for the disabled but advance booking is essential to enable parking space to be reserved. The Centre is open 7 days a week from the February half-term until November although it may be closed on occasional Mondays early and late in the season. It's open all year round for booked parties.

like Peter Allen, for example, whose **Lynmouth Pottery** is very much a pottery with a difference. For one thing, it's a working pottery and one of the few places where you can try out your own skills at the potter's wheel. (Children too are encouraged to have a go). If you're not totally ashamed of the result, Peter Allen will then fire the finished item and post it on to you. Many a visitor to Lynmouth Pottery has discovered an unsuspected talent for turning slippery clay into a quite presentable decorative piece.

If you continue along Watersmeet Road you will come to the popular beauty spot of **Watersmeet**, where the East Lyn river and Hoar Oak Water come together. An 1832 fishing lodge, Watersmeet House, stands close by. A National Trust property, it

Lynmouth

is open during the season as a café, shop and information centre where you can pick up leaflets detailing some beautiful circular walks, starting here, along the East Lyn valley and to Hoar Oak Water.

Lynmouth's setting beside its twin rivers is undeniably beautiful, but it has also proved to be tragically vulnerable. On the night of August 16th, 1952, a cloudburst over Exmoor deposited nine inches of rain onto an already saturated moor. In the darkness, the normally placid East and West Lyn rivers became raging cataracts and burst their banks. Sweeping tree trunks and boulders along with it, the torrent smashed its way through the village, destroying dozens of houses and leaving 31 people dead. That night had seen many freak storms across southern England,

but none had matched the ferocity of the deluge that engulfed this pretty little village.

An earlier exceptional storm, in 1899, involved the Lynmouth lifeboat in a tale of epic endurance. A full-rigged ship, the *Forest Hall*, was in difficulties off Porlock, but the storm was so violent it was impossible to launch the lifeboat at Lynmouth. Instead, the crewmen dragged their three and a half ton boat, the *Louisa*, the 13 miles across the moor. Along the way they had to negotiate Countisbury Hill, with a gradient of 1000ft over two miles, before dropping down to Porlock Weir where the *Louisa* was successfully launched and every crew member of the stricken ship saved. Hooray!

List of Tourist Information Centres

AXMINSTER

The Old Courthouse, Church Street,
Axminster, Devon EX13 5AQ

Tel: 01297 34386

BARNSTAPLE

36, Boutport Street, Barnstaple,
Devon EX31 1RX

Tel: 01271 375000 Fax: 01271 374037

BIDEFORD

Victoria Park, The Quay, Bideford,
Devon EX39 2QQ

Tel: 01237 477676 Fax: 01237 421853

BRAUNTON

The Bakehouse Centre, The Car Park,
Braunton, Devon EX33 1AA

Tel: 01271 816400 Fax: 01271 816947

BRIXHAM

The Old Market House, The Quay,
Brixham, Devon TQ5 8TB

Tel: 0906 680 1268

BUDLEIGH SALTERTON

Fore Street, Budleigh Salterton,
Devon EX9 6NG

Tel: 01395 445275

COMBE MARTIN

Cross Street, Combe Martin,
Devon EX34 ODH

Tel/Fax: 01271 883319

CREDITON

Old Town Hall, High Street, Crediton,
Devon EX17 3LF

Tel/Fax: 01363 772006

DARTMOUTH

The Engine House, Mayor's Avenue,
Dartmouth, Devon TQ6 9YY

Tel: 01803 834224 Fax: 01803 835631

DAWLISH

The Lawn, Dawlish, Devon EX7 9EL

Tel: 01626 863589 Fax: 01626 865985

EXETER

Civic Centre, Paris Street, Exeter,
Devon EX1 1JJ

Tel: 01392 265700 Fax: 01392 265260

EXMOUTH

Alexandra Terrace, Exmouth,
Devon EX8 1NZ

Tel: 01395 222299

GREAT TORRINGTON

Castle Hill, South Street Car Park, Great
Torrington, Devon EX38 8AA

Tel: 01805 626140 Fax: 01805 626141

HONITON

Lace Walk Car Park, Honiton,
Devon EX14 8LT

Tel/Fax: 01404 43716

ILFRACOMBE

The Landmark, The Seafront,
llfracombe, Devon EX34 9BX

Tel: 01271 863001 Fax: 01271 862586

IVYBRIDGE

South Dartmoor TIC, Leonards Road,
Ivybridge, Devon PL21 0SL

Tel: 01752 897035 Fax: 01752 690660

KINGSBRIDGE

The Quay, Kingsbridge, Devon TQ7 1HS

Tel: 01548 853195 Fax: 01548 854185

LYNTON

Town Hall, Lee Road, Lynton,
Devon EX35 6BT

Tel: 01598 752225 Fax: 01598 752755

MODBURY

5 Modbury Court, Modbury,
Devon PL21 OQR

Tel: 01548 830159 FAx: 01548 831371

NEWTON ABBOT

6 Bridge House, Courtenay Street,
Newton Abbot, Devon TQ12 4QS

Tel/Fax: 01626 367494

OKEHAMPTON

3 West Street, Okehampton,
Devon EX20 1HQ

Tel: 01837 53020 Fax: 01837 55225

OTTERY ST MARY

10b Broad Street, Ottery St Mary,
Devon EX11 1BZ

Tel/Fax: 01404 813964

PAIGNTON

The Esplanade, Paignton,
Devon TQ4 6ED

Tel: 01906 680 1268

PLYMOUTH

Island House, 9 The Barbican, Plymouth,
Devon PL1 2LS

Tel: 01752 304849 Fax: 01752 257955

or

Plymouth Discovery Centre, Crabtree,
Plymouth, Devon PL3 6RN

Tel: 01752 266030 Fax: 01752 266033

SALCOMBE

Council Hall, Market Street, Salcombe,
Devon TQ8 8DE

Tel: 01548 843927 Fax: 01548 842736

SEATON

The Underfleet, Seaton,
Devon EX12 2TB

Tel: 01297 21660 Fax: 01297 21689

SIDMOUTH

Ham Lane, Sidmouth,
Devon EX10 8XR

Tel: 01395 516441 Fax: 01383 519333

SOUTH MOLTON

1 East Street, South Molton,
Devon EX36 3BU

Tel: 01769 574122 Fax: 01769 574044

TAVISTOCK

Town Hall, Bedford Square, Tavistock,
Devon PL19 OAE

Tel: 01822 612938 Fax: 01822 618389

TEIGNMOUTH

The Den, Sea Front, Teignmouth, Devon
TQ14 8BE

Tel/Fax: 01626 779769

TIVERTON

Phoenix Lane, Tiverton,
Devon EX16 6LU

Tel: 01884 255827 Fax: 01884 257594

TORQUAY

Vaughan Parade, Torquay,
Devon TQ2 5JG

Tel: 01906 680 1268

TOTNES

The Town Mill, Coronation Road,
Totnes, Devon TQ9 5DF

Tel: 01803 863168 Fax: 01803 865771

WOOLACOMBE

The Esplanade, Woolacombe,
Devon EX34 7DL

Tel: 01271 870553

Index of Towns, Villages and Places of Interest

Hidden Places Order Form

To order any of our publications just fill in the payment details below and complete the order form *overleaf*. For orders of less than 4 copies please add £1 per book for postage and packing. Orders over 4 copies are P & P free.

Please Complete Either:

I enclose a cheque for £ [   ] made payable to Travel Publishing Ltd

Or:

Card No: [   ]

Expiry Date: [   ]

Signature: [   ]

NAME: [   ]

ADDRESS: [   ]

POSTCODE: [   ]

TEL NO: [   ]

Please either send or telephone your order to:

Travel Publishing Ltd   Tel : 0118 981 7777
7a Apollo House   Fax: 0118 982 0077
Calleva Park
Aldermaston
Berks, RG7 8TN

	PRICE	QUANTITY	VALUE
Hidden Places Regional Titles			
Cambridgeshire & Lincolnshire	£7.99	....	....
Channel Islands	£6.99	....	....
Cheshire	£7.99	....	....
Chilterns	£7.99	....	....
Cornwall	£8.99	....	....
Derbyshire	£7.99	....	....
Devon	£8.99	....	....
Dorset, Hants & Isle of Wight	£7.99	....	....
East Anglia	£8.99	....	....
Essex	£7.99	....	....
Gloucestershire & Wiltshire	£7.99	....	....
Heart of England	£7.99	....	....
Hereford, Worcs & Shropshire	£7.99	....	....
Highlands & Islands	£7.99	....	....
Kent	£8.99	....	....
Lake District & Cumbria	£7.99	....	....
Lancashire	£7.99	....	....
Norfolk	£7.99	....	....
Northumberland & Durham	£6.99	....	....
North Wales	£7.99	....	....
Nottinghamshire	£6.99	....	....
Potteries	£6.99	....	....
Somerset	£7.99	....	....
South Wales	£7.99	....	....
Suffolk	£7.99	....	....
Surrey	£6.99	....	....
Sussex	£7.99	....	....
Thames Valley	£7.99	....	....
Warwickshire & West Midlands	£6.99	....	....
Yorkshire	£7.99	....	....
Hidden Places National Titles			
England	£9.99	....	....
Ireland	£9.99	....	....
Scotland	£9.99	....	....
Wales	£9.99	....	....
Hidden Inns Titles			
West Country	£5.99	....	....
South East	£5.99	....	....
South	£5.99	....	....
Wales	£5.99	....	....

For orders of less than 4 copies please add £1 per book for
postage & packing. Orders over 4 copies P & P free.

Hidden Places Order Form

To order any of our publications just fill in the payment details below and complete the order form *overleaf*. For orders of less than 4 copies please add £1 per book for postage and packing. Orders over 4 copies are P & P free.

Please Complete Either:

I enclose a cheque for £ [   ] made payable to Travel Publishing Ltd

Or:

Card No: [   ]

Expiry Date: [   ]

Signature: [   ]

NAME: [   ]

ADDRESS: [   ]

POSTCODE: [   ]

TEL NO: [   ]

Please either send or telephone your order to:

Travel Publishing Ltd   Tel : 0118 981 7777
7a Apollo House   Fax: 0118 982 0077
Calleva Park
Aldermaston
Berks, RG7 8TN

	PRICE	QUANTITY	VALUE
Hidden Places Regional Titles			
Cambridgeshire & Lincolnshire	£7.99	....	....
Channel Islands	£6.99	....	....
Cheshire	£7.99	....	....
Chilterns	£7.99	....	....
Cornwall	£8.99	....	....
Derbyshire	£7.99	....	....
Devon	£8.99	....	....
Dorset, Hants & Isle of Wight	£7.99	....	....
East Anglia	£8.99	....	....
Essex	£7.99	....	....
Gloucestershire & Wiltshire	£7.99	....	....
Heart of England	£7.99	....	....
Hereford, Worcs & Shropshire	£7.99	....	....
Highlands & Islands	£7.99	....	....
Kent	£8.99	....	....
Lake District & Cumbria	£7.99	....	....
Lancashire	£7.99	....	....
Norfolk	£7.99	....	....
Northumberland & Durham	£6.99	....	....
North Wales	£7.99	....	....
Nottinghamshire	£6.99	....	....
Potteries	£6.99	....	....
Somerset	£7.99	....	....
South Wales	£7.99	....	....
Suffolk	£7.99	....	....
Surrey	£6.99	....	....
Sussex	£7.99	....	....
Thames Valley	£7.99	....	....
Warwickshire & West Midlands	£6.99	....	....
Yorkshire	£7.99	....	....
Hidden Places National Titles			
England	£9.99	....	....
Ireland	£9.99	....	....
Scotland	£9.99	....	....
Wales	£9.99	....	....
Hidden Inns Titles			
West Country	£5.99	....	....
South East	£5.99	....	....
South	£5.99	....	....
Wales	£5.99	....	....

For orders of less than 4 copies please add £1 per book for postage & packing. Orders over 4 copies P & P free.

Hidden Places Reader Reaction

The *Hidden Inns* research team would like to receive reader's comments on any visitor attractions or places reviewed in the book and also recommendations for suitable entries to be included in the next edition. This will help ensure that the *Hidden Inns* series continues to provide its readers with useful information on the more interesting, unusual or unique features of each attraction or place ensuring that their stay in the local area is an enjoyable and stimulating experience.

To provide your comments or recommendations would you please complete the forms below and overleaf as indicated and send to:

The Research Department, Travel Publishing Ltd,
7a Apollo House, Calleva Park, Aldermaston, Reading, RG7 8TN.

Your Name:

Your Address:

Your Telephone Number:

Please tick as appropriate: Comments ☐   Recommendation ☐

Name of *"Hidden Place"*:

Address:

Telephone Number:

Name of Contact:

Hidden Places Reader Reaction

Comment or Reason for Recommendation:

Hidden Places Reader Reaction

The *Hidden Inns* research team would like to receive reader's comments on any visitor attractions or places reviewed in the book and also recommendations for suitable entries to be included in the next edition. This will help ensure that the *Hidden Inns* series continues to provide its readers with useful information on the more interesting, unusual or unique features of each attraction or place ensuring that their stay in the local area is an enjoyable and stimulating experience.

To provide your comments or recommendations would you please complete the forms below and overleaf as indicated and send to:

The Research Department, Travel Publishing Ltd,

7a Apollo House, Calleva Park, Aldermaston, Reading, RG7 8TN.

Your Name:

Your Address:

Your Telephone Number:

Please tick as appropriate: Comments ☐   Recommendation ☐

Name of *"Hidden Place"*:

Address:

Telephone Number:

Name of Contact:

Hidden Places Reader Reaction

Comment or Reason for Recommendation:

Hidden Places Reader Reaction

The *Hidden Inns* research team would like to receive reader's comments on any visitor attractions or places reviewed in the book and also recommendations for suitable entries to be included in the next edition. This will help ensure that the *Hidden Inns* series continues to provide its readers with useful information on the more interesting, unusual or unique features of each attraction or place ensuring that their stay in the local area is an enjoyable and stimulating experience.

To provide your comments or recommendations would you please complete the forms below and overleaf as indicated and send to:

The Research Department, Travel Publishing Ltd,
7a Apollo House, Calleva Park, Aldermaston, Reading, RG7 8TN.

Your Name:

Your Address:

Your Telephone Number:

Please tick as appropriate: Comments ☐ Recommendation ☐

Name of *"Hidden Place"*:

Address:

Telephone Number:

Name of Contact:

Hidden Places Reader Reaction

Comment or Reason for Recommendation:

Hidden Places Reader Reaction

The *Hidden Inns* research team would like to receive reader's comments on any visitor attractions or places reviewed in the book and also recommendations for suitable entries to be included in the next edition. This will help ensure that the *Hidden Inns* series continues to provide its readers with useful information on the more interesting, unusual or unique features of each attraction or place ensuring that their stay in the local area is an enjoyable and stimulating experience.

To provide your comments or recommendations would you please complete the forms below and overleaf as indicated and send to:

The Research Department, Travel Publishing Ltd,
7a Apollo House, Calleva Park, Aldermaston, Reading, RG7 8TN.

Your Name:

Your Address:

Your Telephone Number:

Please tick as appropriate: Comments ☐   Recommendation ☐

Name of *"Hidden Place"*:

Address:

Telephone Number:

Name of Contact:

Hidden Places Reader Reaction

Comment or Reason for Recommendation: